D1550271

Constructing a Sociology of Translation

Benjamins Translation Library (BTL)

The BTL aims to stimulate research and training in translation and interpreting studies. The Library provides a forum for a variety of approaches (which may sometimes be conflicting) in a socio-cultural, historical, theoretical, applied and pedagogical context. The Library includes scholarly works, reference books, post-graduate text books and readers in the English language.

EST Subseries

The European Society for Translation Studies (EST) Subseries is a publication channel within the Library to optimize EST's function as a forum for the translation and interpreting research community. It promotes new trends in research, gives more visibility to young scholars' work, publicizes new research methods, makes available documents from EST, and reissues classical works in translation studies which do not exist in English or which are now out of print.

Volume 74

Constructing a Sociology of Translation
Edited by Michaela Wolf and Alexandra Fukari

Constructing a Sociology of Translation

Edited by

Michaela Wolf
University of Graz

Alexandra Fukari
University of Graz

John Benjamins Publishing Company

Amsterdam / Philadelphia

™ The paper used in this publication meets the minimum requirements of
American National Standard for Information Sciences – Permanence of
Paper for Printed Library Materials, ANSI z39.48-1984.

Library of Congress Cataloging-in-Publication Data

Constructing a sociology of translation / edited by Michaela Wolf, Alexandra Fukari.
    p.   cm. (Benjamins Translation Library, ISSN 0929-7316 ; v. 74)
Includes bibliographical references and index.
1. Translating and interpreting--Social aspects. I. Wolf, Michaela. II. Fukari, Alexandra.
P306.97.S63C66   2007
418'.02--dc22   2007033946
ISBN 978 90 272 1682 3 (Hb; alk. paper)

John Benjamins Publishing Co. · P.O. Box 36224 · 1020 ME Amsterdam · The Netherlands
John Benjamins North America · P.O. Box 27519 · Philadelphia PA 19118-0519 · USA

Table of contents

Part IV. Constructing a sociology of translation studies: Overview and perspectives

Introduction

The emergence of a sociology of translation

Michaela Wolf
University of Graz, Austria

Any translation, as both an enactment and a product, is necessarily embedded within social contexts. On the one hand, the act of translating, in all its various stages, is undeniably carried out by individuals who belong to a social system; on the other, the translation phenomenon is inevitably implicated in social institutions, which greatly determine the selection, production and distribution of translation and, as a result, the strategies adopted in the translation itself. What is at stake here, therefore, are the various agencies and agents involved in any translation procedure, and more specifically the textual factors operating in the translation process. The interrelational and interactive character of these factors is fundamental to understanding their functioning, and makes up the view of translation as a "socially regulated activity" (Hermans 1997:10). The social function and the socio-communicative value of a translation can best be located within the contact zone where the translated text and the various socially driven agencies meet. These characteristics of a translation can be revealed through a complex description of the relations that exist between the author of the text, the transfer agencies, the text, and the public in their societal interlacements. Accordingly, the subjectivity of the participants in this "global play" is of paramount importance. Drawing on Anthony Giddens's concept of agency, Venuti argues that this subjectivity is constituted by cultural and social determinations that are diverse and even conflicting:

> Human action is intentional, but determinate, self-reflexively measured against social rules and resources, the heterogeneity of which allows for the possibility of change with every self-reflexive action. (Venuti 1996:206)

In this context, analysing the social implications of translation helps us to identify the translator and the translation researcher as a constructing and constructed subject in society. This, of course, means we need to conceptualize a methodological framework, a task which has been repeatedly undertaken in the last few years. In this introduction, the efforts to methodologically frame translation and its contexts as a social practice will be discussed. A more important purpose of this volume, however, is to improve the conjunction of translation studies and sociology and thus foster the development of a methodological basis. The volume intends to further the debate on the role of an emergent sociology of translation within the broader context of translation studies, while taking into account the discourses constructing a "sociology of translation studies". The potential of such a discussion can best be shown by drawing on the concept of interdisciplinarity.

Interdisciplinarity, or: Translation between culture and society

Interdisciplinarity – understood as a differentiated, multidimensional epistemological concept which, according to Roland Barthes, "consists in creating a new object which does not belong to anybody" (Barthes 1984: 100, my translation) – has, not surprisingly, been a claim put forward by translation studies more or less from its beginnings. In his detailed discussion of the role of interdisciplinarity in research, Klaus Kaindl argues that the discipline of translation studies must reconsider its current practice of instrumentalising the research methods of other disciplines, and instead encourage cooperation on a reciprocal basis (Kaindl 2004: 71). The various results of such a move would include the consideration of cultural studies, linguistics, literary studies, historiography, philosophy and sociology within translation studies. To be sure, while interdisciplinarity may offer opportunities for deeper epistemological insights, such collisions always include some form of friction. In particular, the delimitation from other disciplines, and from various special subjects with their origins in the formation of a modern academic system, gives rise to continuous polemics, albeit without seriously prejudicing the production of knowledge and its methodological processing. As a result, the controversial debates and even erroneous ideas resulting from interdisciplinary work cannot be regarded as troublesome or avoidable inconveniences, but are an expression of the differences that exist between scientific disciplines with regard to their structural characteristics.[1]

In the humanities, interdisciplinary projects are an especially important contribution to the rise and subsequent establishment of "turns", which question both existing paradigms and allegedly definitive certainties, and additionally offer innovative potential for productive new research areas and methodologies. As was shown by what has been labelled the "cultural turn" (see Bassnett and Lefevere

---

1.   See Bourdieu (2004) for the discussion of these structural characteristics in the fields of historiography and sociology and the problems arising from interdisciplinary thinking.

1990), translation studies seems particularly inclined towards the shift of paradigms.[2] This results partly from the fact that its subject is by nature located in the contact zones "between cultures", and is therefore exposed to different constellations of contextualisation and structures of communication, but also from the make-up of the discipline itself. The multifaceted forms of communication which shape the issues undertaken within translation studies call for us to go beyond disciplinary boundaries. It cannot be denied that the "cultural turn" brought about a lasting expansion of the frames of research and demanded the elaboration of very broad questions. This enabled a thorough discussion of historical perspectives, contextual situations and translation conventions, thus foregrounding the macro-context of translation and different forms of representation. If as a first step questions of "transfer" were dealt with as culturally specific facets of single phenomena, this dimension was soon extended to the level of discourse (see e.g. Müller-Vollmer 1998) before being reformulated in terms of new approaches drawn primarily from cultural studies. The methodological procedures resulting from these approaches explicitly questioned modes of representation and redefined translations as "inventions" or "constructions" of the "Other" (see Bachmann-Medick 2004: 450-451; Wolf 2005b: 106-107).

The rupture with exclusively text-bound approaches not only allows translation studies to dislocate fixed entities and reveal asymmetrical transfer conditions, but also focuses on those modes of translation which "concretise translation as an interactive social event" (Fuchs 1997: 319, my translation). This helps draw attention to the cultural *and* social formations which fundamentally characterize the translation phenomenon: processes of mediation are thus implicated in frameworks which involve both negotiating cultural differences and exploring the forms of action that belong to the translation process. Consequently, mediating agents operate – in Clifford Geertz' sense – as a sort of "web"[3] that exists between the various cultures. They are bound up in social networks which allow them to be viewed as socially constructed and constructing subjects.

In the wake of the "cultural turn", these observations open up several questions. On the one hand, they shed a radically new light on the notion of "translation", and thus on the discipline's research object. From this perspective, translation is a concept that opposes the view of culture as an agency preserving static views of tradition and identity, and instead highlights the dynamic transforma-

---

2. See Mary Snell-Hornby's recent book *The Turns of Translation Studies. New Paradigms or Shifting Viewpoints?* (Snell-Hornby 2006) and Doris Bachmann-Medick's seminal study *Cultural Turns. Neuorientierungen in den Kulturwissenschaften* (Bachmann-Medick 2006).

3. Geertz says, "Believing, with Max Weber, that man is an animal suspended in webs of significance he himself has spun, I take culture to be those webs [...]" (Geertz 1993: 5).

tions resulting from continual confrontations of cultural formations. This change of viewpoint requires us to engage with the potential of a metaphorically conceptualized notion of translation. Such a theory of translation would not only consider the intersecting spaces within the translation process, but would also give voice to the translators and other agents of this process as subjects ensuing from particular cultural dynamics. In addition, it would reveal problems of cultural representation[4] and the contribution made by translation to the construction of cultures. On the other hand, these insights introduce a research area which so far has been touched upon only unsystematically and which, under the label of a "sociology of translation", deals with the issues that arise when viewing translation and interpreting as social practice as well as symbolically transferred interaction. As will be shown, the implications of these interactions are being analysed in an increasingly sophisticated range of issues and methodological refinements.

The process of translation seems, to different degrees, to be conditioned by two levels: the "cultural" and the "social". The first level, a structural one, encompasses influential factors such as power, dominance, national interests, religion or economics. The second level concerns the agents involved in the translation process, who continuously internalize the aforementioned structures and act in correspondence with their culturally connoted value systems and ideologies. There is, however, a danger of dichotomising these two levels. Anthony Pym has recently claimed that "[w]e talk, too readily, about 'sociocultural' or 'social and cultural' approaches, contexts, factors, whatever. [...] No doubt the 'social' is also the 'cultural', in the sense that both are opposed to the 'eternal' or the 'ontological'. But why then do we need the two terms?" (Pym 2006: 14). This question has troubled other disciplines as well. Certainly, society cannot be adequately described without culture nor culture without society. As part of the classical heritage, the Roman terms *cultura* and *societas* survived for several centuries in the common language of education, Latin, without suffering considerable changes in meaning. It was only around 1800, with the rise of radical social changes, that these terms were integrated into the European vernaculars and became key terms in public as well as private discourses. This indicates that the terms "culture" and "society" symbolized radical re-orientations. In their various connotations they not only reflected social transformation over time and space but also encompassed new perceptions by adopting a certain "social vocabulary" as a tool for developing new concepts of society and culture (Tenbruck 1990: 21-22). The subsequent dichotomisation of the two terms denotes that two distinct aspects of "reality" were taking shape.

---

4.   For the "crisis of representation" in cultural studies, see Berg and Fuchs (1993) and Chartier (1992).

By way of illustration, a glance at the discussions on the evolution of "cultural sociology" within German speaking academia reveals the dilemma inherent in this dichotomisation – a dilemma which is ultimately reflected in the questions put forth on the subject of a "cultural" and/or "social turn" currently being discussed within translation studies. The founders of German sociology, Max Weber and Georg Simmel, considered that all social action embedded in cultural settings had to be explored both in its historical contexts and in its institutional representations. Subsequently, the concept of culture was denied its analytical potential and was ascribed a notion of value: culture in itself was thus resubstantialized, dismantling the postulate of "freedom of value" within scientific research (Gebhardt 2001). This view survived until the end of the 1970s, when – in the wake of individualising, pluralising and globalising processes – critics of cultural anthropology pointed out the essentialisation of culture operating in dualisms such as "representative" versus "popular" culture or "high" versus "everyday life" culture, and ultimately called for a redefinition of the concepts involved in cultural and social practices (ibid.). These developments were taken up through various initiatives, for example the publication of a thematic volume of the *Kölner Zeitschrift für Soziologie und Sozialpsychologie* entitled "Kultursoziologie" in 1979 and the publication of a special issue on "Kultur und Gesellschaft" by the same journal in 1986, as well as a conference of sociologists from German-speaking countries, held in 1988 in Zurich and dedicated to the topic (Lichtblau 2003). One of the key questions dealt with in these projects was how "present-day societies constitute themselves as culture" (Rehberg 1986: 106). The discussion mainly focused on how to avoid mutual exclusion when defining the two concepts, and alternatively suggested viewing culture and society as interdependent, a definition which would help to transcend a deterministic view and foster an integrative approach.

Once it becomes obvious that all the elements contributing to the constitution of society are conditioned by specific cultural abilities of language and symbolisation (ibid.: 107), the concepts of "society" and "culture" are both revealed as constructions: culture "creates social structures and is shaped by existing ones" (Neidhardt 1986: 15, my translation). In these construction processes, translation undoubtedly plays a major role. Especially in the translational analysis of recent world-wide developments, such as migration or globalisation, where cultural, social and societal problems in the narrower sense are at stake, it becomes clear on the one hand that there is no benefit in encouraging the elaboration of separate analytical tools (stemming, among other sources, from sociology and cultural studies[5]), and, on the other, that some of the methodologies developed in the

---

5.   On this topic, see Heilbron and Sapiro (in this volume).

wake of the "cultural turn" seem to no longer suffice for a thorough analysis of the contribution of translation within these multifaceted processes. An emphasis on the relationship between culture and society would help to avoid dichotomisation and allow us to transcend traditional deterministic views. In institutional terms, the question of whether we are witnessing the emergence of a new "turn" – the "sociological turn" – no longer seems relevant: cultural and social practices – and consequently their theoretical and methodological conceptualization – cannot be regarded as detached from one another. If we focus on "the social" yet neglect the conditions that mould translation as a cultural practice in terms of power, ideology and similar issues, the creation of a new sub-discipline within translation studies called "sociology of translation" would sidestep the problem of methodology. The questions pertinent to translation viewed as a social practice should instead be placed at the core of the discipline. Last but not least, such a position has the potential to better conjoin existing approaches with a "sociology of translation", as well as to discuss more efficiently the interface of methodologies developed in sociology and cultural studies.

First glances at "translation as a social practice"[6]

The question of "the social" within translation had been dealt with throughout the history of translation studies in various forms and from varying perspectives. Here, I will give only an overview of the main considerations arising from such approaches. Although it has been recognized that the translation process is socially conditioned and that "the viability of a translation is established by its relationship to the cultural and social conditions under which it is produced and read" (Venuti 1995: 18), no comprehensive research seems yet to have been conducted with regard to the social implications of translation.

While system-oriented approaches do not insist on the theoretical conceptualization of the social implications of translation, they do – more than any other research designs – offer numerous links to socially oriented questions. Polysystem theory, for instance, has brought about fruitful insights into the functioning of translated literature within broader literary and historical systems of the target culture. This was a decisive move beyond the prescriptive models prevailing at the time when polysystem theory was elaborated, and placed the phenomenon of translation within broader "socio-cultural" contexts. The theory proposes that literature be understood as a dynamic, functional and stratified system; 'system' be-

---

6.   For an overview on the "state of the art" of an emerging "sociology of translation" see also Prunč, in this volume.

ing defined as "the network of relations that can be hypothesized for a certain set
of assumed observables ([or] 'occurrences'/'phenomena')" (Even-Zohar 1990: 27).
In Even-Zohar's view, systems are highly hierarchical and are determined by their
struggle for the primary position in the literary canon. Canonical repertoires tend
to be consumed and conventionalized through repetition and are gradually driven
towards the system's periphery, whereas peripheral repertoires push towards the
centre and, in this process, are often used as a means to enrich aesthetic values.
Criticisms of polysystem theory emphasize, among other aspects, the dichotomic
stance inherent in its "toolbox" of binary oppositions, such as "canonized" versus "non-canonized" literature or "centre" versus "periphery". From a sociological
point of view, however, it seems particularly relevant that throughout polysystem
theory it is never made clear what driving forces are behind the ongoing dynamics
in a system. According to Even-Zohar, it

> suffices to recognize that it is the *interdependencies* between these factors which
> allow them to function in the first place. Thus, a CONSUMER may "consume" a
> PRODUCT produced by a PRODUCER, but in order for the "product" (such as
> "text") to be generated, a common REPERTOIRE must exist, whose usability is
> determined by some INSTITUTION. A MARKET must exist where such a good
> can be transmitted. None of the factors enumerated can be described to function
> in isolation, and the kind of relations that may be detected run across all possible
> axes of the scheme.   (Even-Zohar 1990: 34, original emphasis)

What seems to be implicitly "meant", but not openly expressed, are the conditions
of the social interactions in question. What is the nature of the political and social
relationships between the groups involved in these processes? And what are the
criteria underlying the "generation" of a product or the "existence" of a market?
These and other questions illustrate that Even-Zohar's words remain directly related to the text – as Edwin Gentzler points out: "Even-Zohar seldom relates texts
to the 'real conditions' of their production, only to hypothetical structural models
and abstract generalizations" (Gentzler 1993: 123). Even-Zohar thus fails to integrate his "factors" (i.e. agents and institutions) into the frameworks of polysystem
theory, and prefers to focus on the description of the existing relationships between them.

  With regard to the mechanisms underlying the dynamics of the literary polysystem, which are supposed to condition the translation production process,
Even-Zohar claims that some of the reasons for the continual shifts between periphery and centre – which, he says, can enable the introduction of translated
literature into the system – are found in the "lack of repertoire" in the target literature (Even-Zohar 1990: 47). This seems to be a category of polysystem theory
which has the potential to disclose the driving conditions of the literary system.

Even-Zohar defines repertoire as "the aggregate of rules and materials which govern both the making and use of any given product" (ibid.: 39; see also ibid.: 17 and 207ff.) and as "shared knowledge necessary for producing [...] various [...] products for the literary system". He also postulates that there might be a repertoire for "behaving as one should expect from a literary agent" (ibid.: 40).[7] Although the notion of repertoire is often linked to grammar or lexicon, it implicitly bears the social, cultural, economic or other aspects which generate cultural products, among them translations. Even-Zohar, however, never discusses these aspects explicitly, and fails to consider the agents operating at the base of "repertoire".

Within the wider realm of systemic-oriented translation studies, a descriptive, empirical approach was developed which emphasizes a translation's function within the target culture and strongly draws on the concept of translation norms – norms that govern the relations between source and target text. In sociology, norms are a rather disputed category, as they only gain relevance once they have been generally accepted by a given community and can answer the following questions: what norms are applicable to whom and in what context, in what way are norms accepted, and how does a change in norms operate (Bahrdt 2000: 48). However, if we accept the significance of norms in moulding social structures, they become paramount to the discussion of social forces in translation. Norms operate in each phase of the translation process: in the selection of texts, by determining what source languages and what (literary) models should be selected for the target literature, and in the selection of translation strategies that reveal the relationships between the two translation cultures involved. A detailed analysis of all translation norms effective at a specific time within a specific society would ideally enable insights into that society's ideas on translation as a cultural phenomenon.

Toury calls attention to the relevance of norms for translator training institutes, and remarks on the importance of feedback. Translators undergo a socialisation process during which feedback procedures, motivated by norms, are assimilated. This helps them to develop strategies for coping with the various problems they encounter during actual translation, and in some cases translators might even adopt automatized techniques to resolve specific problems. This internalisation

---

7. Rakefet Sheffy, too, recognizes the social potential of "repertoires": "Certainly, such [a repertoire-oriented] approach to systems is amenable to sociological perspectives" (Sheffy 1997: 36). For his part, Theo Hermans denounces the aspect of automatism in these processes of change, which "become self-propelling and cyclical: the canonized centre does what it does, and when it is overrun a new centre repeats the pattern, as if the whole thing were on automatic pilot" (Hermans 1999: 118).

process is reminiscent of the translator's *habitus*, introduced by Bourdieu and is conceptualized by Toury as follows:

> It may also be hypothesized that to the extent that a norm has indeed been internalized and made part of a modified competence, it will also be applied to the production of more spontaneous translated utterances, in situations where no sanctions are likely to be imposed. [The translator's] behavioural varieties [...] may therefore prove a useful tool for checking not only the prevailing norms as such, but also their assimilation by individuals and, in the long run, the universals of the process of assimilation itself.   (Toury 1995: 250)

The "agreements and conventions" underlying the practice of translation are continuously negotiated by the people and institutions involved. When considering translation as a norm-governed activity we must take into account the status held by translators within their specific setting and the references they make to the norms they constantly create, agree upon, maintain and break, applying them to different translation situations (Toury 1999: 20).

In his theoretical work, Toury gives the social role of norms a major position – but without conceptualizing them in terms of their socially conditioned context and of the factors involved. Consequently, a sociological framework based on a concept of norms should include the analysis of both the contingent elements responsible for the reconstruction of norms and the internalisation of norms, which ultimately contribute to a specific "translational behaviour" partly based on the negotiation skills between the various subjects involved in the translation procedure. Most of these elements are pointed out by Toury, but he has not so far linked them to a socially driven methodology. Nevertheless, Toury seems quite aware of the need to accentuate societal questions more strongly:

> I believe it is about time [to supply] better, more comprehensive and more flexible explanations of the translational behaviour of individuals within a social context.
> (Toury 1999: 28–29)

Theo Hermans further develops the norm concept by focusing on its broader, social function, and particularly stresses its relevance in relation to power and ideology. Hermans has, perhaps more explicitly than any other scholar, concentrated on the social constraints by which norms, in turn, shape the translation process and effect. He claims that translation today is seen "as a complex transaction taking place in a communicative, socio-cultural context" (Hermans 1996: 26). This means the agents involved are placed at the fore of these transfer processes, with special attention paid to the "interactive form of social behaviour, involving a degree of 'interpersonal coordination' among those taking part (selecting and attuning an appropriate code, recognising and interpreting the code, paying attention, eliminating 'noise', etc.)" (ibid.: 29; see also Hermans 1997: 7). In addition, the relative positions and interests of the participants have to be taken into account in order to contextualize the social dimension of the creation and reception of translation.

Hermans finds that empirical studies have yet to elaborate a theoretical framework which encompasses both the social and ideological impact of translation. In his opinion, emphasis on the analysis of norms could be a first step towards such a framework. Norms are, after all, involved in all stages of the translation procedure and thus define "the contours of translation as a recognized, social category" (ibid.: 42). A further step into the conceptualization of "the social" within translation – which would include the concept of norms – could be the elaboration of methodological instruments to help give detailed insight into the social conditions of the translator's and other agents' labour, and into the social forces that drive the translation process. Systemic approaches to translation have taken these questions into account, but have not yet managed to elaborate them within a coherent theoretical framework.

The view of translation as social practice is also central to the work of André Lefevere. In particular, the notion of "rewriting" is one that denotes both the manipulative interventions on the level of the text and the cultural (literary) devices which direct and control the production procedure in the interplay of social forces. The patronage system at work within this interplay embraces individuals, collectives and institutions, which are determined mainly by ideology. Lefevere not only ascribes a social dimension to this notion (Lefevere 1998: 48), but also extends it by means of Bourdieu's concept of "cultural capital", which he sees as the driving force for the distribution of translations within a specific culture, as "cultural capital is transmitted, distributed and regulated by means of translation, among other factors, not only between cultures, but also within one given culture" (ibid.: 41).[8] The rewriting concept also draws on other concepts closely linked to Bourdieusian categories – economic capital as an important contribution to the final shape of a translation, and "status" (viz "social and/or symbolic capital"), which is responsible for positioning the "patrons" in their respective literary system and is vital for the conceptualization of a sociology of translation.

Through their concentration on the role of various participants in the translation enterprise (initiator, commissioner, source and target text producer, user, receiver, etc.) with the aim of accomplishing the declared *skopos*, a good deal of the functional approaches can be regarded as sociologically motivated, having shifted their main focus from texts to the mediators of these texts. Attempting to

---

8. The slightly fuzzy use of the notion "cultural capital" by Lefevere cannot be fully associated with the Bourdieusian notion. See in detail Wolf (2005b: 103).

transcend the equivalence postulate, functionalism-oriented scholars explore the professional domain of translation, which is linked with a view of translation as an intercultural communication act (Nord 1991:9). For skopos theory in the narrower sense, however, it seems that a vague notion of culture is rather an obstacle to a sociological perspective, because the concept of culture – idio, dia and para-culture (Vermeer 1990:32) – suggests social restraint yet does not fully consider it as an object of investigation. The social forces behind the communicative acts that select and prepare the *skopos*-ready cultural product for reception in the target culture are not conceptualized in a discursive net. Doing so, would ultimately allow us to foreground the constraints informing the decisions taken in favour (or against) a declared *skopos*.

Justa Holz-Mänttäri's "translational action model" might *a priori* serve as a better basis for a sociologically driven translation analysis. Her model seeks to develop a framework that would allow for the cooperation of the subjects participating in the social make-up of translation. The model poses as its parameters the specific qualification of the persons involved, the necessity of cooperation, and the agents' professionalism resulting from these requirements. All these factors enforce the idea of translation as social practice. Yet when Holz-Mänttäri claims that a translation – at least ideally – is produced according to prior agreement of all subjects involved, we are reminded of Hans Hönig, who argues that this kind of notion is based on a horizontally conceptualized model of society, one which in fact does not correspond to the hierarchical relationships that exist between the agents in Holz-Mänttäri's model (Hönig 1992:3; see also Wolf 1999). These hierarchies could be revealed by studying both the connections existing between the various agents and the conditions underlying their relationships.

The category of the power relationships operating in translation has become an important research topic over the last few decades. Apart from certain informative articles, such as Peter Fawcett's "Translation and Power Play" (1995), which can be regarded as one of the first systematic investigations into the implications of power and translation, the collection of essays edited by Román Álvarez and Carmen-África Vidal (1996) set the course for a more detailed examination of translation viewed as a politically motivated activity. Álvarez and Vidal seek to analyze the relationship between the production of knowledge in a given culture and its transfer, as well as the location of knowledge within the target culture. They concentrate on the figure of the translator, "who can be the authority who manipulates the culture, politics, literature, and their acceptance (or lack thereof) in the target culture" (ibid.:2). As for Lawrence Venuti, the central value he gives to the question of power relations in translation is already revealed in his view of translation itself. He conceives of translation as "cultural political practice, constructing or critiquing ideology-stamped identities for foreign cultures, affirming or transgressing discursive values and institutional limits in the target-language culture" (Venuti 1995: 19), and articulates the implications of these limits for the translator's position in society alongside the social implicatedness of translation (Venuti 1998: 3).[9] The link between the manifestation of power and domination in the creation of a translation and the phenomenon of the translator's "invisibility" seems obvious. Once we acknowledge that this invisibility has been (and still is) an essential requirement of acceptability, there are undoubtedly aspects of power at work as long as the translator's presence in the target text is masked by "fluent" strategies, or so Venuti would argue (1995: 22). The more visible the translator is within the text, the less likely it is that he or she can be ignored, marginalized or insufficiently rewarded (Arrojo 1997: 130).

"Power" is thus not only – as stated by Edwin Gentzler and Maria Tymoczko – "the key topic that has provided the impetus for the new directions that translation studies have taken since the cultural turn" (Gentzler and Tymoczko 2002: XVI), but also one of the driving forces of a social view of the translation process, and as such a key issue to be analysed in what has been labelled "sociology of translation". As will be shown, Pierre Bourdieu offered one of the most influential frameworks for studying of the factors which condition the power relations inherent in both the practice and theory of translation. Those factors help to shed light on questions such as the impact that translation can have or actually has on social change, or the relation of social factors of dominance to the selection and ultimately the shaping of translations.

To sum up this short survey, the assertion of Gentzler and Tymoczko that translation is "a deliberate and conscious act of selection, assemblage, structuration, and fabrication" (ibid.: XXI) hints at the paramount importance of analysing social aspects in translation and calls for discussion of both the translator's task creating knowledge and his/her contribution to the shaping of culture *and* society. In addition, poststructuralist concepts produce deeper insights into these procedures, as they tend to question basic categories of social sciences such as action, subject, society or social structure (Stäheli 2000). This opens up new perspectives on the functioning of translation and interpreting as a social practice, including self-reflexivity as a crucial issue in the development of the analytical instruments of a sociology of translation. The next section will explore the major questions that have so far been asked concerning the development of a sociology

---

9.   See also Venuti (1992: 10). The association of "power" and the social implications of translation is also discussed by Erich Prunč. As he points out in this volume, a social practice approach to translation calls attention to the process of negotiation based on agencies of power, since the differentials between cultures in terms of power and prestige correlate with the prestige and social position of the agents involved in the translation process.

of translation, and will look at the sociological methods that have been adopted to deal with these questions within a translational context.

The methodological framing of a sociology of translation

Traditional approaches to translation studies have shown a certain awareness of socially driven questions in translation. They have not, however, coherently synthesized the various issues raised, and little work has been done on the theorisation of these questions. Obviously, there is quite a difference between a more or less vague consciousness of research deficits and systematic research on social aspects of translation.

In a recently published paper "Translation and Society: The Emergence of a Conceptual Relationship", Daniel Simeoni (2005) aims to disclose the reasons for the delayed attention given to social issues in translation studies. He states that although, over the centuries, discourses characterising the practice of translation have always been fundamentally social in nature, the observations remained mostly limited to the particular text under discussion. Even in the 1980s, with an increasing emphasis on the environment of translation, the major contributions "remained attached to a primarily formal, and only secondarily social, worldview" (ibid.: 4). One of Simeoni's major arguments is that a "sociological eye" was regarded as secondary in the establishment of the academic field, which in the course of a more "contextualising" comprehension of translation rather accentuated the culturalist paradigm; he argues that this has to be seen in the broader context of scientific conceptions which traditionally have been nationalistically induced (ibid.: 12).[10]

Nevertheless, the "sociological eye" has been sharpened in the last few years. This section will look into these developments which can be discussed under the umbrella notion of a "sociology of translation". It seems as though several different "sociologies" can be identified so far: one which, in the classical sociological tradition, focuses on the agents active in translation production, another which emphasizes the "translation process", while a "sociology of the cultural product" scrutinizes the construction of social identities. A cluster of approaches delivers the theoretical and methodological groundwork for a view of translation and interpreting as a social practice, drawing on the works of various sociologists, and,

---

10. Simeoni also argues that on the institutional level, academic tradition in Europe has been influenced by a "proverbial provincialism of research in national institutions" which, for a long time, did not consider acceptable the entire cultural-studies paradigm as developed in North America (Simeoni 2005: 7).

very recently, some articles have also engaged in what can be subsumed under the label of a "sociology of translation studies".[11]

Sociology of agents

Theories that bring social action to the fore conceive of social life from the perspective of individually acting persons who are involved in social processes. In such a context, agents participating in the translation procedure are highlighted from various aspects. Their activity is, for example, discussed in light of the sociology of profession and the sociology of literature (Silbermann and Hänseroth 1985) or in their role in the constitution of a unified Europe (Barret-Ducrocq 1992). Cornelia Lauber (1996) attempts to reconstruct self-portraits of French translators by evaluating their sociological profiles through gender, labour, and source-text specific questions, an approach which can also be applied to other geographical or cultural contexts. Gender-specific issues in the area of sociological frameworks are dealt with in detail by Wolf (2006) in her study on women translators working in German-speaking countries for women publishers or women's book series. This study, on the opinions of translators and publishers and on pertinent editorial policies, is supplemented by a historical dimension in a volume edited by Grbić and Wolf (2002), which examines the practice of translation by female translators from the point of view of their social networks, thus revealing their positions in society and the struggle for social recognition.

Individual figures of translators have frequently been investigated in historically oriented works. To begin with, the influential volume *Translators Through History* edited by Delisle and Woodsworth (1995)[12] examines the role of translators in the formation of national literatures, the transfer of knowledge, and the dissemination of religion, giving detailed information on their social and cultural contexts. With his innovative work *Method in Translation History*, Anthony Pym (1998) fills a long-felt need to conceptualize historical studies on translation within a methodological framework. Pym calls for a shift of emphasis from texts and contexts to the individual figures of translators as central objects of research, and aims to reconstruct the domain of socially conditioned subjectivity as a basis for understanding the translators' history. His three-stage model includes a "translation archaeology", a set of discourses which single out the fundamental sociological facts; a "historical critique", which examines the role of translations in their

---

11. Given the flourishing state of the art of the subject in question, in the context of this survey only the key works can be taken into account.

12. See also Delisle (1999, 2002).

ideological dimension; and the "explanation", which discusses the causation of how translations come into being. In this last step, translators are self-reflexively called upon as agents whose subjectivity is socially conditioned – as indeed is that of the researchers (Pym 1998: 5–6).

Some works address the agents in the translation process by theoretically modelling them on some of Pierre Bourdieu's main categories. An outline of the "mediation space" for the translation of *Harry Potter and the Philosopher's Stone* into German, for example, attempts to unravel the power relations inherent in the translational production process by identifying the massive capitals invested in the "Harry Potter" field (Wolf 2002). In another study, Wolf discusses the constraints that prevailed in the translation domain during the Nazi regime, where the role of translators in translation production and the translation phenomenon was instrumentalized in order to foster the regime's ideology (Wolf 2003). Similarly, Jean-Marc Gouanvic draws on Bourdieusian concepts in order to shed light on the agents' activities in the translation field. In his various studies on the importation of US-American science fiction literature into France between 1945 and 1960 (see e.g. Gouanvic 1997, 1999), he claims that a translation is basically exposed to the same logics as an original and that, in the case of his empirical studies, the stakes (*enjeux*) of the agents involved (critics, editors, publishers, translators) enabled the establishment of a new literary field of science fiction in France. This field was created as a sort of compromise between the US-American field's structures and part of the corresponding French tradition. Gouanvic explores in detail the power struggles in the field conditioned by the differing interests of the various social agents, and their impact on the textual form of the translations. He also takes into account the mechanisms of legitimation to which the social groups were exposed in the course of their struggle for symbolic, economic and political power.

Sociology of the translation process

As has already been shown, descriptive approaches offer particularly fertile ground for the development of a "sociology of the translation process". Calling for a more coherent consideration of historical and cultural factors and the processes of identity formation through translation, Clem Robyns's paper "Towards a Sociosemiotics of Translation" (1992) reveals its connections with systemic approaches. Robyns views both source and target texts as constructions embedded in social discourses, and develops a translation model with three interactive aspects. First, the metadiscourse on translation poses questions such as what type of discourse exists in political or other debates. A second aspect deals with the selection and distribution of the elements imported through translation, thus indirectly evoking the concept of norms: which mechanisms do these elements follow, and what is their status? In which discursive formations are they located, and what is their particular function? Finally, the "integration and transformation of those elements" affects the adoption of concrete translation strategies which depend on the envisaged position in the target system and are submitted to doctrine, taboo, political pressure or explicit censorship (ibid.: 220). Despite its lack of reflection on the agents participating actively and discursively in the interaction of the various spheres of action, this dynamic model – not least through its attempt to reconstruct translation as "social discourse" – represents a decisive step towards the conceptualization of a sociology of translation.

Translation viewed as a set of discourses is also studied by Annie Brisset. *Sociocritique de la traduction* (Brisset 1990), a study on theatre translation in Quebec, pursues the idea that literature is per se a discursive act and a representation of other discourses. The question resulting from this insight is "how and under what conditions the 'discourse' of the foreign text becomes an integral part of the 'discourse' of the target society" (Brisset 1996: 4). In the discussion of this question, Brisset claims that like any other discursive practice, translation is governed by norms. She investigates institutionally relevant norms and tries to find regularities in certain translators' decisions, which lay bare the "discursive make-up" of the relevant institutions of the target literature.

Translation as a socially driven process is central to Klaus Kaindl's study on the introduction of comics into the literary field of German-speaking countries (Kaindl 2004). To develop a theoretical framework for a sociologically relevant study of the translation of comics, Kaindl systematically adopts Bourdieu's main concepts and comes to the conclusion that the failure of an elaborated field of comics to come about is due both to the lack of adequate parameters for translators to draw on and to the low symbolic capital of comics in the German-speaking cultural space. This confirms Bourdieu's assertion that the position of a certain cultural product and its relative value in a given society are responsible for the product's "success".

Sociology of the cultural product

The majority of the approaches discussed so far cannot be exclusively ascribed to only one of the categories of "sociology", but should rather be located in some overlapping spaces. This is particularly true for the publications I will now discuss, which emphasize not only the agents in the production and reception of translation, but also their shaping role in the respective power relations and the relevance of the translation as a cultural product which circulates in inter- and transnational transfer. The works pertinent to this section discuss translation – more or less explicitly – by highlighting its contribution to the construction of social identity, image, social roles, or ideology. The factors which operate in these construction processes are, to a large degree, socially driven and re-organised within social networks that condition the very specific interplay of the different mediation agencies. Two volumes will be discussed here in detail: the special issue "Traduction: Les Échanges littéraires internationaux" of *Actes de la Recherche en Sciences Sociales*, edited by Johan Heilbron and Gisèle Sapiro (2002), and the thematic issue "Soziologie der literarischen Übersetzung" of *Internationales Archiv für Sozialgeschichte der deutschen Literatur*, edited by Norbert Bachleitner and Michaela Wolf (2004). Both volumes include studies based on comprehensive corpora, adopting the analytical tools offered by Pierre Bourdieu to inspect the translation flows on the global translation market and the conditions of production and distribution with the aim of analysing the various transfer mechanisms.

In a first step, Heilbron and Sapiro argue that inspecting the practice of translation implies a double rupture: with hermeneutical methods on the one hand – since these neglect the analysis of social conditions in the production process as well as the plurality of the agents involved – and with strictly economically oriented views of international transactions on the other. Sociological approaches, in contrast, can shed light on the logics which determine the circulation of symbolic goods. One such logic operates within the political relationships between the countries involved, another within the international book market, and yet another within the domains of cultural exchange. The conceptualization of this international space of translation exchange, along with the discussion of its various constituents, is understood as the basis of the volume's articles. These discuss transfers between various geographical spaces, both in the nineteenth century and in a contemporary context. Two shortcomings might diminish the informative value of the volume: first, the failure to acknowledge translation studies as an autonomous discipline,[13] which might explain the hesitant inclusion of translation studies approaches in the various papers, and second, the concentration on translation phenomena on an extra-textual level without taking into consideration text structures or translation strategies. In fact Bourdieu himself stressed the necessity of combining these two levels, a methodological move which enables a comprehensive explanation of the functional logics in the field (Bourdieu 1999: 326).[14]

---

13. It is seen as a "research domain in search of academic legitimacy" (Heilbron and Sapiro 2002: 4).

14. The works by Johan Heilbron cannot be discussed in detail here. He elucidates the international flow of translation between "centre" and "periphery" focusing on translations to and

The editors of the second volume (Bachleitner and Wolf 2004) could also be reproached for their lack of integration between textual and extra-textual analyses. In their introduction they assert, however, that their intention to elaborate the first stage of a programme for the development of a "sociology of literary translation" deliberately does not include text-level analyses. A sociological theory of translation is seen as an essential device for the international transfer of knowledge. The conceptualization of a translation market that is hierarchically structured according to the weight of the various languages, a view substantiated by data on translated works in the international market, is complemented by illustrations of the forces operating on this market and contributing to the promotion, prevention and manipulation of translations. In the "field", for instance, centres generated by power relations are created around agents who dispose of massive capitals. Not only do these centres have ideological and aesthetic interests, but they also engage in the struggle for acceptance of translation products, for example if translators attempt to anticipate the ideas of critics and the reading public, or if they change their publishing house for a new book in order to increase their economic and symbolic capital. The contributions in this special issue focus on the study of these questions in the literary translation domain in the German-speaking countries.

Sociological contributions to a sociology of translation

This section will look into those theoretical and methodological approaches coming from the discipline of sociology which in the last few years have been progressively adopted by translation studies scholars for the discussion of translation and interpreting as a social practice. The sociologists whose work could form the basis of a theoretical framework for a sociology of translation are Pierre Bourdieu, Bernard Lahire, Bruno Latour and Niklas Luhmann.

Jean-Marc Gouanvic points out that Pierre Bourdieu's theory of cultural action can be widely applied to translation studies, as it is a "sociology of the text as a production in the process of being carried out, of the product itself and of its consumption in the social fields, the whole seen in a relational manner" (Gouanvic 2005: 148). I have already discussed several works which employ Bourdieu's

---

from Dutch and views these translation flows as part of an ample globalisation process. With a critical eye on Even-Zohar's *polysystem theory*, he stresses that target cultures have to be considered as part of a global constellation of national and supranational cultures. As a result, "a more complete sociological analysis may therefore seek to connect the dynamics of the international translation system with the actual working of the book market and its various segments" (Heilbron 1999: 441).

key concepts to conduct specific translation analyses; this section deals with the explicit efforts by translation studies scholars to include Bourdieu's theory of cultural production in their elaboration of a sociology of translation.

One of the first scholars who attempted to highlight Bourdieu's importance for the study of translation was Jean-Marc Gouanvic. He claims that Bourdieu does not include translations in his field theory because "far from constituting a field of their own, translated texts are submitted to the same objective logic as the indigenous texts of the target space" (Gouanvic 2002: 160). This homology[15] is also apparent between the position of the translating agent within a field and his or her concrete way of translating (ibid.: 162), both being equally subject to the power play of the field. In his various studies, Gouanvic gives a detailed account of the factors and agents responsible for the production of translation in specific institutions (critics, translators, publishing houses, etc.) and comes to the conclusion that the stakes of translation are strongly legitimised practices, endowed with power on the basis of which the terms of translation operating between the various social spaces are continually renegotiated (ibid.: 167; Gouanvic 1997: 146). Gouanvic stresses that there is an aesthetic pleasure in playing this game, which Bourdieu calls *illusio*. *Illusio* is viewed as the object of the translator's work. During the translation process, a (literary) text reinvents the rules of the literary genre to which it belongs, and subsequently is reinterpreted, according to its own logic, by the agents involved (Gouanvic 2005: 163). Gouanvic claims that adept readers adhere to the idea of *illusio* and the specific stakes in the field by internalising them for the duration of the reading (ibid.: 164). He stresses that the principle of *illusio* is primarily actualised through the agents' *habitus*, another Bourdieusian concept already mentioned. During the translation procedure, the act of translating is incorporated through, and at the same time influenced by, the translator's *habitus*, which can be identified by reconstructing the translator's social trajectory. In his contribution to the present volume, Gouanvic distinguishes between the translator's *habitus* as a result of his or her practice, and a specific *habitus* which is constructed while the cultures involved encounter one another during the transfer process (Gouanvic, in this volume). Consequently, translation strategies, according to Gouanvic, are generally not to be understood as deliberate choices conforming to or breaking norms, but rather as the translator's *habitus*, which, together with that of other agents, structures the respective field and, in turn, is structured by the field itself (Gouanvic 2005: 157–158).

In his regularly quoted article "The Pivotal Status of the Translator's Habitus" (1998) Daniel Simeoni gives the notion of *habitus* another role. Simeoni claims

---

15. For the discussion of this homology as illustrated by Gouanvic, see Wolf's contribution in this volume.

that over the centuries the translatorial *habitus* has contributed to the internalisation of a submissive behaviour, thus generating low social prestige for translators. As a result of the continuous, historically conditioned acceptance of norms by translators, Simeoni argues, the translators' willingness to accept these norms has significantly contributed to the secondariness of their activity (ibid.: 6). He stresses the key role of this internalized position in the "field of translation". Simeoni tries to integrate the category of the translatorial *habitus* into systemic translation models, not least by reframing Toury's concept of norms "on the assumption of a translating *habitus* understood as: (culturally) pre-structured and structuring agents mediating cultural artefacts in the course of transfer" (ibid.: 1). Ultimately, a *habitus*-led consideration of translation practices would encourage more finely-grained analyses of the "socio-cognitive emergence of translating skills and their outcome".

The question of the translator's alleged subservience is also discussed by Moira Inghilleri. On the basis of Bourdieu's concepts of field and *habitus*, as well as Basil Bernstein's theory of pedagogic discourse, Inghilleri elaborates a theoretical framework for the analysis of community interpreting as a norm-driven activity (Inghilleri 2003). With this framework Inghilleri proposes not only to reveal the constructivist nature of norms, but also to analyse the principles which generate the practice of public service interpreting in its various contexts. She pays special attention to reconstructing the interpreters' *habitus*, which Inghilleri is not willing to locate within the subordination of the translators' and interpreters' activity under norm systems. She points instead to the interplay of the distinctive, conflictual and contradictory *habitus* of the agents participating in the process of community interpreting, which eventually make up the dynamics of the interpreting situation and have the potential to change existing social relationships and social practices. In another paper, Inghilleri further explores the interpreting *habitus*. She first investigates the phenomenon of interpreting in the political asylum application procedure adopting ethnographic questions which address the "representation of the other"[16] in interpreting. She then stresses Bourdieu's idea of the "zones of uncertainty in social space" where problematic gaps are opened up between individual expectation and actual experience (Inghilleri 2005a: 70). The discordance evident within these zones, however, creates the potential for agents to redefine their role, thus enabling a change "from within". This also entails a change of the interpreting *habitus*, generating new forms of interpreting practices. In her introduction to the special issue of *The Translator* "Bourdieu and the Sociology of Translation and Interpreting", Inghilleri discusses the ethnographic

---

16. For the relationship between "representation techniques" in translation and ethnographic methodologies, see also Agorni, in this volume.

dimension in translation and the relationship between Bourdieu's reflexive sociology and ethnographic approaches relevant for the practice of translation; she is particularly interested in Clifford Geertz's work on interpretive anthropology. Inghilleri argues that the major insights to be gained from Bourdieu's cultural sociology for the study of translation can be found in his theorisation of "the social". This suggests that the acts of translating and interpreting should be understood through the social practices in the fields where they are generated. Of particular relevance are the translators and interpreters as agents who are involved in the forms of practice in which they operate and yet also capable of transforming these practices through the working of their *habitus* (Inghilleri 2005b: 143).

Another scholar who draws on the *habitus* is Rakefet Sela-Sheffy. She critically takes up Simeoni's arguments on the relatedness of *habitus* and norms, and argues for a re-examination of these two notions, calling attention to the principles of divergence and conformity as constructed entities and their relevance for the practice of translation in the translation field. Sela-Sheffy views this field as a space of stratified positions, regulated by its own internal repertoires and competitions and equipped with an exclusive symbolic capital. The translation field's dynamics can be detected in the "potential for perceiving the tension between the predictability and versatility of translators' preferences and choices, as determined by their group affiliation" (Sela-Sheffy 2005: 19).

The possibility of reconstructing a translation field is viewed rather sceptically by Michaela Wolf. It seems that the fundamental differences between the functional mechanisms operating in the production processes of "originals" and "translations" respectively do not enable the formation of a field in Bourdieu's sense.[17] On the one hand, the agents involved cannot create enduring positions in the "field" due to the temporary character of their contacts so that the transfer conditions necessary for translation production need to be constantly re-constituted. On the other hand, the various instruments for the consecration of translators and their products are much less established than those of "original" writers and their works; this results in a generally lower share of symbolic capital. Consequently, Wolf attempts to broaden Bourdieu's notion of field through Homi Bhabha's theorem of the *Third Space*. This theorem corresponds more closely to the requirements of continuous re-negotiations and accentuates the dynamics

---

17. According to Jean-Marc Gouanvic (in this volume), it seems difficult to conceptualize a "translation field", because translated texts are inscribed by various configurations which make them belong to different specific fields, such as the economic, the judicial, etc.

of the transfer aspect, which are particularly relevant for translation production (Wolf, in this volume).[18]

Pierre Bourdieu's sociology of the production of cultural goods seems particularly fertile for deepening understanding of the social relevance and responsibility of the translation process. For the conceptualization of a sociology of translation, important insights have already been gained from the reflection and adoption of these methodological tools. It now, however, seems time to go beyond a predominantly heuristic employment of Bourdieu's social theory, and to look more closely into the theorising potential of his framework for a more comprehensive understanding of translation. This will involve critical questioning of the limits of his theoretical and analytical work for the development of a sociologically oriented translation studies.

One of Bourdieu's major critics in France is Bernard Lahire. In the introductory article of his seminal volume *Le travail sociologique de Pierre Bourdieu* (2001), Lahire asserts that respectful use of a work and its author resides in a methodical discussion and evaluation, and not in an endless repetition of his concepts and prefabricated arguments (ibid.: 18). Lahire invites a number of scholars from various disciplines to critically re-discuss Bourdieu's work by entering into a constructive dialogue with the sociologist. In his most recent book, *La culture des individus* (Lahire 2004), the author takes up his own invitation to re-read Bourdieu and, on the basis of more than one hundred interviews presented in the form of portraits, scrutinizes several of Bourdieu's concepts, among them the *habitus*. For Lahire, the individual is not trapped in the tight web of the *habitus*, as Bourdieu suggests, but determined by multiple social experiences which influence him or her during a whole lifetime.[19] He particularly criticizes the universalist stance of the notion and claims that individuals can draw on a vast array of dispositions which allow for a more differentiated view of their socialisation. Consequently, when Lahire argues for a sociology "at the level of the individual" (Lahire 2003), he is seeking to foreground the plurality of the individual's dispositions – for example, dispositions vary in stability and strength (ibid.: 339) – and the multiplicity of different situations in which the agents interact. The focus on the diverse modalities which prompt the *habitus* could provide a better route to explain the conditions underlying translation strategies, and reconstruct the unconscious and conscious motives which trigger specific translation situations. Lahire's assertion that "dispositions

---

18. For the problematic reconstruction of a "translation field" see also Wolf (2005a); in Wolf (2005b) these observations are demonstrated by using the functioning of translation processes in the domain of production and reception in the late Habsburg Empire.

19. There has not yet been any discussion of the distinction made by Lahire concerning Bourdieu's notion of *habitus* and its validity in the translation procedure.

become active *under specific conditions* only" (ibid.: 342, original emphasis), can help reveal the manifold character of the discursive practices operating in translation, both on the level of the adoption of specific translation methods in time and space based on "tradition", and on the level of the constraints which – sometimes temporarily – effect the translator's decisions. Despite its high degree of dynamism, however, it seems clear that Lahire's "sociology of dispositions" puts too much emphasis on the individual's subjectivity.[20] Applied to translation studies contexts, this theory neglects the powerful circumstances in which agents interact among one another, shaping, in our case, the emerging translation product.

Social studies as developed in France seem to be particularly pertinent when reflecting upon translation as a social practice. Another theorist who has recently been mentioned by several scholars in light of his applicability to translation studies is Bruno Latour. His Actor-Network Theory (ANT), an interdisciplinary approach to the social sciences and technology studies, describes the progressive constitution of a network of both human and non-human "actants" whose identities and qualities are defined according to prevailing strategies of interaction. Constantly redefining each other, actor and network are mutually constitutive and are not to be equated with individual and society, but should be considered as two faces of the same phenomenon. One of the main elements in the formation of an actor-network is "translation", a process in which actors construct common meanings and need continuous negotiation to achieve individual and collective objectives by means of the driving force of "interessement" (Bardini 2003). New networks emerge out of already existing ones, and their dynamics are revealed as "negotiation",[21] which works to counteract what Latour, referring to the size of networks, calls the "tyranny of distance" and has the potential to change the network's structure. The "two extremes, local and global, are much less interesting than the intermediary arrangements that we are calling networks" (Stalder 1997).

---

20. Regarding the over-estimation of the individual, Lahire argues that today's societies are strongly characterized by individualisation, and that therefore a sociology needs to reflect on "what is social in a [given] society" (Lahire 2003: 352).

21. The notion of "negotiation" has been conceptualized by Homi Bhabha within the framework of his hybridity theory (Bhabha 1994). To my knowledge, the interface of the notion used respectively by the two scholars has not yet been discussed. Such an interface could prove particularly informative in the perspective of its value for the translation process.
"Negotiation" is also highlighted by Lieven Tack in his attempt to conceptualize the distinctions and borders in gender relations, generation ties, oppositional social classes, competing professional groupings, etc., by which translation is fundamentally structured (Tack 2000).

The common goal of the "actants" who make up the network might, for instance, be the development of a (cultural) product, such as a translation in the traditional sense of the word. When Latour describes the nature of the actants, it becomes clear that the individual is no longer at the centre of this theoretical conception:

> The distinction between humans and non-humans, embodied or disembodied skills, impersonation or "machination", are less interesting than the complete chain along which competences and actions are distributed.
>
> (Latour and Cussins 1992: 243)

Instead, the accent is on a process-oriented research, as underlined recently by Hélène Buzelin (2005). According to Buzelin, such studies of translation "in the making" (see Buzelin, in this volume), could usefully generate data that tends to be hidden when the translation process is examined retrospectively. This can disclose the various stages of translation production, for instance the specific consultations or debates between the agents involved, the respective strategies of persuasion and dissuasion, and so on. The potential of such an approach using ethnological methodology is obvious: it brings to the fore those moments of the translation's "genesis" that document "from within" the selection and promotion of a foreign text as well as the translation and editing procedures.

Quite different perspectives on translation within a societal context than those discussed so far are introduced with Niklas Luhmann's social theory. Theo Hermans states that in light of Luhmann's theory, translation can be conceptualized as an autonomous and heteronomous category; he draws attention to those theorems which improve awareness of the internal organisation and development of the social and intellectual space of translation (Hermans 1999: 138).[22] Luhmann conceives of social organisation as self-producing, self-regulating systems, which operate according to functional differentiation. Literature, in such a perspective, is constituted by polycontextural systems which permanently re-produce the elements they consist of. These elements are understood as communicative acts whose "sense" is made up of the "code" of communication (Luhmann 1987: 197) and the criteria of selection. This also applies to translation: its "sense" is based on the principle of selectivity and its circumstances, as well as on the "translational mode" selected for a specific translation situation (Hermans 1997: 12). Another important aspect of Luhmann's social theory with some relevance for a socially driven understanding of translation is the complex of "expectations". Luhmann describes social structures as "structures of expectation" (Luhmann 1987: 362–

---

22. See also Hermans' contribution in this volume, where he takes up the issue of Luhmann's relevance for the understanding of translation as a social system.

364), and such expectations are fundamental to the structure of the "translation system". As, according to Luhmann, the various formations of expectations and "expectations of expectations" are permanently re-negotiated (ibid.: 364), translation can be seen as located within such a set of expectations which try to re-define themselves through continuous "translatorial" discourses: conversations in everyday life, in the scientific community, in translators' training institutions, or in critiques and paratexts. By taking into consideration the category of continually operating expectations in the "translation system", a Luhmannian approach to an emerging sociology of translation can thus disclose the dynamics of the changes experienced by a given translation phenomenon in its initiating stage and in its context of reception.[23]

The construction of a "sociology of translation studies"

A type of "sociology" that has recently been taking shape, and that is particularly present in various contributions of this volume, is the "sociology of translation studies". To start in more general terms it is paramount to mention that in the sociology of science, science is conceived of as a social system which, in respecting its own rules and norms, regulates the activities of the individual; simultaneously, scientific reflection operating "from within" determines social structures (Knoblauch 2005: 237). Claiming to unveil the relationship of science to society, the sociology of science distinguishes between "institutional" aspects that include the cluster of interactions stemming from the embeddedness of science in economic, political, ideological or religious configurations and from "historical" aspects. This historical perspective follows Thomas Kuhn's *The Structure of Scientific Revolutions* (1962) in addressing the progressive expansion of certain scientific branches; it leads to a history of science which proceeds in various phases of

---

23. Luhmann's key concept "system", is also central to Anthony Giddens's social theory, though from a different perspective. With the exception of Venuti's brief remarks on Giddens's concept of agency (see Venuti 1996: 210), his sociology has so far not been explored in translation studies. Giddens's structuration theory (Giddens 1979: 59–60) – especially its claim to transcend dualisms which essentialize cultural practices – could foreground the mechanisms underlying the relatedness between the translator's individual decisions and the constraints conditioning them. For the purpose of conceptualizing the translation activity within a sociological framework, Giddens's view of how human action is generated not only could help us understand the principles that drive translational behaviour in specific contexts and induce the translator to adopt certain translation strategies over others, but also indicates the historical, political or ideological patterns which condition or restrain the translation activity over long periods of time, forming the groundwork of "translation norms".

development, each representing a particular "paradigm".[24] Emphasising the role played by social factors in scientific development has thus accentuated both the close relationship of science with society and the history of scientific disciplines.

In translation studies, recent works have asserted the necessity of reflecting on the discipline's mapping from a historical and institutional perspective. They discuss both the emergence of various sub-fields and their position in the scientific community, foregrounding the social conditions that underlie the relation of translation studies to other disciplines. These explorations have extended into a further reflection on translation studies as an area of research, beginning to analyse the paradigms that have determined the discipline's paths since its establishment (see, e.g., Snell-Hornby 2006 and Bachmann-Medick 2006). Recently, Daniel Simeoni (2005) has discussed the reasons for the delay in dealing with socially inspired questions of translation. His sketch of the discipline's multifaceted history calls for the investigation of socially relevant factors conditioning the discipline's constitution over the decades. In his contribution to this volume, Simeoni takes up that thread. He distinguishes between the various traditions underlying the discipline's formation in Europe, in North America, and in other areas where "world Englishes prevail", and stresses that the institutional map being reconstructed does not coincide with the complex positions of scholars active in these institutions. He tries to avoid essentialism by questioning the way that differences among scholars have been classified in terms of aggregates and by adopting a comparative analysis in the hope of achieving "a kind of *Homo academicus* of translation studies" (Simeoni, in this volume). In order to re-enact the intellectual processes conditioning the establishment of translation studies, he proposes to think in terms of "scholarly localisms", a notion which unveils the decentredness and multiplicity of the factors shaping a scientific community and its objects of investigation.

The conceptualization of a "field of translation studies" has been pivotal to Jean-Marc Gouanvic's research interests. Drawing on Bourdieu's methodology, Gouanvic suggests that the constitution of a specific field of translation studies with its own structures, rules and stakes is only feasible through the work of those agents who have a symbolic or material interest in positioning themselves in this field, investing their "*libido sciendi*", their *habitus* and their scientific *illusio*. For Gouanvic, conceptualizing a sociology of translation will require reinforcement of the field's legitimation, by continuing to promote the institutionalising processes that enable the discipline to gain an autonomous status in Bourdieu's sense. The

---

24. In the last few decades, Kuhn's model of historical paradigms was severely criticized (see, e.g., Hess 1997), particularly its presumption of a closed view of scientific community as well as its lack to take into account the processual character of any type of development.

foundation and consolidation of translation studies programmes, the formation of scholarly associations, journals and book series, and the organisation of international conferences and workshops create the premises for questioning and, at the same time, directing the discourse on translation that dominates the scientific community (Gouanvic, in this volume, and 1999:146).

Similarly, Yves Gambier is concerned with questions regarding the institutionalisation of translation studies. He analyses the sociological dynamics contributing to the constitution and practice of the discipline and particularly deplores the lack of a historiography of translation studies that would take account of the scholars' representation in the field and investigate the archaeology of the discourses which have made up the discipline during its constitution process (Gambier, in this volume).

To sum up, it seems that the self-reflexive inspection of the social moves moulding the history of science has also been taking ground in translation studies, thus contributing not only to the shape of the discipline and of its objects "from within", but also of the discourses on the field. One must therefore agree with Raymond Aron when he says that "science is inseparable from the republic of scholars".

The show goes on

The various thoughts, approaches and elements of theoretical groundwork presented in this introduction are both divergent and competing. However, they all, from varying perspectives and with different methods, aim to foreground the relevance of translation as social practice functioning in a social field or social system, and constituting an operative force within it. Embracing methodologies from sociology and integrating them into our discipline does, of course, question some of the established categories of translation studies, and calls for a thorough re-definition and re-constitution of long-assumed principles and values inscribed in these conceptions. The text-bound paradigm which began to be transcended in the approaches that followed the "cultural turn" seems, in the course of an evolving sociology of translation, to have slipped out of sight of the translation researcher, bringing about the danger of a sociology of translation existing without translation.[25] The complexity of the societal "realities" of the practice of translation and its implications for translational decisions mean we must address macro clusters, such as the politics of media concerns, the publishing industry, or insti-

---

25. For this discussion see also Buzelin, in this volume.

tutional principles of the translation profession, which cannot be dismissed as single phenomena specific to individual transfer situations. A systematic identification of the problems that condition and influence the selection, production and reception of translation seems to be underway – involving both questions about the integration of translational action with all its agencies into the broad societal context and questions that, in a narrower sense, concern the functional mechanisms of translation markets or the socially relevant character of translation strategies. However, the impact of this on concrete translation practice should not be ignored. It is also vital to discuss the interactional relations that exist between the external conditions of a text's creation and the adoption of the various translation strategies, not least so that we can challenge those approaches claiming to hold a monopoly on text comprehension and those sustaining a sociologistic reduction to external factors.

The papers included in this volume reveal the potential for responding to some of the questions illustrated above. Several of these papers were read and discussed at the conference *Translating and Interpreting as a Social Practice*, held at the University of Graz in May 2005. They show that to further develop and refine the outlined approaches, several directions seem appropriate.

The first section, *The Debate on the Translator's Position in an Emerging Sociology of Translation*, is opened by **Erich Prunč**. At the centre of his article "Priests, Princes and Pariahs. Constructing the Professional Field of Translation" is the figure of the translator in the course of history to the present day. He retraces in great detail the importance that has been attributed to the translator in translation theory and practice. Prunč analyses the historical, social and cultural reasons underlying the image of the translator either as a "genius" or as a self-sacrificing, anonymous figure. Additionally focusing on the translator's image as created in numerous works in translation studies, the author shows the researchers' responsibility for creating and perpetuating these misleading, but nevertheless enduring conceptions.

In his contribution "Translation, Irritation and Resonance", **Theo Hermans** "abolishes" the figure of the translator. Hermans brings the text as translation product back to the core of the debate and thoroughly discusses the role of translation within society, drawing both on recent research in translation studies and on the works of Niklas Luhmann. According to Hermans, the view of translation as a social system in Luhmann's sense – a system seen as both autonomous and heteronomous – seems to offer fertile ground for further methodological developments in translation studies and therefore needs more attention in current research. Hermans insists in particular upon the importance of what Luhmann calls "second-order observation", which reveals the way in which the observer observes: in the translation context, translators engage in this sort of observation when they comment upon other translations through the form of their own translations.

With his paper "Objectivation, réflexivité et traduction. Pour une re-lecture bourdieusienne de la traduction" **Jean-Marc Gouanvic** opens the second section, *Bourdieu's Influence in Conceptualising a Sociology of Translation*. According to Gouanvic, one of the central questions in the analysis of translation as social practice is "quelles sont les conditions d'une réflexion sur la traduction en tant que pratique sociale". By linking up this question with Bourdieu's concept of "double reflexivity" – which, for Gouanvic, should be a *conditio sine qua non* for all researchers in translation studies – and by also integrating the notion of *illusio* in his reflections, Gouanvic considerably enlarges the field of Bourdieu-based translation research.

The main categories of Pierre Bourdieu's field theory are also the basis of the article by **Johan Heilbron** and **Gisèle Sapiro**, "Outline for a Sociology of Translation. Current Issues and Future Prospects". They discuss the contribution of the discipline of sociology to social questions in translation studies, and claim to provide a systematic overview and a programmatic discussion of recent Bourdieu-inspired sociological contributions to the discipline of translation studies. Against the background of the social practice of literary translation, the authors give insights into the power relations between language groups and the international hierarchy of languages, adopting, among other ideas, Pascale Casanova's concept of "literary capital". They deliver specific parameters allowing for the detailed analysis of the field of reception and take particular account of the various agents and institutions which shape this field.

With her paper "The Location of the 'Translation Field'. Negotiating Borderlines between Pierre Bourdieu and Homi Bhabha", **Michaela Wolf** meets a need which has recently been felt in sociologically oriented research in translation studies. Although insisting upon the outstanding relevance and importance of Bourdieu's work for an emerging sociology of translation, she draws attention to some of the major weaknesses which appear in the application of his concepts to translation as a social practice, especially with regard to the specific characteristics of translation. She argues that Homi Bhabha's notion of *Third Space* might be one of the elements which allow for better analysis, particularly of the processual character of translation, whatever its stakes and functioning might be in a given society and culture at a certain time.

The section *Mapping the Field: Issues of Method and Translation Practice* begins with **Mirella Agorni**'s paper "Locating Systems and Individuals in Translation Studies". Agorni points out an important direction for further research in sociologically oriented translation studies. Her major tool is localism, a concept that, in her words, mediates "between systems and individuals", which are no longer considered as two opposing poles. An approach to translation research based on the notion of localism yields a view of translation in its specific environment, accentuating its connections with other translation or translation-like phenomena. Such a view not only makes judgments like "correct" or "faulty" translation practice superfluous, but also, on a methodological level, breaks up dichotomies like descriptive versus explanatory or quantitative versus qualitative approaches.

Hélène Buzelin's contribution "Translations 'in the Making'" is mainly inspired by the Actor-Network Theory developed by the French philosopher and anthropologist Bruno Latour. Arguing for a process-oriented view of translation, Buzelin claims that this would highlight the numerous stages of the translation process, including documents of correspondence between the various agents involved and also oral negotiation. In her paper, she demonstrates this approach by sketching out an ongoing project which retraces some literary translation projects 'in the making', launched by publishing houses in Paris and Montréal. Methodologically, Buzelin's combination of Latour's Actor-Network Theory and various ethnographic methods allows her to follow each step in the translation process very closely.

In view of the multiple approaches to the conceptualization of a sociology of translation, the need for "bridge concepts" to link them up is urgently felt. **Andrew Chesterman** ("Bridge Concepts in Translation Sociology") identifies this need on a more general level as well, where the discipline of translation studies has passed through a series of paradigms – linguistic, cultural, cognitive and, more recently, social. The author focuses on notions like *habitus*, translation practice and causality, and discusses Edward O. Wilson's term "conscilience", used in the sense of the unity of all knowledge. This issue seems to be of particular relevance for translation studies which is still struggling to find a way to better analyse the relations between texts, languages, cultures, societies and individuals.

In the concluding section *Constructing a Sociology of Translation Studies: Overview and Perspectives*, the two contributions focus on a sociologically oriented meta-discussion of translation studies. **Daniel Simeoni** ("Between Sociology and History. Method in Context and in Practice") reflects upon methods in translation studies in the light of some precedents in the social and human sciences, particularly sociology and history. Linking up the developments of history and sociology with the respective evolutions within translation studies, he adds to our understanding of questions such as why it took so long to pay attention to the "social" in translation. With regard to the discussion of the first translation of Shakespeare's *Julius Caesar* into Italian (1756) by Domenico Valentini, Simeoni advocates a view of translation which no longer prioritizes the macro-contextual impact in the adoption of norms (institutions, ideology, patronage), but instead a micro-contextual level, where agents act through their socialisation and their *habitus*.

The volume is concluded by **Yves Gambier**'s programmatic question "Y a-t-il place pour une socio-traductologie?". With regard to his aim of sketching the prerequisites for the development of what he calls "socio-translation studies", understood as a kind of sociology of translation studies, the author identifies the lack not only of a detailed historiography of translation studies, but also of a kind of self-analysis of translation researchers, an issue already stressed by Jean-Marc Gouanvic. Structuring his paper as a series of questions, Gambier suggests future domains of research and particularly highlights the need to thoroughly explore the institutions as well as the various kinds of publications which have allowed for the modelling of the discipline of translation studies.

The majority of the contributions included in this volume adopt the notion of "sociology of translation". Most papers conceive of this notion as an umbrella term for the issues that arise when viewing translation as a social practice and as symbolically transferred interaction. A "social perspective" on translation concepts in general, and on the translation process in particular, is reflected in the term "socio-translation studies" proposed by Daniel Simeoni. He sheds light on the background of sociological orientations in translation studies by comparing the evolution of history and sociology with that of recent translation studies. Yves Gambier, on the other hand, introduces the term "socio-traductologie", which indicates a sociologically driven reflection on the historical development of translation studies and an analysis of the discipline's field. As can be seen, the terminology is quite inconsistent, and, accordingly, the research area itself happens to be still "in the making". It seems likely that only further insights into the socially conditioned workings of translation and translation studies will be able to specify both the terminology and the research area of a "sociology of translation" and a "sociology of translation studies".

In a broader context, the sociology of translation may well become "a new branch of the sociology of culture and a promising domain for the study of the cultural world-system" (Heilbron 1999: 440). However, the social constraints and dynamics which are inscribed in the materiality of the translated text and in its discursive strategies mean that in order to examine Heilbron's claims, we need, first and foremost, to refine our methodologies. Looking at the questions raised and discussed in this volume not only reveals translation's processual character, but also allows us to conceptualize the agencies and agents involved in an open system that depends on the negotiation of symbolic forms in a world of global societal changes. This book aims to show that even if the domain of "translation as a social practice" is still under construction, its outlines are most certainly beginning to come into view.

References

Álvarez, Román and Vidal, M. Carmen-África (eds). 1996. *Translation, Power, Subversion*. Clevedon and Philadelphia etc.: Multilingual Matters.
Arrojo, Rosemary. 1997. "Die Endfassung der Übersetzung und die Sichtbarkeit des Übersetzers". Trans. Helga Ahrens. In *Übersetzungswissenschaft in Brasilien. Beiträge zum Status von „Original" und Übersetzung*, M. Wolf (ed). Tübingen: Stauffenburg. 117–132.
Bachleitner, Norbert and Wolf, Michaela (eds). 2004. *Internationales Archiv für Sozialgeschichte der deutschen Literatur* 29 (2). Special Issue "Soziologie der literarischen Übersetzung".
Bachmann-Medick, Doris. 2004. "Übersetzung als Medium interkultureller Kommunikation und Auseinandersetzung". In *Handbuch der Kulturwissenschaften. Band 2. Paradigmen und Disziplinen*, F. Jaeger, B. Liebsch, J. Rüsen and J. Straub (eds). Stuttgart and Weimar: Metzler. 449–465.
Bachmann-Medick, Doris. 2006. *Cultural Turns. Neuorientierungen in den Kulturwissenschaften*. Reinbek bei Hamburg: Rowohlt.
Bahrdt, Hans Paul. ⁸2000. *Schlüsselbegriffe der Soziologie*. München: Beck.
Bardini, Thierry. 2003. "What is Actor-Network Theory?". M. Ryder (ed). http://carbon.cudenver.edu/~mryder/itc_data/ant_dff.html. Visited May 2007.
Barret-Ducrocq, Françoise (ed). 1992. *Traduire l'Europe*. Paris: Payot.
Barthes, Roland. 1984. *Le bruissement de la langue*. Paris: Seuil.
Bassnett, Susan and Lefevere, André. 1990. "Introduction: Proust's Grandmother and the Thousand and One Nights: The 'Cultural Turn' in Translation Studies". In *Translation, History and Culture*, S. Bassnett and A. Lefevere (eds). London and New York: Pinter. 1–13.
Berg, Eberhard and Fuchs, Martin (eds). 1993. *Kultur, soziale Praxis, Text. Die Krise der ethnographischen Repräsentation*. Frankfurt am Main: Suhrkamp.
Bhabha, Homi K. 1994. *The Location of Culture*. London and New York: Routledge.
Bourdieu, Pierre. 1999. *Die Regeln der Kunst. Genese und Struktur des literarischen Feldes*. Trans. Bernd Schwibs and Achim Russer. Frankfurt am Main: Suhrkamp.
Bourdieu, Pierre. 2004. *Schwierige Interdisziplinarität. Zum Verhältnis von Soziologie und Geschichtswissenschaft*. E. Ohnacker and F. Schultheis (eds). Münster: Westfälisches Dampfboot.
Brisset, Annie. 1990. *Sociocritique de la traduction: théâtre et altérité au Québec (1968–1988)*. Montréal: Les Éditions du Préambule.
Brisset, Annie. 1996. *A Sociocritique of Translation: Theatre and Alterity in Quebec, 1968–1988*. Trans. Rosalind Gill and Roger Gannon. Toronto and Buffalo etc.: University of Toronto Press.
Buzelin, Hélène. 2005. "Unexpected Allies: How Latour's Network Theory Could Complement Bourdieusian Analyses in Translation Studies". *The Translator* 11 (2): 193–218.
Chartier, Roger. 1992. *Die unvollendete Vergangenheit. Geschichte und die Macht der Weltauslegung*. Frankfurt am Main: Fischer.
Delisle, Jean (ed). 1999. *Portraits de traducuers*. Ottawa: Les Presses de l'Université d'Ottawa.
Delisle, Jean (ed). 2002. *Portraits de traductrices*. Ottawa: Les Presses de l'Université d'Ottawa.
Delisle, Jean and Woodsworth, Judith (eds). 1995. *Translators through History*. Amsterdam and Philadelphia: John Benjamins.
Even-Zohar, Itamar. 1990. *Poetics Today* 11 (1). Special Issue "Polysystem Studies".
Fawcett, Peter. 1995. "Translation and Power Play". *The Translator* 1 (2): 177–192.

Fuchs, Martin. 1997. "Übersetzen und Übersetzt-Werden: Plädoyer für eine interaktionsanaly-tische Reflexion". In *Übersetzung als Repräsentation fremder Kulturen*, D. Bachmann-Medick (ed). Berlin: Schmidt. 308–328.

Gebhardt, Winfried. 2001. "Vielfältiges Bemühen. Zum Stand kultursoziologischer Forschung im deutschsprachigen Raum". http://www.uni-koblenz.de/~instso/kuso-dgs/debatte/gebhardt. htm. Visited May 2007.

Geertz, Clifford. 1993. *The Interpretation of Cultures. Selected Essays*. Hammersmith and London: FontanaPress.

Gentzler, Edwin. 1993. *Contemporary Translation Theories*. London and New York: Routledge.

Gentzler, Edwin and Tymoczko, Maria. 2002. "Introduction". In *Translation and Power*, M. Tymoczko and E. Gentzler (eds). Amherst and Boston: University of Massachusetts Press. XI–XXVIII.

Giddens, Anthony. 1979. *Central Problems in Social Theory. Action, Structure and Contradiction in Social Analysis*. London: Macmillan.

Gouanvic, Jean-Marc. 1997. "Translation and the Shape of Things to Come. The Emergence of American Science Fiction in Post-War France". *The Translator* 3 (2): 125–152.

Gouanvic, Jean-Marc. 1999. *Sociologie de la traduction. La science-fiction américaine dans l'espace culturel français des années 1950*. Arras: Artois Presses Université.

Gouanvic, Jean-Marc. 2002. "The Stakes of Translation in Literary Fields". *Across Languages and Cultures* 3 (2): 159–168.

Gouanvic, Jean-Marc. 2005. "A Bourdieusian Theory of Translation, or the Coincidence of Practical Instances: Field, 'Habitus', Capital and 'Illusio'". *The Translator* 11 (2): 147–166.

Grbić, Nadja and Wolf, Michaela (eds). 2002. *Grenzgängerinnen. Zur Geschlechterdifferenz in der Übersetzung*. Graz: Institut für Translationswissenschaft.

Heilbron, Johan. 1999. "Towards a Sociology of Translation. Book Translations as a Cultural World-System". *European Journal of Social Theory* 2 (4): 429–444.

Heilbron, Johan and Sapiro, Gisèle (eds). 2002. *Actes de la recherche en sciences sociales* 144. "Les échanges littéraires internationaux".

Hermans, Theo. 1996. "Norms and the Determination of Translation: A Theoretical Framework". In *Translation, Power, Subversion*, R. Álvarez and M. C.-Á. Vidal (eds). Clevedon and Philadelphia etc.: Multilingual Matters. 25–51.

Hermans, Theo. 1997. "Translation as institution". In *Translation as Intercultural Communication. Selected Papers from the EST Congress Prague 1995*, M. Snell-Hornby, Z. Jettmarová and K. Kaindl (eds). Amsterdam and Philadelphia: John Benjamins. 3–20.

Hermans, Theo. 1999. *Translation in Systems. Descriptive and System-oriented Approaches Explained*. Manchester: St Jerome Publishing.

Hess, David J. 1997. *Science Studies. An Advanced Introduction*. New York: New York University Press.

Hönig, Hans. 1992. "Von der erzwungenen Selbstentfremdung des Übersetzers – Ein offener Brief an Justa Holz-Mänttäri". *TextConText* 7 (1): 1–14.

Inghilleri, Moira. 2003. "Habitus, field and discourse. Interpreting as a socially situated activity". *Target* 15 (2): 243–268.

Inghilleri, Moira. 2005a. "Mediating Zones of Uncertainty. Interpreter Agency, the Interpreting Habitus and Political Asylum Adjudication". *The Translator* 11 (1): 69–85.

Inghilleri, Moira. 2005b. "The Sociology of Bourdieu and the Construction of the 'Object' in Translation and Interpreting Studies". *The Translator* 11 (2): 125–145.

Kaindl, Klaus. 2004. *Übersetzungswissenschaft im interdisziplinären Dialog. Am Beispiel der Comicübersetzung*. Tübingen: Stauffenburg.

Katschuba, Wolfgang. 1995. "Kulturalismus: Kultur statt Gesellschaft?". *Geschichte und Gesellschaft. Zeitschrift für Historische Sozialwissenschaft* 21 (1): 80–95.

Knoblauch, Hubert. 2005. *Wissenssoziologie*. Konstanz: UVK Verlagsgesellschaft.

Kölner Zeitschrift für Soziologie und Sozialpsychologie. 1979. Special Issue "Kultursoziologie" 31 (3).

Kölner Zeitschrift für Soziologie und Sozialpsychologie. 1986. Special Issue "Kultur und Gesellschaft" 27.

Lahire, Bernard (ed). 2001. *Le travail sociologique de Pierre Bourdieu. Dettes et critiques*. Édition revue et augmentée. Paris: La Découverte.

Lahire, Bernard. 2003. "From the habitus to an individual heritage of dispositions. Towards a sociology at the level of the individual". *Poetics* 31: 329–355.

Lahire, Bernard. 2004. *La culture des individus. Dissonances culturelles et distinction de soi*. Paris: La Découverte.

Latour, Bruno and Cussins, Adrian. 1992. *Registration marks: metaphors for subobjectivity*. London: Pomeroy Purdy Gallery.

Lauber, Cornelia. 1996. *Selbstporträts. Zum soziologischen Profil von Literaturübersetzern aus dem Französischen*. Tübingen: Narr.

Lefevere, André. 1998. "Translation Practice(s) and the Circulation of Cultural Capital: Some Aeneids in English". In *Constructing Cultures. Essays on Literary Translation*, S. Bassnett and A. Lefevere. Clevedon and Philadelphia etc.: Multilingual Matters. 41–56.

Lichtblau, Klaus. 2001. "Soziologie als Kulturwissenschaft? Zur Rolle des Kulturbegriffs in der Selbstreflexion der deutschsprachigen Soziologie (1)". http://www.uni-koblenz.de/~instso/kuso-dgs/debatte/lichtblau.htm. Visited May 2007.

Luhmann, Niklas. 1987. *Soziale Systeme. Grundriß einer allgemeinen Theorie*. Frankfurt am Main: Suhrkamp.

Müller-Vollmer, Kurt. 1998. "Übersetzen – Wohin? Zum Problem der Diskursformierung bei Frau von Staël und im amerikanischen Transzendentalismus". In *Übersetzung als kultureller Prozeß. Rezeption, Projektion und Konstruktion des Fremden*, B. Hammerschmid and H. Krapoth (eds). Berlin: Schmidt. 11–31.

Neidhardt, Friedhelm. 1986. "Kultur und Gesellschaft. Einige Anmerkungen zum Sonderheft". *Kölner Zeitschrift für Soziologie und Sozialpsychologie* 27: 10–18.

Nord, Christiane. 1991. *Text Analysis in Translation. Theory, Methodology, and Didactic Application of a Model for Translation-Oriented Text Analysis*. Amsterdam and Atlanta: Rodopi.

Pym, Anthony. 1998. *Method in Translation History*. Manchester: St Jerome Publishing.

Pym, Anthony. 2006. "On the social and cultural in Translation Studies". In *Sociocultural aspects of translating and interpreting*, A.Pym, M. Shlesinger and Z. Jettmarová (eds). Amsterdam and Philadelphia: John Benjamins. 1–25.

Rehberg, Karl-Siegbert. 1986. "Kultur versus Gesellschaft". *Kölner Zeitschrift für Soziologie und Sozialpsychologie* 27: 92–115.

Robyns, Clem. 1992. "Towards a Sociosemiotics of Translation". *Romanistische Zeitschrift für Literaturgeschichte. Cahiers d'Histoire des Littératures Romanes* 16: 211–226.

Sela-Sheffy, Rakefet. 2005. "How to be a (recognized) translator. Rethinking habitus, norms, and the field of translation". *Target* 17 (1): 1–26.

Sheffy, Rakefet. 1997. "Models and Habituses: Problems in the Idea of Cultural Repertoires". *Canadian Review of Comparative Literature* 24 (1): 35–47.

Silbermann, Alphons and Hänseroth, Albin. 1985. *Der Übersetzer. Eine berufs- und literatur-soziologische Untersuchung.* Wiesbaden: Harrassowitz.

Simeoni, Daniel. 1998. "The Pivotal Status of the Translator's Habitus". *Target* 10 (1): 1–39.

Simeoni, Daniel. 2005. "Translation and Society: The Emergence of a Conceptual Relationship". In *In Translation. Reflections, Refractions, Transformations*, P. St-Pierre and P.C. Kar (eds). Delhi: Pencraft International. 3–14. Also published as: Simeoni, Daniel. 2007. "Translation and Society: The Emergence of a Conceptual Relationship". In *In Translation. Reflections, Refractions, Transformations*, P. St-Pierre and P.C. Kar (eds). Amsterdam and Philadelphia: John Benjamins. 13–26.

Snell-Hornby, Mary. 2006. *The Turns of Translation Studies. New Paradigms or Shifting Viewpoints?* Amsterdam and Philadelphia: John Benjamins.

Stäheli, Urs. 2000. *Poststrukturalistische Soziologien.* Bielefeld: transcript.

Stalder, Felix. 1997. "More on Bruno Latour". http://amsterdam.nettime.org/Lists-Archives/nettime-1-9709/msg00012.html. Visited May 2007.

Tack, Lieven. 2000. "Translation and the Dialectics of Difference and Equivalence: Some Theoretical Propositions for a Redefinition of the Source-target Text Relation". *Meta* XLV (2): 210–227.

Tenbruck, Friedrich H. 1990. "Repräsentative Kultur". In *Sozialstruktur und Kultur*, H. Haferkamp (ed). Frankfurt am Main: Suhrkamp. 20–53.

Toury, Gideon. 1995. *Descriptive Translation Studies and beyond.* Amsterdam and Philadelphia: John Benjamins.

Toury, Gideon. 1999. "A Handful of Paragraphs on 'Translation' and 'Norms'". In *Translation and Norms*, C. Schäffner (ed). Clevedon and Philadelphia etc.: Multilingual Matters. 9–32.

Venuti, Lawrence. 1992. "Introduction". In *Rethinking Translation. Discourse, Subjectivity, Ideology*, L. Venuti (ed). London and New York: Routledge. 1–17.

Venuti, Lawrence. 1995. *The Translator's Invisibility. A history of translation.* London and New York: Routledge.

Venuti, Lawrence. 1996. "Translation as a Social Practice: or, The Violence of Translation". *Translation Perspectives* IX: 195–213.

Venuti, Lawrence. 1998. *The Scandals of Translation. Towards an ethics of difference.* London and New York: Routledge.

Vermeer, Hans J. 1990. *Skopos und Translationsauftrag – Aufsätze.* Frankfurt am Main: IKO Verlag für Interkulturelle Kommunikation.

Wägenbaur, Thomas. 1999. "Beobachter beim Zähneputzen. Niklas Luhmann, Pierre Bourdieu, Anthony Giddens und die Leitdifferenzen ihrer Kulturtheorien". In *Interkulturalität. Zwischen Inszenierung und Archiv*, S. Rieger, S. Schamma, Schahadat and M. Weinberg (eds). Tübingen: Narr. 29–45.

Wolf, Michaela. 1999. "Zum 'sozialen Sinn' in der Translation. Translationssoziologische Implikationen von Pierre Bourdieus Kultursoziologie". *Arcadia* 34 (2): 262–275.

Wolf, Michaela. 2002. "Translation Activity between Culture, Society and the Individual: Towards a Sociology of Translation". In *CTIS Occasional Papers* 2, K. Harvey (ed.). Manchester: UMIST. 33–43.

Wolf, Michaela. 2003. „ÜbersetzerInnen – verfangen im sozialen Netzwerk? Zu gesellschaftlichen Implikationen des Übersetzens". *Studia Germanica Posnaniensia* XXIX: 105–119.

Wolf, Michaela. 2005a. "'Der Kritiker muß ein Verwandlungsmensch sein, ein ... Schlangenmensch des Geistes'. Ein Beitrag zur Dynamisierung der Feldtheorie von Pierre Bourdieu am Beispiel von Hermann Bahr". In *Entgrenzte Räume. Kulturelle Transfers um 1900 und in der Gegenwart*, H. Mitterbauer and K. Scherke (eds). Wien: Passagen. 157–171.

Wolf, Michaela. 2005b. *Die vielsprachige Seele Kakaniens. Translation als soziale und kulturelle Praxis in der Habsburgermonarchie 1848 bis 1918*. Graz: Habilitationsschrift.

Wolf, Michaela. 2006. "The female state of the art: Women in the 'translation field'". In *Sociocultural aspects of translating and interpreting*, A. Pym, M. Shlesinger and Z. Jettmarová (eds). Amsterdam and Philadelphia: John Benjamins. 129–141.

PART I

The debate on the translator's position in an emerging sociology of translation

Priests, princes and pariahs*

Constructing the professional field of translation

Erich Prunč
University of Graz, Austria

In translation, the power to control texts and to attribute meaning to them is either decreed in an authoritarian manner or agreed upon democratically. This depends upon the hierarchical structure of the society, and especially on the extent to which a ruling elite attempts and is able to maintain control over cross-cultural communication. Against this background, this paper aims at investigating the various reasons for the discrepancy between the rather marginal status of the translator, on the one hand, and his or her crucial role in the construction of meaning in transcultural exchange, on the other. It will be shown that to view translation as a social practice helps to identify the processes of negotiation based on positions of power. We will highlight these processes as being both consolidated locally due to the shrinking importance of time and space in a globalised society, and in a fuzzy network of meanings that transcend national cultural boundaries.

Every translation is re-creation and elevates the good translator to the level of poet. Duméril goes even further and maintains that the act of translation requires greater genius than the creation of an original poem. […] A good translation requires a willingness for self-sacrifice, for depersonalisation and complete devotion to the text. A good translator should remain anonymous, like the medieval artist, and accept that his honour and reputation derive from his ability to recreate a foreign master in a new form.

(Gipper 1966:69, translated by U. Stachl-Peier)

These two diametrically opposed statements from a book with the telling title *Linguistic and mental metamorphoses in poetry translation* reflect the almost schizophrenic expectations typically associated with translation and translators,

---

* My special thanks go to Ursula Stachl-Peier who was kind enough to translate my paper into English.

which – despite a substantial body of research – are still engrained in the minds of clients, users and observers and reproduced in fictional texts (Kurz 1987; Bardeleben 1997; Strümper-Krobb 2003; Kurz and Kaindl 2005) and films (Morascher 2004). Before exploring in detail the historical and socio-cultural reasons for this paradoxical situation, I will take a critical look at translation studies and their role in generating and keeping alive this misconception. I am aware that I am generalising here and also of the risks associated with a purely European perspective. However, given the multitude of diverse cultures of translation, which was recently highlighted by Hermans (Hermans 2006), it seems legitimate and appropriate to focus on the evolution of European approaches, even if they represent only one of many possible forms of the autopoeitic system of translation. Another reason why concentrating on Europe seems justified is that a critical appraisal of the other is possible only when we first critically review the self.

From the ideal to the real translator

Before exploring in detail the historical and socio-cultural reasons for the discrepancy between the marginal status of translators and their central role in the construction of meaning in transcultural exchange, we take a critical look at translation studies and their role in generating and perpetuating the notion of the subalternity of translators. Originating as a sub-discipline of contrastive linguistics, translation "theory" for many years chose to ignore the cognitive, social and cultural constraints under which translators operate. The notion of the ideal translator which was modelled on the systemic linguistic notion of the ideal speaker, and the logocentric construct of the decontextualised "sacred original" (Arrojo 1997a), the translation of which of course can only be its similarly decontextualised copy, forced the translators into invisibility, reducing them to the status of transcoders and translation machines (cf. Venuti 1992, 1995; Hewson 1997).

As translation studies established themselves as a separate academic (inter)discipline (Snell-Hornby 1995), the basic concepts were given a wider interpretation, yet the social framework within which translators act was only partially defined. This applies to Levy's (1963, 1969) notion of the finality of translation, Holz-Mänttäri's (1984) application of action theory to translation, the dethroning of the source text by Vermeer (1986) – ten years after the proclamation of the death of the author by Roland Barthes (1977) and Michel Foucault (1977 : 130f.) – as much as to the dominance of the purpose in the stronger form of skopos theory (Reiß and Vermeer 1984; Vermeer 1996).

Although Descriptive Translation Studies indirectly uncovered power structures (Toury 1995), the concept of norms defined the social space in which the translators acted ex negativo, i.e. as a reactive space that is subject to constraints and restrictions, and not as an interactive space in which the translators as social beings act and interact. The reference values employed by DTS were the literary systems (Even-Zohar 1990) and not the agents and agencies that generate conventions and norms as a product of social negotiation (cf. Hermans 1999:117ff., 124ff.).

It was not until the 1990s and the cultural turn in translation studies (Bassnett/ Lefevere 1990) that translation studies finally also included the translators in its purview, as well as the translators' search for a way to cut through the labyrinth of socio-cultural constraints and their active role in the construction of cultures (Bassnett and Lefevere 1998).

A similar development can be observed in cognitive science-based translation studies. For a long time, the study of translational processes relied heavily on mentalistic concepts which had little to do with translational practice (Krings 1986; Lörscher 1991), and on psycholinguistic experiments. The metaphor for this approach was the famous "black box" in the mind of translators. It was not until the 1990s that cognitive science-based theories acknowledged that world knowledge, which is acquired through experience and socialisation and is therefore culture-specific, and which reflects the translator's individual and collective interactions with his/her social environment, forms part of the cognitive processes in translation. To model the translation process Hönig (1995) used a connectionist approach, while a few years later Risku (1998) employed constructivist methodology. The question arose to what extent efforts to make different world views compatible actually relied on the interaction of self-referential cognitive systems or to what extent they entailed the integration of the cognitive worlds of the translator in the interpretation process.

The notion of situated cognition proposed by Risku (2000, 2004), which sees the professional interactions between cooperating subjects and the interactions between translation as an artefact and all other artefacts, for the first time included the social determinants that affect the interacting subjects and institutions within the purview of cognitive-science based translation studies.

The critical post-modernist approaches, especially deconstruction (Davis 2001), which translation studies increasingly drew on in the 1990s (Arrojo 1992; Arrojo 1994, 1997b), refuse to acknowledge that there may be an objective reality beyond textuality, and merely admit the free play of signifiers. Translation became a metaphor for deconstruction and deconstruction a metaphor for translation. The space of freedom that this approach defined has seemingly reached its outer limits, yet translators stumble through it lost in aporias. The never-ending play with the signifiers which opened up – at least in theory – an infinite room for play in the deconstruction of established meaning and text worlds, was, however, limited in social practice by prevalent power constellations. According to this model, it was again the social context which determined whether or not the deconstruction of traditional meaning worlds would degenerate to an intellectual game or be able to exploit the emancipatory force of deconstruction. The latter was at the heart of the feminist (Lotbinière-Harwood 1991; Simon 1996; Massardier-Kenney 1997; Grbic and Wolf 1997; Flotow 1991, 1997) and post-colonial (Robinson 1997; Bassnett and Trivedi 1999; Tymoczko 1999; Simon and St-Pierre 2000) discourse in translation studies, which challenges "the unproblematic, naively representational theory of language" (Niranjana 1992:48), makes the power driven construction of identities visible and investigates the impact of cultural and political hegemonies as well as the role of translation in the global power play of cultures (Álvarez and Vidal 1996; Tymoczko and Gentzler 2002). The same concept also underlies culture-studies-based research which deconstructs the traditional unity of representation and sees translation as a medium for representing foreign cultures (Bachmann-Medick 2004:452) and thus as the "representation of representations" (Bachmann-Medick 1996).

The situation is similar in interpreting studies (Pöchhacker 2004). As long as interpreting studies focussed only on the noblest subject, i.e. simultaneous interpreting in the setting of international conferences, where the interpreter, isolated in a booth, was able to ignore social and moral issues, social and related ethical problems were of no interest to interpreting researchers. As researchers began to study other settings, including community interpreting, where translators are directly involved in the communication process, where unequal power relations and diverging interests are pitted against each other, they began to gradually shake off the idea that translation is only an objectivistic transformation of the text, and shifted to a discursive (Hatim and Mason 1990, 1997) and emancipatory approach. Whether or not these new tenets will also have an impact on the many codes of ethics which are currently being written, depends less on intellectual reflection and a thorough analysis of the different communicative settings and situations than on the definition of roles and functions of interpreters and translators on one hand, and the negotiation of meaning between all interactants, their agents and agencies in the social field of translation on the other.

The sociological turn in translation studies in the late 1990s completes the circle, which began with the exclusion of the real translators and the cognitive, cultural and social resources they brought to the translation task. In addition to James Holmes (1988/1972), Itamar Even Zohar (1990), Peter Newmark (1993), José Lambert (1994, 1995) and André Lefevere (1998), who largely made only vague comments, it was above all Theo Hermans, who tried to define translation

as a self-referential institution (1997) and emphasised the need for a more systematic sociological approach in his criticism of DTS (Hermans 1999).[1]

At roughly the same time, Parks (1998), Gouanvic (1997), Simeoni (1998)
and Wolf (1999) began to look into issues of a sociology of translation. Following
Lefevere (1992) and Venuti (1992), Gerald Parks (1998) raised some programmatic questions, yet never outlined detailed parameters. Daniel Simeoni (1998)
tried to use Bourdieu's concept of the *habitus* in translation studies; Jean Marc
Gouanvic (1997, 1999) applied Bourdieu's sociology in his socio-historic study of
the translations of US-American science-fiction into French and how these were
received by French readers, using aesthetic and social parameters to examine the
establishment of this new literary genre in France. In her article on the "social
meaning" of translation, Michaela Wolf (1999) first sought to identify aspects
which were of interest to translation studies in Bourdieu's work. Then she tried to
apply these in several studies, including an analysis of translations of Harry Potter
(2002a), of ideological contexts (Wolf 2002b, 2003), feminist translation (Wolf
2006) and literary translation in general (Bachleitner and Wolf 2004a). Johann
Heilbron (1999, 2000) developed a model for describing translation preferences.
He tried to establish a hierarchical system with central, semi-peripheral and peripheral languages and sought to find regular patterns underlying the uneven flow
of book translations. Together with Gisèle Sapiro (Heilbron and Sapiro 2002), he
also edited a special edition on translation *Les échanges littéraires internationaux*
of the *Actes de la recherche en sciences sociales,* a journal started by Bourdieu in
which Bourdieu's concepts and analytical instruments are used to discuss a wide
range of issues.

The provisional end of this development is the (re)incarnation of the ideal
translator who has now become the real translator and his/her reintegration into
the social and historic spaces in which they are both allies and rivals of other
agents, both puppets and central actors hoping to secure their position in the
social field of translation.

Transcultural communication and translation

Before discussing the constraints acting in the social field of translation in detail,
it is appropriate to give a definition of the concept of translation and to show how
it differs from inter- and transcultural communication. Inter- and transcultural
communication comprise all symbolic and non-symbolic interactions which a

---

1. For a comprehensive overview of the research history see the introduction by Wolf to this
volume.

given society has to accomplish with other societies with a different culture and a different language. A first possible differentiation is that of symbolic interactions between immediate interactants on one hand and specialised forms of interaction by language bound mediation on the other. For the first type we use the term interculturality, for the second transculturality (cf. Prunč 2004). The field of transcultural communication may be further subdivided into mediation processes, where the communicative goals are established and negotiated by more or less professional mediators, who are commissioned by a third party, whereas translation (and interpreting), in a narrower sense, can be defined as an activity, where mediation is achieved by conventionalised text transformations.

The types of transcultural communication that a given society engages in and their enactment is culture-specific. At an abstract level, which has yet to be supported by empirical data, we can determine several parameters of distinction. First, the number of different communicative roles a society acknowledges depends on available resources and also on the division of labour and social differentiation of the respective culture.[2] A complex society with abundant resources that can and/or is willing to invest in transcultural communication, will have more habitualised types of transcultural communication than a less complex society that lacks resources. In the case of text-bound mediation less wealthy cultures prefer allrounders, who can work as authorised interactants, mediators, translators and interpreters, whereas more prosperous cultures can afford greater differentiation of jobs and job profiles. The first time such a differentiation was introduced was in Ancient Egypt where the Princes of Elephantine were the "overseers of dragomans" (Kurz 1985). The Princes were members of the nobility and endowed with power and prestige and were responsible for organising transcultural communication. The dragomans, by contrast, had to complete the different tasks ordered by the Princes, ranging from interpreting to acting as guides.

A second parameter, which can be determined, is an imbalance of power and unequal prestige between cultures. The power balance between interacting cultures determines how much is being translated and also the preferred translation flows (cf. Heilbron 1999, 2000). The findings will depend on our perspective. Seen from the perspective of the more prestigious cultures, it can be said that the greater the power imbalance between two cultures, the smaller the number of texts that are translated into the language of the more prestigious culture. Hegemonic and prestigious cultures, on the other hand, are reluctant to invest in translation because they believe in the dominance of their culture and expect that weaker

---

2. If I refer to cultures and not to societies or civilisations, it is because from the perspective of transcultural communication, I consider culture as the *differentia specifica* of interacting societies.

cultures will undertake the translations if they want access to information and cultural goods. Again, we can see relevant examples of this in Ancient Egypt and Greece. A culture which is aware of its dominant position and which considers other cultures merely as "*barbaroi*" who need to be "pacified" is unlikely to support translation into its own language. A more recent example is the US-American translation culture which, as Venuti (1995) showed, is highly ethnocentric and marginalises other cultures (cf. also Bachleitner and Wolf 2004b:2). The opposite is true of the less prestigious cultures. Amongst the options which they have available to secure the presence of their culture abroad and the enjoyment of what Casanova described as "the mechanisms of consecration of translation" (Casanova 1999:188f.), low-prestige cultures chose those translation flows which they hope will economically be profitable and also give them maximum symbolic value. This results in more translations being done into the languages of the more prestigious cultures which in turn reinforces their dominant position. However, these translations will overcome the marginalisation of the less prestigious cultures only in rare cases. Most often, the translations into more prestigious languages facilitate translation into other non-prestigious cultures (cf. Heilbron 2000:14f.).

There is another facet, closely related to the power relations between cultures, which is relevant in the context of translation. It seems that in addition to aspects such as the intensity of transcultural relations and the legal status of translation (cf. Dollerup 2000) there is also a correlation between the prestige of cultures and the social status of translators. This correlation is perhaps best captured in the famous relief on the walls of the tomb of Haremhab in which the figure of the interpreter is the same size and also on the same level as the foreign subjects, while the figures depicting the god-like pharaoh and the powerful king Haremhab are larger and also on a higher level (Kurz 1986).

But not only the negative prestige that is attached to a culture affects the status of translators and interpreters. Translators may also gain significant symbolic capital if they choose prestigious languages as their working languages – even if this may run counter to the requirements of the market and the dominance of supply and demand. A good example is the demand for the less widely spoken and less widely taught languages and the prestige of translators, working in these languages. Although with EU enlargement the demand for these languages has significantly increased, the translators and interpreters with more widely spoken languages generally still enjoy greater public prestige than their colleagues with less widely spoken languages such as Slovene or Lithuanian.

If the political will exists to translate from a prestigious culture then the necessary resources are made available and at the same time, the prestige of the translators doing the translation also increases, irrespective of the economic power of the source culture. A good example for this correlation is the – true or invented –

story about the famous translator Hunain ibn Ishaq who was paid an amount in gold equal to the weight of his translations from Greek into Arabic (cf. Delisle and Woodsworth 1995:113f.).

If transcultural communication is the exclusive remit of the political, economic, cultural and military elites who want their interests guarded, then the differentiation of translational activities closely follows the inclinations of these elites. If they have the linguistic skills to cope with all types of transcultural communication then they will not need translation. If there are enough bilingual speakers or if the members of the elite can rely on an international lingua franca, like Latin in the Middle Ages or French as the language of diplomacy, then translators will only be active in those areas that have little symbolic capital, i.e. in those domains where members of the elite had to communicate with the "common people". For example, the conquerors with the conquered, the colonial masters with the colonised, the generals with the soldiers. In these contexts, translators are typically slaves and prisoners of war or lowly scribes and subaltern officials in the service of feudal lords and colonial masters.

This typical correlation between translation activities and the bilingual potential of a society and its elites can be overturned by ideological factors. As the non-German speaking peoples as the Slovenes and the Croats in the Austro-Hungarian Empire developed their national ideologies, at first the more prestigious literary genres were not translated into the national languages. Publishers, authors and literary critics agreed that the "world literature" did not need to be translated into the national languages because bilingual middle-class citizens could easily read the texts in German. For the process of national integration it was necessary, however, to include the predominantly monolingual rural population in the nation-building process by supporting organisational measures such as, for instance, the establishment of reading circles to provide these groups with literature in their national languages. The texts, which were translated into the national languages, did not qualify as "serious literature" but included, above all, religious texts, practical instructions for farming and cattle breeding, and simple narrative genres. This situation did not change until the late nineteenth century when the profile of genres was gradually expanded, and more complex and demanding literary texts were translated (cf. Hladnik 1993; Prunč 2005). In this process the first literary genre that were translated were plays. Here the focus was on the representative function of language, not on the bi- or multilingual competence of the audience and the aim was to provide translated scripts to help develop theatre as a national institution.

This last example highlights the correlation between the amount of translation and the degree of democracy and literacy in a society. As transcultural processes are becoming increasingly democratic and globalised, not only the demand for translations increases, but also the need for greater specialisation and for co-operation with the other agents in the communicative act. This greater degree of democracy can have both a horizontal and a vertical effect. Horizontally, it affects the power balance between cultures and vertically, the access to transcultural information flows for a wider range of people. The process of horizontal democratisation is reinforced by the ideological and politically motivated re-evaluation of some languages which become symbolic vehicles for ethnic and national identity affirmation. A current example is the elevation of the official languages of the new EU member states to the status of official languages of the European Union.

The vertical democratisation of transcultural communication can be achieved with an old or new lingua franca, if limited financial resources make this necessary. However, the use of a lingua franca can be subject to – occasionally completely unexpected – functional restrictions. Immediately after the disintegration of the Soviet Union, Russian ceased to be a lingua franca, for both ideological and psychological reasons. At the same time, the seemingly unstoppable rise of English was slowed down when the internet, the most international of all media, started to use regional languages. This new competition forced the international companies to adapt their language and culture to the needs of the consumers. Evidence for this development is the rapidly growing number of bi- and multilingual websites.

The internet is the most recent medium for transcultural communication. Its technical parameters determine its extent and structure. Before the development of writing, translation as a special type of transcultural communication occurred only in the here and now of the communicative act. As writing emerged and made available a complex symbolic system that allowed the recording of language on more permanent media, and as communication beyond the confines of interpersonal encounters became possible and the constraints of space and time were overcome, we also see a differentiation of translational activity into translating and interpreting. Interpreting was the translational activity that was still tied to the spatio-temporal context in which the communicative act was performed, while translators produced artefacts that could be recontextualised in an endless chain of meaning construction. The consequence is that the durability of translations and interpretations differs.

The situative and social coordinates of interpreting did not change, in theory until the invention of the sonograph, in actual fact until the arrival of the media of mass communication. Translation, by contrast, developed along with the media that were available for the dissemination of texts, and was subject to technical, social and economic constraints. Access to texts on stone, parchment and paper was limited and the prerogative of the rich and powerful. Writing and reading and, thus, also the production and dissemination of translations were limited to small social groups. Writing by itself was a highly prestigious activity. The invention of the printing press triggered a revolution which turned translation into a market factor. Shortly after Gutenberg invented movable type in 1450, the first major translations of the bible were undertaken and increasing number of genres were being translated and printed. This development reached its first climax in the translation factories of the nineteenth century which fragmented the translation process thus imitating industrial production processes (Bachleitner 1989). In addition to the doyens and patrons of translators, who tried to derive symbolic capital from translations, and the institutions and holders of power, who tried to gain influence through translations, now a new group evolved, namely the publishers who were keen to maximize their profits. This development eventually brought forth a translation market where speed and quantity were the main competitive parameters. This trend further intensified in the nineteenth century as the number of readers and the number of lending libraries increased and the libraries became a powerful factor in the field of translation. Mass production and competition also resulted in negative side effects like price dumping, poor quality translations and loss of image for the translators.

The last stage in this development was initiated by recent advances in the printed media, the development of electronic media as well as the emergence of global networks which led to an exponential rise in the number of published translations and gave translation as a field of action its current form.

The use of audiovisual media, however, initiated yet another development. Because interpretations can now also be reproduced and recontextualised, the once clear dividing line between translation and interpreting is once becoming blurred.

The *habitus* of translators

A review of the history of translation from a sociological perspective shows that the *habitus* of translators not only involves the internalisation of subalternity and marginality (Simeoni 1998) but that there is now a wide range of prototypical *habitus*, located on a cline between the *habitus* of the priest and the *habitus* of the self-effacing pariah.

The translator-priests see themselves as the guardians of the word and as the gate keepers and constructors of culture. They know that they have the power to select, to transform and to define, which also provides them with the key to socially accepted values and truths. The *habitus* of the translator-priest first emerged in Mesopotamia where the priests guarded and interpreted the interlinear translations of the Akkadian texts (Vermeer 1992:52). It was later adopted by the great bible translators St. Jerome and Luther and also by literary translators whose creations have become an integral part of national literary canons. Today, this *habitus* may survive amongst the interpreters and translators of transnational and international organisations such as the UNO or the EU. However, not all seem to be aware that they have the power to act as mediators in delicate negotiations and to create concepts, meaning worlds and value communities (cf. Koskinen 2000:87f.).

The *habitus* of the pariah is the most extreme version of the *habitus* of the "quintessential servant", as Simeoni (1998:12) puts it. This *habitus* is the relic of the historic marginalisation of translators and the result of their other or self-imposed invisibility. Translators who adopt this *habitus* consider the author and poet as their master, the customer as the king. They continue to work for ever lower prices and rates and are both the victims and originators of the current price-cutting spiral (cf. Prunč 2003) which threatens not only their own existence but also the reputation of the translation profession. The pariah *habitus* is so engrained in their character that they ignore the fact that interpreters and translators "may and do find themselves in the middle of potentially conflicting agendas" (Inghilleri 2003:255) and that they are involved in the power game of interpretation, whether they like it or not.

The power game over interpretation

A look at the history of translation as the production of text and meaning worlds quickly reveals that the dispute over whether "literal" or "free" translation is more appropriate, largely reflects the social debate over the power and impotence of the translators, which in turn reflects the power games between all those social forces that have a vested interest in or even a monopoly over the interpretation of a text.

Ancient Greek has no special term for translation. The verb *hermeneun* can be translated as "to explain", "to interpret" or "to translate" and only the cotext will disambiguate its meaning. Translation and (hermeneutic) interpretation are quasi-synonymous terms.

Translation for the Latin authors-poets like Cicero and Horace not only meant integrating the concepts and textual structures of the ancient Greek texts into the Latin texts, thus providing a cultural power-base for the expanding Roman Empire. It also meant that they interpreted the texts and adapted them through *emendatio* to the target culture system. They did not doubt that they had the right to interpret and adapt the original texts. They wielded absolute power and had no rivals with sufficient cultural capital to vie with them for their exclusive right to interpretation. The polyphonous concert of the deities was incompatible with monolithic claims to the truth.

The integration of Platonic Christian concepts and ideas into Roman conceptual systems not only favoured monotheism, it also required the interpretation and disambiguation of ambiguous texts. The simplest way to achieve this was to assume that the word was equal to truth, and to offer a transcendental explanation. Following John 1.1. "*In the beginning was the Word, and the Word was with God, and the Word was God*" the church constructed a logocentric system the accuracy of which was guaranteed by God, in which the "*ordo verborum*" was declared a mystery by St. Jerome. Word-for-word translation was thus the only admissible since ideologically sanctified strategy. In the battle between orthodoxies and heresies, i.e. between the winners and losers in the fight for ideological and political supremacy, this strategy proved a potent instrument to support the claims by each party that they alone had the right to interpret the original text. Logocentrism offered God's powerful representatives on earth the opportunity to postulate that they alone owned the truth and check the production of anti-truths. By pretending that their interpretations closely followed the original text, they were able to include extra-textual aspects and set up control agencies that assumed responsibility for the interpretation (cf. Delisle and Woodsworth 1995: 139f.). Professional exegetes were appointed whose task was to disseminate truth in the name of God but in the spirit and on behalf of rulers. They were helped by censors and inquisitors. The translators had only limited scope for creative freedom. Essentially, interpretations were possible only within the narrow confines permitted by the exegetes, and approved by God's representatives on Earth. Jan Hus, Etienne Dolet and William Tyndale who transgressed these confines, paid for it with their lives. Martin Luther would have suffered the same fate if he had not successfully claimed for himself the status of exegete and won the support of the Imperial ruler.

Enlightenment brought with it not only the deconstruction of the theo-centric model but also the abandonment of claims that only a literal translation approach was appropriate (Schneiders 1995). The aim was to give truth a more human, rational face. During the Absolutist Period, the *belles infidèles* constructed new textual worlds, value systems and truths at the heart of which were the absolutist rulers and their elites (Zuber 1968; Stackelberg 1988).

A major new trend started in the Romantic Era and its cult of the genius. The logocentric belief in truth which was upheld by mythical associations, was secularised and re-located to the level of the author-reader. The divine spark of creation that guaranteed the author's geniusness became a mere metaphor and was gradually replaced by a belief in the creativity of the genius which was very much based on earthly accomplishments and principles. It was this genius that was believed to have the power to create unique intellectual products. The God-Author and the authorised Word of God were replaced by the Author-God, as Roland Barthes called him, not without irony (Barthes 1977: 146). The task of the translator consequently was to copy this unique intellectual product. Schleiermacher's concept of alienation added a further dimension. Here literalness also paves the way to the otherness of the other which is reflected in the linguistic *habitus* (Berman 1992).

There was little change with regard to the social position and power of translators, however. Having adopted the *habitus* of the servant and invisible communicator they had ended up in a situation from which there was no way out. The status of the Author-God derived not only from his intellectual genius but also from the positive formulation of the concept of intellectual property. While authors eventually, in the nineteenth century, won the ideological, social and legal battle for the sole rights to their texts, the translators clearly lacked the social backing, as well as the cultural and symbolic capital and even more so the financial capital, that would have allowed them to secure the right to be an equal partner in the signification process. They were under political, ideological and financial pressure from clients and publishers, and also had to battle against the monopolisation of interpretations. While in the past it was the church that controlled the interpretation of texts, in the secularised world this control is exerted by the new and professional exegetes in translator-mediated interactions who claim this interpretive monopoly for themselves: the hermeneutists for fictional and philosophical texts, lawyers for legal texts, therapists in therapeutical sessions etc. What they all have in common is that they believe in the identity of the word and truth and that transparent transcoding will give them access to the meaning of texts.

Although it is precisely this belief in the identity of the word and truth which is cast into doubt in our post-modern world, while the notion of the interpretive openness of the text is generally accepted, translators still hide behind the illusion of objectivity. This leads to an almost schizophrenic constellation of self-constructed translator identities which combine the pariah *habitus* and the self sacrifice and self-mutilation demanded by others.

This may also explain why translators who are involved in the creation of textual worlds, of meaning and value constructions, are loathe to admit their creative involvement in the current codes of ethics. Neither their other nor their self-construed identities allow translators to overcome the *habitus* of the servant so as to self-confidently confront the circle of social meaning and value constructions. This brief overview of the history of translation theory and translation shows that due to the underlying socio-historical restrictions translators hardly ever succeeded in overcoming their self-construed or imposed pariah status and orientating themselves by historical configurations, metaphors and personalities in their search for an adequate self-image, which would allow them to make visible their own intellectual efforts and take into account the social-constructivist nature of values and truth. So they are not able to test out the emancipatory dimension of the dictum "He who has the power, has the word. And he who has the word, has the power" in order to initiate a debate about their past and present role in the construction of meaning worlds and to gain an equal position with the other agents in the social field of translation.

References

Álvarez, Román and Vidal, M. Carmen-África (eds). 1996. *Translation, Power, Subversion*. Clevedon and Philadelphia etc.: Multilingual Matters.

Arrojo, Rosemary. 1994. "Deconstruction and the teaching of translation". *TextConText* 9 (1): 1–12.

Arrojo, Rosemary. 1997a. "The 'death' of the author and the limits of the translator's visibility". In *Translation as Intercultural Communication. Selected Papers from the EST Congress Prague 1995*, M. Snell-Hornby, Z. Jettmarová and K. Kaindl (eds). Amsterdam and Philadelphia: John Benjamins. 21–32.

Arrojo, Rosemary. 1997b. "Gedanken zur Translationstheorie und zur Dekonstruktion des Logozentrismus". Trans. Hans J. Vermeer. In *Übersetzungswissenschaft in Brasilien. Beiträge zum Status von "Original" und Übersetzung*, M. Wolf (ed). Tübingen: Stauffenburg. 63–70.

Arrojo, Rosemary (ed). 1992. *O Signo Desconstruído. Implicações para a tradução, a leitura e o ensino*. Campinas: Pontes.

Bachleitner, Norbert. 1989. "Übersetzungsfabriken. Das deutsche Übersetzungswesen in der ersten Hälfte des 19. Jahrhunderts". *Internationales Archiv für Sozialgeschichte der deutschen Literatur* 14 (1): 1–50.

Bachleitner, Norbert and Wolf, Michaela (eds). 2004a. *Internationales Archiv für Sozialgeschichte der deutschen Literatur* 29 (2). Special Issue "Soziologie der literarischen Übersetzung".

Bachleitner, Norbert and Wolf, Michaela. 2004b. "Auf dem Weg zu einer Soziologie der literarischen Übersetzung im deutschsprachigen Raum". *Internationales Archiv für Sozialgeschichte der deutschen Literatur* 29 (2): 1–25.

Bachmann-Medick, Doris. 1996. "Texte zwischen den Kulturen: ein Ausflug in 'postkoloniale Landkarten'". In *Literatur und Kulturwissenschaften. Positionen, Theorien, Modelle*, H. Böhme and K.R. Scherpe (eds). Reinbeck bei Hamburg: Rowohlt. 60–77.

Bachmann-Medick, Doris. 2004. "Übersetzung als Medium interkultureller Kommunikation und Auseinandersetzung". In *Handbuch der Kulturwissenschaften. Band 2. Paradigmen und Disziplinen*, F. Jaeger, B. Liebsch, J. Rüsen and J. Straub. Stuttgart and Weimar: Metzler. 449–465.

Bardeleben, Renate von. 1997. "The Translator as Mediator and Metaphor. Joyce Carol Oates' 'Détente', Eva Hoffman's Lost in Translation and Ward Just's The Translator". In *Transfer. Übersetzen – Dolmetschen – Interkulturalität. 50 Jahre Fachbereich Angewandte Sprach- und Kulturwissenschaft der Johannes Gutenberg-Universität Mainz in Germersheim*, H.W. Drescher (ed). Frankfurt am Main and Berlin etc.: Peter Lang. 325–345.

Barthes, Roland. 1977. *Image, Music, Text*. Trans. V. Stephen Heath. New York: Hill and Wang.

Bassnett, Susan and Lefevere, André (eds). 1990. *Translation, History and Culture*. London and New York: Pinter.

Bassnett, Susan and Lefevere, André. 1998. *Constructing Cultures. Essays on Literary Translation*. Clevedon and Philadelphia etc.: Multilingual Matters.

Bassnett, Susan and Trivedi, Harish (eds). 1999. *Post-colonial Translation. Theory and Practice*. London and New York: Routledge.

Berman, Antoine. 1992. *The Experience of the Foreign. Culture and tanslation in romantic Germany*. Albany (NY): State University of New York Press.

Casanova, Pascale. 1999. *La république mondiale des lettres*. Paris: Seuil.

Davis, Kathleen. 2001. *Deconstruction and Translation*. Manchester and Northampton: St Jerome Publishing.

Delisle, Jean and Woodsworth, Judith. 1995. *Translators through History*. Amsterdam and Philadelphia: John Benjamins.

Dollerup, Cay. 2000. "The status of translation and translators". *Lebende Sprachen* 45 (4): 145–149.

Even-Zohar, Itamar. 1990. *Poetics Today* 11 (1). Special Issue "Polysystem Studies".

Flotow, Luise von. 1991. "Feminist translation. Contexts, practices and theories". *TTR* IV (2): 69–84.

Flotow, Luise von. 1997. *Gender and Translation. Translation in an Era of Feminism*. Manchester: St Jerome Publishing.

Foucault, Michel. 1977. *Language, Counter-memory, Practice*. Ithaca: Cornell University Press.

Gipper, Helmut. 1966. *Sprachliche und geistige Metamorphosen bei Gedichtübersetzungen. Eine sprachvergleichende Untersuchung zur Erhellung deutsch-französischer Geistesverschiedenheit*. Düsseldorf: Pädagogischer Verlag Schwamm.

Gouanvic, Jean-Marc. 1997. "Pour une sociologie de la traduction: le cas de la littérature américaine traduite en France après la Seconde Guerre mondiale (1945–1960)". In *Translation as Intercultural Communication. Selected Papers from the EST Congress Prague 1995*, M. Snell-Hornby, Z. Jettmarová and K. Kaindl (eds). Amsterdam and Philadelphia: John Benjamins. 33–44.

Gouanvic, Jean-Marc. 1999. *Sociologie de la traduction. La science-fiction américaine dans l'espace culturel français des années 1950*. Arras: Artois Presses Université.

Grbić, Nadja and Wolf, Michaela. 1997. "Feministische Translationswissenschaft". *Information der Interuniversitären Koordinationsstelle für Frauenforschung (Graz)* 3(1): 23–26.

Hatim, Basil and Mason, Ian. 1990. *Discourse and the Translator*. London and New York: Longman.

Hatim, Basil and Mason, Ian. 1997. *The Translator as Communicator*. London and New York: Routledge.

Heilbron, Johan. 1999. "Towards a Sociology of Translation. Book Translations as a Cultural World-System". *European Journal of Social Theory* 2(4): 429–444.

Heilbron, Johan. 2000. "Translation as a cultural world-system". *Perspectives: Studies in Translatology* 8 (1): 9–26.

Heilbron, Johan and Sapiro, Gisèle (eds). 2002. *Actes de la recherche en sciences sociales* 144. "Les échanges littéraires internationaux".

Hermans, Theo. 1997. "Translation as institution". In *Translation as Intercultural Communication. Selected Papers from the EST Congress Prague 1995*, M. Snell-Hornby, Z. Jettmarová and K. Kaindl (eds). Amsterdam and Philadelphia: John Benjamins. 3–20.

Hermans, Theo. 1999. *Translation in Systems. Descriptive and System-oriented Approaches Explained*. Manchester: St Jerome Publishing.

Hermans, Theo (ed). 2006. *Translating Others. Vol. 1, 2*. Manchester, UK and Kinderhook, USA: St Jerome Publishing.

Hewson, Lance. 1997. "Change in Translation and the Image of the Translator". In *Translating Sensitive Texts: Linguistic Aspects*, K. Simms (ed). Amsterdam and Atlanta: Rodopi. 47–56.

Hladnik, Miran. 1993. "Der Einfluss des Bilinguismus auf die Auswahl der zu übersetzenden narrativen Gattungen". In *Übersetzen, Verstehen, Brücken bauen. Geisteswissenschaftliches und literarisches Übersetzen im internationalen Kulturaustausch*, A.P. Frank, J. Gulya, U. Mölk et al. (eds). Berlin: Erich Schmidt. 801–810. http://www.kakanien.ac.at/beitr/fallstudie/Mhladnik4.pdf. Visited May 2007.

Holmes, James S. 1988/1972. "The Name and Nature of Translation Studies". In *Translated! Papers on Literary Translation and Translation Studies*, J. S. Holmes. 1988. Amsterdam and Atlanta: Rodopi. 67–80.

Holz-Mänttäri, Justa. 1984. *Translatorisches Handeln. Theorie und Methode*. Helsinki: Suomalainen Tiedeakatemia.

Hönig, Hans G. 1995. *Konstruktives Übersetzen*. Tübingen: Stauffenburg.

Inghilleri, Moira. 2003. "Habitus, Field and Discourse: Interpreting as a Socially Situated Activity". *Target* 15 (2): 243–68.

Koskinen, Kaisa. 2000. *Beyond Ambivalence. Postmodernity and the Ethics of Translation*. Tampere: University of Tampere.

Krings, Hans P. 1986. *Was in den Köpfen von Übersetzern vorgeht. Eine empirische Untersuchung zur Struktur des Übersetzungsprozesses an fortgeschrittenen Französischlernern*. Tübingen: Narr.

Kurz, Ingrid. 1985. "The Rock Tombs of the Princes of Elephantine. Earliest references to interpretation in Pharaonic Egypt". *Babel* 31 (4): 213–218.

Kurz, Ingrid. 1986. "Das Dolmetscher-Relief aus dem Grab des Haremhab in Memphis. Ein Beitrag zur Geschichte des Dolmetschens im alten Ägypten". *Babel* 32 (2): 73–78.

Kurz, Ingrid. 1987. "Conference interpreting – myth and reality". In *American Translators Association Conference – 1987. Proceedings of the 28th Annual Conference of the American Translators Association. Albuquerque, New Mexico, October 8–11, 1987*, K. Kummer (ed). Medford (NJ): Learned Information. 315–319.

Kurz, Ingrid and Kaindl, Klaus (eds). 2005. *Wortklauber, Sinnverdreher, Brückenbauer. DolmetscherInnen und ÜbersetzerInnen als literarische Geschöpfe*. Münster and Hamburg etc.: LIT.

Lambert, José. 1994. "Ethnolinguistic Democracy, Translation Policy and Contemporary World (Dis)order". In *Transvases culturales: Literatura, cine y traducción. Actes du Congreso Internacional sobre Transvases Culturales, 20 y 22 de mayo 1993*, F. Eguíluz, R. Merino, V. Olsen, E. Pajares and J.M. Santamaría (eds). Vitoria: Universidad del Pais Vasco. 23–33.

Lambert, José. 1995. "Translation, Systems and Research. The Contribution of Polysystem Studies to Translation Studies". *TTR* VIII (1): 105–152.

Lefevere, André. 1992. *Translation, Rewriting, and the Manipulation of Literary Fame*. London and New York: Routledge.

Lefevere, Andre. 1998. "Translation Practice(s) and the Circulation of Cultural Capital. Some Aeneids in English". In *Constructing Cultures. Essays on Literary Translation*, S. Bassnett and A. Lefevere. Clevedon and Philadelphia etc.: Multilingual Matters. 41–56.

Levý, Jiří. 1963. *Umění překladu*. Praha: Československý spisovatel.

Levý, Jiří. 1969. *Die literarische Übersetzung. Theorie einer Kunstgattung*. Frankfurt am Main und Bonn: Athenäum.

Lörscher, Wolfgang. 1991. *Translation Performance, Translation Process and Translation Strategies. A Psycholinguistic Investigation*. Tübingen: Narr.

Lotbinière-Harwood, Susanne de. 1991. *Re-Belle et infidèle. La traduction comme pratique de réécriture au féminin. The body bilingual. Translation as a rewriting in the feminine*. Québec/Toronto: Lés édition du remue-ménage/Women's Press.

Massardier-Kenney, Françoise. 1997. "Towards a redefinition of feminist translation practice". *The Translator* 3 (1): 55–69.

Morascher, Arnold. 2004. *The Good, the Bad and the Ugly. Rolle und Image von DolmetscherInnen und ÜbersetzerInnen in amerikanischen und europäischen Spielfilmen*. Graz: Diplomarbeit.

Newmark, Peter. 1993. *Paragraphs on translation*. Clevedon and Philadelphia etc.: Multilingual Matters

Niranjana Tejaswini. 1992. *Siting Translation. History, Post-Structuralism, and the Colonial Context*. Berkeley and Los Angeles etc.: University of California Press.

Parks, Gerald. 1998. "Towards a Sociology of Translation". *Rivista internazionale di tecnica della traduzione* 3: 25–35.

Pöchhacker, Franz. 2004. *Introducing Interpreting Studies*. London and New York: Routledge.

Prunč, Erich. 2003. "Óptimo, subóptimo, fatal: refelexiones sobre la democracia etnolingüística en la cultura europea de traducción". In *La direcconalidad en traducción e interpretación: perspectivas teóreticas, profesionales y didácticas*, D. Kelly, A. Martin, M.-L. Nobs et al. (eds). Granada: Editorial Atrio. 67–89.

Prunč, Erich. 2004. "Zum Objektbereich der Translationswissenschaft". In *Und sie bewegt sich doch... Translationswissenschaft in Ost und West. Festschrift für Heidemarie Salevsky zum 60. Geburtstag*, I. Müller (ed). New York and Oxford etc.: Peter Lang. 263–285.

Prunč, Erich. 2005. "Hypothesen zum Gattungsprofil deutsch-slowenischer Übersetzungen im Zeitraum 1848–1918". In *Beyond Equivalence – Jeinseits der Äquivalenz – Oltre l'equivalenza – Onkraj ekvivalence*, N. Kocijančič-Pokorn, E. Prunč and A. Riccardi (eds). Graz: Institut für Translationswissenschaft. 19–37.

Reiß, Katharina and Vermeer, Hans J. 1984. *Grundlegung einer allgemeinen Translationstheorie*. Tübingen: Niemeyer.

Risku, Hanna. 1998. *Translatorische Kompetenz*. Tübingen: Stauffenburg.

Risku, Hanna. 2000. "Situated Translation and Situated Cognition: Ungleiche Schwestern". In *Translationswissenschaft. Festschrift für Mary Snell-Hornby zum 60. Geburtstag*, K. Kaindl, F. Pöchhacker, M. Kadric (eds). Tübingen: Stauffenburg. 81–92.

Risku, Hanna. 2004. *Translationsmanagement. Interkulturelle Fachkommunikation im Informationszeitalter*. Tübingen: Narr.

Robinson, Douglas. 1997. *Translation and Empire. Postcolonial Theories Explained*. Manchester: St Jerome Publishing.

Schneiders, Hans-Wolfgang. 1995. *Die Ambivalenz des Fremden. Übersetzungstheorie im Zeitalter der Aufklärung (Frankreich und Italien)*. Bonn: Romanistischer Verlag.

Simeoni, Daniel. 1998. "The Pivotal Status of the Translator's Habitus". *Target* 10 (1): 1–39.

Simon, Sherry. 1996. *Gender in Translation. Cultural identity and the politics of transmission*. London and New York: Routledge.

Simon, Sherry and St-Pierre, Paul (eds). 2000. *Changing the Terms. Translating in the Postcolonial Era*. Montréal: University of Ottawa Press.

Snell-Hornby, Mary. 21995. *Translation Studies. An integrated approach. Revised Edition.* Amsterdam and Philadelphia: John Benjamins.

Stackelberg, Jürgen von. 1988. "Blüte und Niedergang der 'Belles infidèles'". In *Die literarische Übersetzung. Stand und Perspektiven ihrer Erforschung,* H. Kittel (ed). Berlin: Erich Schmidt. 16–29.

Strümper-Krobb, Sabine. 2003. "The Translator in Fiction". *Language and Intercultural Communication* 3 (2): 115–121.

Toury, Gideon. 1995. *Descriptive Translation Studies and beyond.* Amsterdam and Philadelphia: John Benjamins.

Tymoczko, Maria. 1999. *Translation in a Postcolonial Context.* Manchester: St Jerome Publishing.

Tymoczko, Maria and Gentzler, Edwin (eds). 2002. *Translation and power.* Amherst and Boston: University of Massachusetts Press.

Venuti, Lawrence (ed). 1992. *Rethinking Translation: Discourse, Subjectivity, Ideology.* London and New York: Routledge.

Venuti, Lawrence. 1995. *The Translator´s Invisibility. A history of translation.* London and New York: Routledge.

Vermeer, Hans J. 1986. "Übersetzen als kultureller Transfer". In *Übersetzungswissenschaft – eine Neuorientierung. Zur Integrierung von Theorie und Praxis,* M. Snell-Hornby (ed). Tübingen: Francke. 30–53.

Vermeer, Hans J. 1992. *Skizzen zu einer Geschichte der Translation. Band 1.* Frankfurt am Main: Verlag für Interkulturelle Kommunikation.

Vermeer, Hans J. 1996. *A skopos theory of translation (Some arguments for and against).* Heidelberg: TcT-Verlag.

Wolf, Michaela. 1999. "Zum 'sozialen Sinn' in der Translation. Translationssoziologische Implikationen von Pierre Bourdieus Kultursoziologie". *Arcadia* 34 (2): 262–75.

Wolf, Michaela. 2002a. "Translation Activity between Culture, Society and the Individual: Towards a Sociology of Translation". In *CTIS Occasional Papers 2,* K. Harvey (ed). Manchester: UMIST. 33–43.

Wolf, Michaela. 2002b. "Censorship as Cultural Blockage: Banned Literature in the Late Habsburg Monarchy". *TTR* XV (2): 45–61.

Wolf, Michaela. 2003. "Translating – A Social Event. Towards a Sociological Approach to Translation". In *Língua, Literatura e Cultura em Diálogo,* H. Bonito Couto Pereira and M.L. Guarnieri Atik (eds). São Paulo: Editora Mackenzie. 47–67.

Wolf, Michaela. 2006. "The female state of the art: Women in the 'translation field'". In *Sociocultural aspects of translating and interpreting,* A. Pym, Z. Jettmarová and M. Shlesinger (eds). Amsterdam and Philadelphia: John Benjamins. 129–141.

Zuber, Roger. 1968. *Les "belles infidèles" et la formation du goût classique.* Paris: Collins.

Translation, irritation and resonance

Theo Hermans
University College London, United Kingdom

I seek to work from a textual approach to a view of translation as a social system. I start by positing a strong notion of equivalence and show that translations cannot be equivalent to their originals unless they are recognized as authenticated versions, at which point they have ceased to be translations. Because translations, unlike originals or equivalent authentic versions, are repeatable, they have a translator's subject position inscribed in them. Reading translations for what they say about translation, i.e. for their translation-specific intertextuality, opens up an historical and social dimension, a social system in Niklas Luhmann's sense. As a system, translation has its autonomy, in the form of operational closure, autopoiesis and self-reference, and its heteronomy, in that it caters for other systems and adapts to their topics and discursive forms as its other-reference. Its function is meta-representational, the production of representations of representations, and typically verbal re-enactments of pre-existing discourses. In that sense it contributes to society's construction of reality.

Can we imagine translation without translators? However perverse it may seem in the context of understanding translation as a social practice, I should like to sketch a sociological perspective on translation that chooses to write translators out of the picture. Still, let me begin with translators. We can then watch them disappear, not once, but twice.

Equivalence and intertextuality

First, here are three scenarios, assembled around the well-worn issue of equivalence. I present them very briefly, because they serve merely as the run-up to other things.

Everyone who is even remotely familiar with the history of translation in the West will know the story of the ancient Septuagint. Told many times since the famous letter of Aristeas in the second century BCE, it revolves around the seventy Greek translators of the Hebrew Bible in Alexandria who all worked independently of each other yet produced identical renderings. God had apparently breathed the one correct version into the translators' ears, hence the remarkable result. The story of the miracle evidently serves the purpose of investing the Greek rendition with a status equal to that of the Hebrew original. For Saint Augustine, God spoke with the same intent and with equal authority in both versions.

Perhaps not everyone who has read around in more recent translation history has come across the story of the Book of Mormon, very similar to that of the Septuagint but even more spectacular. The detail of how in the 1820s Joseph Smith managed to translate an unknown script from a collection of gold plates which he had dug up following the directions of the angel Moroni, would take too long here (see Hill 1977; Persuitte 1985; Robinson 2001: 54–61). The defining moment of this intriguing tale occurred when, in July 1829, the translation was ready and Joseph Smith's associates were allowed to see and touch the mysterious gold plates as the assembled company witnessed another visitation from Moroni. During these proceedings a voice descending from heaven declared that "the book is true and the translation accurate", whereupon the angel took the original plates under his wing and vanished with them, for good. They have not been seen since. The physical removal of the original emphatically sealed the divine pronouncement, the proclamation from on high which endowed the translation with a value equal to that of the original. The pronouncement, that is, made translation and original equivalent. In so doing it enabled the translation to displace the original, which indeed was no longer needed and could be taken away without loss.

If not everyone interested in the recent and current history of translation knows about the Convention of Vienna, this is unfortunate, because in one way or another it affects every country on the globe, and therefore every one of us as citizens. The United Nations' Vienna Convention on the Law of Treaties, first adopted in 1969, governs international treaties. Such treaties normally exist in the form of parallel texts in several languages. If some of these versions have come into existence as translations, they cease to be translations as soon as the multilingual treaty is agreed by the relevant parties as constituting one single legal instrument. "Agreeing" here means that the parallel texts of the treaty are authenticated, that is, recognized as equivalent sources for the interpretation of the treaty. From that moment onwards the translations become versions which all possess equal value in law and are, on that basis, presumed to have the same meaning. Indeed paragraph 3 of article 33 of the Vienna Convention states that "The terms of a treaty are presumed to have the same meaning in each authentic text" (Reuter 1995: 261). All the key documents of the European Union, for instance, are in this sense equal, equivalent and definitive versions in all of the

EU's twenty official languages, even though, with the organisation's successive expansions over the years, we can be certain that most of them started out as translations.

The perspective I am adopting here is that a translation that, in a particular institutional context, has successfully been declared equivalent with its parent text, is no longer a translation. It has graduated to a version on a par with other versions (among them the original original), all of which are deemed to be equally authoritative, animated by the same authorial intent and therefore presumed to have the same meaning. The Book of Mormon dramatized the point by spiriting away the now redundant original. The Convention of Vienna forbids those interpreting authenticated versions of an international treaty from privileging a version known to have served at an earlier stage as a source of translation for the other version(s). Doing so would undermine authentication, which institutes legal parity.

One obvious consequence of authentication is that, having instituted equivalence, it does away with translation. And where there is no translation, there cannot be a translator. A successful declaration of equivalence spells the end of translation and evicts the translator. Joseph Smith and the seventy who penned the Septuagint acted as mere conduits for divine messages. The twenty versions of the amalgamated EU treaty do not have names of translators appended to them. Here we witness the translator's first disappearance.

At least three things follow from this. Firstly, translations cannot be equivalent to their originals. They may pursue equivalence, as many translations do, but if they attain it they cease to be translations. Upon fulfilling their most ambitious aim, at the moment of sublimation, they self-destruct, and the translator vanishes with them.

Secondly, for as long as translations fall short of their highest ambition and continue to function as translations, they cannot be definitive. In contrast to the EU Treaty, which exists in a single definitive version in each of the organisation's official languages, there always remains room, in any given language, for more than one translation of any particular document. Translations are repeatable, they can be attempted again and again.

Thirdly, because translations are repeatable, each has a translator's subject-position written into it. This point needs a brief illustration. Any translation will do for the purpose, so the choice of example is immaterial. Let me pick one that is more explicit than most. Here are a few lines from the diary of Anne Frank as printed in Laureen Nussbaum's section on Anne Frank in a collection called *Women Writing in Dutch* (1994):

> I must keep my head high and be brave, those thoughts will come {all the same},
> not once, but oh, countless times. Believe me, if you have been shut up [confined]

for a year and a half, it can get too much for you some days. In spite of all justice *[fairness]* and thankfulness, you can't crush *[repress]* your feelings.

(Nussbaum 1994: 552; original emphasis)

The unusual typography is due to the fact that, as Nussbaum explains in her preface and notes, she had made her own translation of parts of Anne Frank's diary for *Women Writing in Dutch* but had run into trouble. She had seen the standard translation of the diary, by B. M. Mooyaart-Doubleday, and had felt unhappy with it. Having done what she regarded as a better job, she requested permission from the copyright holder to print her rendering – but was refused. Mightily annoyed but faced with no alternative except that of dropping the entire chapter from the book, she reproduced the Mooyaart-Doubleday rendering. However, she decided to pepper the Mooyaart-Doubleday translation with her own suggestions for improvement. They appear in italics and between square brackets and accolade marks, as shown above.

Now, if Nussbaum had simply reproduced the Mooyaart-Doubleday translation without adding her own suggestions, it would have looked like this:

> I must keep my head high and be brave, those thoughts will come, not once, but oh, countless times. Believe me, if you have been shut up for a year and a half, it can get too much for you some days. In spite of all justice and thankfulness, you can't crush your feelings.

Of course, Nussbaum would have much preferred to be able to print her own rendering. Had she been granted permission to do so, it would have looked like this:

> I must keep my head high and be brave, those thoughts will come all the same, not once, but oh, countless times. Believe me, if you have been confined for a year and a half, it can get too much for you some days. In spite of all fairness and thankfulness, you can't repress your feelings.

My point is simply that this translation, had it been allowed into print in this form, challenges the previous translator's choices just as vigorously as the one sporting accolade marks and square brackets. Even if the polemic is less visibly marked in this last version, it too engages the other translation critically, and it does so over the head of the original. Nussbaum's version hosts an angry debate in which one translator takes issue with a fellow translator about issues of register and accuracy in translation. It inscribes a subject-position that can only be the translator's, not the original author's.

It does more than that. It opens up an intertextual dimension specific to the domain of translation. Beyond the immediate reference to the previous version there is a more generic appeal to other translations of this type, and beyond those resonances there lies what Gérard Genette (1979) would call an architextual appeal to a broad sedimented notion of translation as such, a socially relevant concept of legitimate, proper translation. In other words, the translation invokes not just another translation, but other translations, and, by extension, translation as a generic and historical category.

In addition, and now looking forward rather than backward, Nussbaum's rendering demonstrates the repeatability and provisionality of translation. The criticism of the predecessor that is inscribed in the texture of Nussbaum's version reminds us that any particular rendition offers only one of a number of possible ways of representing the original in translation. A new translation may seek to replace one or more others but it will not be the last in line and it may in turn be overtaken by others. Further alternative renderings remain possible. Let me delve into this issue a little more.

In any given translation there is a latent gesturing towards additional possibilities and alternative renderings. This gesturing accompanies individual translations insofar as they can always be attempted again and differently. The text of a translation as we read it on the page represents a series of choices that in turn point up a large virtual reservoir in which all the unselected, excluded but potentially valid alternative choices are stored. Each re-translation taps into the reservoir, without, of course, ever exhausting it.

While the production of a new translation shows the underlying original to be translatable, the provisionality of the rendering intimates the dimension of the untranslatable, understood here as the impossibility of arriving at a definitive version – because a definitive version, as suggested earlier, would spell the end of translation. The potential for retranslation thus undermines any claim an individual translation may have to be the original's sole representative.

Consequently, while no translation can act as sole representative of a given original, every translation can lay claim to be a representation of it, in the double sense of the word: representation as proxy (as speaking or standing in for, as mouthpiece, delegate, ambassador) and as resemblance (replica, copy, mirror-image, simulation, interpretation). None however can claim to be the original's exclusive mouthpiece or the only possible copy of it. Retranslations can challenge any existing translation.

The modern world possesses an instrument that can put a stop to the potentially endless profusion of retranslations. The instrument has a name. It is called copyright law. It can halt the dissemination of rival versions by granting one version the exclusive right to act as proxy, and therefore as the only permitted (not: the only possible!) replica of a given original. Copyright law can also be used to prevent translation as such. More precisely: it can prevent translations from entering the public domain. But it can do all this for a brief period of time only, currently up to seventy years after the author's death. When copyright expires, the free-for-all resumes. In this way copyright law serves as a reminder that the untranslatability I mentioned above is rolled out over time. It can be held up for a while, for a century or so, but is unstoppable in the longer term, as each translation harbours the potential for retranslations. Put differently: as translation remains forever repeatable and provisional, every particular rendering potentializes others. In the same way the choices made in individual translations merely temporalize the excluded alternatives; it puts them on a reserve list.

Social systems

In talking of things like copyright law and temporalization, social and historical horizons come into view. What does translation look like if viewed as a social practice? To pick one paradigm from among several on offer, what would translation look like if viewed through a social systems lens, the type of lens that has been ground and polished by Niklas Luhmann in particular?

Translators would not be part of such a system. They would be presupposed, as would be all sorts of material preconditions. Here we encounter the translator's second disappearance. In social systems theory, translators are not part of any social system because, like other human beings, they are composed of minds and bodies, and neither minds nor bodies are social. Systems theory as Luhmann developed it[1] conceives of minds as psychic systems and of bodies as biological systems. The human body is encased within its owner's skin, and that is its outer limit. The body needs the outside world because it must take in air and food, but its functioning is an internal matter. In the same way the mind needs sense perceptions but then goes on to process thoughts and feelings in its own way. This processing is again an internal matter, just as digestion is internal to the body. Another way of putting this is to say that both minds and bodies function autonomously. Cells reproduce; thoughts feed on thoughts and trigger further thoughts. None of these processes are social. Minds cannot reach into other minds or transmit thoughts. I cannot read your mind and you cannot read mine.

What we can do is communicate. If we think of what it is that makes the social *social*, we end up with what happens not within but between persons. That is why Luhmann defines social systems as systems consisting of communications. Communication requires thoughtful minds, talking heads and functioning bodies, but its social nature comes to the fore when it happens in the sphere of the inter-

---

1.   All Luhmann's major works outline the ideas on which the following paragraphs are based. The most relevant titles are listed in the bibliography.

personal. The participating bodies and minds are not themselves social. What is social is the to and fro of communicative exchange, as one communication hooks into another and their linkage starts building a chain over time.

This concatenation is an ongoing concern in which the event character of individual communications is crucial. Communication happens. It does not linger. Communications have to connect if the system is to get going and to keep going. Signals have to be picked up, made sense of and responded to.

Communication, the key to it all, is conceived here as the coincidence of utterance, information and understanding. In this description "utterance" (Luhmann's German term is *Mitteilung*) stands for the communicative act, the performative aspect of communication. Information, the constative aspect, concerns what the utterance is about. It refers to something outside the communicative act itself. If information presents a communication's external reference, the utterance is its self-reference. Understanding (*Verstehen*) then means observing the unity of the difference between utterance and information: a receiver construes a speaker as saying something.

It may be worth adding a few footnotes to this idea of communication. First, communication, in this model, begins with understanding. That is, it begins with the receiver, not with the sender. Understanding means that the receiver grasps both utterance and information as selections, ascribing a communicative intention to the sender and assuming that the topic that is broached is of relevance in one way or another. It gets under way when a receiver responds to a communication and in turn finds a responsive receiver. Secondly, the model is inferential. Making sense of a communication is a matter of drawing inferences from a signal. Communication is not transfer, the transmission of pre-existing content via a conduit such as language. Instead, we have the same stimulus and inference model that also underpins Relevance theory. Applying this model to translation will mean sacrificing the metaphors of packaging and transportation dear to traditional conceptualizations of translation. Thirdly, inference leaves room for misunderstanding. Or better: misunderstanding is that apparent mismatch between intended and construed meaning that can only be established by making it the theme of further communicative exchanges, which themselves require inferential interpretation.

Before we return to translation, we need a few additional general points. Here, then, brutally simplified, are some essentials of systems theory, Luhmann on the back of an envelope, so to speak.

1. Communications are fleeting events, therefore they must be connected. To do this, the system scans and latches on to communications selectively. Of all the possible meanings a given communication proffers, only some are retained and used to trigger connecting communications, which are again filtered out

and made sense of selectively. In this way communication generates communication. The system continually recycles and modifies its own elements. It is self-reproducing or "autopoietic" in this sense.

2.   By doing this recursively and self-referentially over a period of time, and by selectively remembering and forgetting, a certain stabilization comes about in that networks and structures are built up that make certain communications more likely and therefore more predictable than others. The structures of a social system are structures of expectation. We need expectations to counter the double contingency that rules all things interpersonal and that consists in our inability to read each other's intentions or to fully predict each other's behaviour. As specific structures and expectations begin to cluster around certain kinds of communication, individual systems differentiate themselves from what is around them.

3.   Luhmann thinks of modern society as consisting of a large number of functionally differentiated social systems. Whereas in earlier periods of history the dominant forms of social organisation were segmentation (as in clan systems) and hierarchical stratification (as in feudal societies), the form of society in the industrial and postindustrial world is characterized by systems which specialize, so to speak, in performing certain socially necessary functions, such as producing collectively binding decisions (politics), the management of scarce resources (the economy), or maintaining social order through the distinction between permissible legal and punishable illegal acts.

4.   The various function systems of modern society that Luhmann has described in detail (the economy, politics, law, education, religion, art, the sciences, the mass media, organisations, but also social and protest movements) are perhaps best thought of as discourse networks. Each concentrates on certain kinds of communication and will process communications in its own way. There is however no superordinate system to keep the various function systems in check. Society as a whole, as the conglomerate of these function systems, manages without a centre, without a common direction and without an overarching purpose.

5.   Each function system is organized around an embedded matrix, a guiding difference or schema – Luhmann speaks of a "code" – that provides a basic orientation for its operations. For instance, the system of science is guided by a schema that distinguishes what it sees as "true", and therefore tenable, from false, and therefore untenable. Everything that happens in the sciences is meant ultimately to revolve around the pursuit of true rather than false statements about the world.

6.   Programmes flesh out a system's code and render it operational. In the sciences, for example, they endow truth with a positive value and furnish cri-

teria to tell truth from falsehood. Because these criteria are not self-evident the programmes of the sciences result in the welter of competing approaches and schools of thought that inspire research and debate. Other systems have their own programmes clustering around and giving substance to their specific codes. Whereas a system's code is highly abstract but fairly stable, programmes are more concrete and more variable.

7. Luhmann thinks of the major function systems of the modern world – the economy, politics, law, science – as rather self-centred networks that read everything that happens around them in their own terms. Politicians translate the church's moral pronouncements into their own vocabulary and interests. The commercial sector puts a price on art on the basis of criteria that are common currency in the business community but may well be at odds with those employed in the artworld. Natural catastrophes trigger very different responses among environmentalists, the news media, medical staff and insurance companies, for instance. Luhmann calls these reflexes "operative closure". Whatever systems take from their environment they convert into their own currency. For their operations systems draw on their own resources.

8. Even though each system has its own currency, systems can irritate one another, and they all do so all the time. Church leaders know their words resonate among politicians, and politicians realize they will do well to monitor developments in the churches. The monetary value of works of art affects the artworld. Irritation is merely another word for the stimulus and inference idea mentioned above. It implies that a system is not impervious to its environment, even though it will make its own sense of any stimulus that comes its way. In other words, it transforms irritation into information. National news media may promote nation-building but they do so through their primary function of garnering and disseminating news stories. This means the environment can intervene only indirectly into the system. It can produce resonance, but direct intervention would erase the difference between system and environment, and that would wipe the system out.

9. Systems are interdependent. Communication needs functioning bodies and minds, just as bodies need communication and minds, and minds need communication and bodies. Social systems, too, interact. The business sector knows that levels of taxation may go up or down following an election, and it plans for such an eventuality, even to the extent of seeking to influence politicians. Schools may start teaching creationism alongside or even instead of evolution theory due to evangelical lobbies. Luhmann calls these correlations "structural coupling". The term means that a system develops structures that also suit the demands of other systems, so that various systems can coexist while retaining their own identity and their specific difference. If operative

closure suggests autonomy, structural coupling points towards heteronomy. Put differently, structural coupling conditions a system's autonomy but does not determine it.

10. A system operates by means of distinctions to obtain and process information, and in this sense a social system is an observing system. When a system observes itself by means of its own constitutive difference – that is, when it re-enters the basic distinction that renders it distinct – it can generate self-descriptions. When such self-descriptions focus on the system as a whole, they become reflection theories. Self-descriptions and reflection theories typically re-enter the system's constitutive difference into their own observation of that system. If the sciences operate with a distinction between true and false, epistemological theories within the sciences re-enter that distinction to reflect on the nature of science. To the extent that this becomes a matter of observing, within the sciences, how the sciences observe the world, we have observation of observation, or second-order observation.

Translation as a social system

Can we describe translation along these lines? Let me stress that I am not interested in claiming that translation *is* a social system. That would mean making an ontological, essentialist claim, and the constructivist nature of systems theory militates against such claims. Systems exist in systems theory. Whether they have an objective existence outside it is a question systems theory cannot resolve. The translation system exists to the extent that a plausible case for this proposition can be made in system-theoretic terms. In other words, we can view translation through a system-theoretic prism with the aim of gaining a fresh perspective, a way of focussing attention. In that sense I want to consider translation as a social system and see what emerges.

What emerges is a system that comprises communications perceived as or concerned with translation, in other words translations and discourses about translation. But communications, as we saw, are events. That means the translation system does not consist so much of translations as objects such as written texts or spoken words but of the innumerable communicative acts that count as translations or contribute to its self-observation. Perhaps the fluidity of interpreting rather than the fixity of translated print offers the prototype of translation.

The system's unity, its own sense of being distinct, derives from its function, the role the system assigns to itself. The function of the translation system, I would suggest, is to extend society's communicative range, typically across natural languages. The system fulfils this function by producing communications that circulate as representations of communications on the other side of an intelligibility barrier such as a natural language.

The system's function also provides its code. As the translation system's code I regard the notion of representation in the double sense indicated above as proxy and resemblance, prototypically in the form of interlingual re-enactment. In other words, representation organizes the system and renders it distinct. You know you are dealing with a communication that belongs to the translation system if it is an instance of or bears on representation as proxy and resemblance, especially if it appears as interlingual re-enactment. "Proxy" refers to the idea of translation as a form of delegated speech, "resemblance" to translation as displaying similarity with the speech being represented. Put differently: translation is second-order discourse, discourse that represents another discourse.

The translation system emerges as communications of the same type begin to cluster. When this chatter gains volume and momentum and the system differentiates itself, programmes – prescriptions, proscriptions, preferences and permission, that is, the whole complex of norms and expectations governing particular modes of representation – flesh it out, provide backbone and structure, and unfold it over time.

As it unfolds, structural coupling ensures the system's ability to interact with the environment and its readiness to absorb the irritations the environment has in store. For example, the translation system may become aware that, as a rule, translations have to slot into existing text types and it will develop appropriate representational modes to ensure its products will fit. The current debates about localization are a case in point: the specific requirements of globalized websites stimulate the translation system into generating adequate forms of representation. The Anne Frank example, too, was about producing the most appropriate kind of representation for a certain type of text. But whether it is dealing with localization or with Anne Frank, the system has to decide for itself, with reference to its own resources and procedures, what kind of communication to bring about. If it did not do this, it would not be self-referential, it would not be autopoietic and it would therefore not be a system.

The basic tension in the system is that between autopoiesis and structural coupling, between autonomy and heteronomy, self-reference and external reference. As the self-reference of translation I regard that aspect of a translated text that refers, more or less self-consciously, to the particular mode of representation it has selected for itself. I will return to this below. The other aspect, a translation's external reference, that which a translation talks about in addition to being a replica of an earlier communication, lends itself to appropriation by other systems. It helps a translated text to live out its life as a translated degree certificate or historical novel, an interpreted speech, a localized website. In other words, and in the modern world, the internal differentiation of the translation system mirrors its differentiated environment, the various client systems with which it interacts. We are dealing with structural coupling in that the translation system copies into itself the differentiation it perceives in its environment so as to be able to mesh with a range of particular client systems – the medical world, the legal profession, finance, literature, journalism, and so on.

Internal differentiation means that the translation system gains in complexity, enabling it to cope with a complex world. Paradoxically, the growth in complexity also reduces the room for manoeuvre, as the system's various subdivisions are tied to particular sets of client demands. Nevertheless, due to the system's own momentum, the fact that it translates into its own terms the demands of its clients and accommodates them into its own structures, there can be no one-to-one correspondence between translation and its client systems. Resonance cannot be dictated. Hence there remains the possibility of friction, mismatch and conflict. The translation system may throw up peculiarities which a client system perceives as noise, as outrageous or obnoxious. These may concern issues of what constitutes a valid representation or a well-formed text but they may equally be ethical matters and normative ideas regarding what translation can be and what translators should do. All of them arise from debates within the translation system. In the same way, of course, a client system may irritate the translation system by voicing particular demands about what kinds of texts it wants to see.

If this is the basic scaffolding for a systems approach to translation, we can go on to investigate several aspects, from translation history to translator training. In what follows I will explore just two dimensions: the "form" of translation, and second-order observation.

The form of translation

To explain what I mean by the form of translation we may go back for a moment to the idea of translation as a specific kind of communication. Relevance theory names this specificity the interpretive (as against the descriptive) use of language. It means that translations are treated as secondary discourse, as metatexts: they report on other texts rather than speaking directly ("descriptively", in Relevance theory parlance) about the world (Gutt 1991).

As metatextual communications, translations invoke the distinction between utterance and information. Information may here be understood as covering what Andrew Chesterman (1996) calls "relevant resemblance". It is what a translation is about, its external reference, its resemblance to another text. The utterance is then the presentation and delivery of that resemblance, the translator speaking for someone else. Note that "translator" here stands for a discursive identity, a point of reference, not a real person: physical bodies belong not to the social system but to its environment.

The utterance points up a double frame: it announces reported speech, and then it performs that reporting. To see this more clearly, we might think of a translation that comes with a translator's preface. The preface frames the translation in the way quotation marks frame a quotation or a main clause an embedded clause. The frame also sets the scene and provides clues on how to read the simulation that follows. Assuming there is no glaring conflict between announcement and simulation, the actual rendition is then merely the dramatization of the particular translative option, the performance of the particular mode of representation announced in the preface. As a result, the performance is altered: we no longer see an underlying text being performed, we see the performance of a text being performed in a particular key. The actor who announces he is going to act Hamlet, acts Hamlet like an actor demonstrating a particular way of acting Hamlet.

I am suggesting that reading translations as translations, that is, as metatexts, with or without a preface, perhaps just using the bare mention of the word "translation" on the title page as a cue, means entering into a contract according to which translation operates as demonstration. The approach accords with the view of translation as quoting, since quotation can readily be thought of as an instance of demonstration (Mossop 1983, 1998; Clark and Gerrig 1990). The demonstration consists of the re-enactment of a pre-existing text and, because it is framed as a demonstration, of the display of a particular re-enacting style. In other words, translations can be read not only with reference to the originals they represent, and not only for what they say about whatever they and their originals speak about outside themselves. They can also be read for what they say about their individual way of re-enacting an original – and also, more generally, about the kind of re-enactment that is called translation.

In this perspective, each individual rendition exhibits a particular mode of representation profiled against the ever-present possibility of alternative modes and other performances. As, over time, translations intertextually endorse or berate one another along the lines we discussed with reference to the Anne Frank example above, the form of translation is condensed and confirmed into a series of patterns for further use. It is condensed in that a particular mode of representation can be applied again at a later moment and it will still be recognized as being the same mode. It is confirmed in that the same mode can be applied in different circumstances and thus extend its range while still remaining the same mode.

The form of translation is then what emerges as the historical set of communicative practices that become recognizable as translation because particular modes of representation are selected again and again. It is performed as translations are produced over time and representational modes are selected and re-selected, and it is reflected in the programmes fleshing out the schema of translation. The programmes are not uniform. Because in the modern world translation caters for an array of differentiated function systems, it is also itself differentiated. Nevertheless the system as a whole remains distinct. It allows itself to be irritated by different systems in its environment, but its resonance comes from within and is determined by its form.

The idea of form I am using here has an inside and an outside. It was Michelangelo, I think, who explained that the statue he wanted to carve was already there waiting within the block of marble in front of him; all he had to do was liberate it by chipping away the redundant stone. Form is two-sided. The inside is what is there; the outside is what had to be cut away for the inside to be revealed. Form is arrived at by selection, that is, by excluding what is not included and then concentrating on what is included as the inside of the form. The exclusions, for their part, are not just "potentialized" as I suggested above, but bracketed in time, temporalized, hence they remain available for future use.

What is the point of trying to think the form of translation along these lines? Just as speaking cuts into silence, what is translated is always profiled against what is left untranslated. But silence can also communicate: it may communicate an inability or an unwillingness to translate. Moreover, just as, in speaking, the words a speaker selects push back other words, those that could have been spoken but were not, a translation offers its particular choice of words by obscuring other choices, as we saw before. In doing so, it activates one mode of representation at the expense of alternative modes. The temporal sequence in which these differential choices are made constructs a past as well as a future. The future is the horizon of possibilities that is conditioned by the present but that may still mine the past in unexpected ways. The past may be thought of as the storeroom in which selections and inclusions are archived, selectively, as part of a process of forgetting as well as remembering. We deselect outmoded ways of translating and let them sink into oblivion so as to retain only a conveniently foreshortened canon of successful past selections as a template for day to day use. But nothing prevents us from occasionally stirring up the sediment and reinstating former rejects, bringing them back from the margins. This is, to name just one instance, what Lawrence Venuti did in *The Translator's Invisibility* (1995) when he extracted from the historical archive a largely forgotten genealogy of non-fluent translation as a way of buying credit for his own programme of "resistant" translation. The past is that selection of forms that the present holds available for future use.

In all these ways, it seems to me, considering form as two-sided allows us to appreciate translation as involving ongoing selection and therefore exclusion as well as inclusion. The series that becomes visible in this way is the evolving social system of translation.

Second-order observation

If selection has a performative and therefore a self-referential dimension, how self-reflexive can the system be? Anthony Pym (2004) and Brian Mossop (1998), among others, have claimed that a translating translator cannot say "I am translating", for at the moment of speaking or even thinking these words the translator cannot be translating. It is a claim I do not want to tackle head-on, but I will nibble at its edges. I would argue that because self-reference shadows the performance of translation, the translator, as translating subject, is actually written into the enactment. Grasping translation as utterance means being alive to the fact that a particular and no other mode of representation is being selected.

Perhaps the real problem lies deeper. We may be able to appreciate it better when we reflect that, while translating translators can write their own subject-positions as selectors into their performance as it proceeds, they cannot, in their own performance, survey or assess the conditions of possibility of their performance. It takes another viewpoint to see that conditioning.

The situation I am describing has a parallel in hermeneutics. There, understanding is seen as dependent on the pre-knowledge and self-understanding that come from being part of a cultural context and tradition, including what Hans-Georg Gadamer calls "the tyranny of hidden prejudices" (1989:270), the things one takes for granted as a child of one's age. The tyranny means that the understanding a person can achieve results from occupying a vantage point that s/he cannot fully appreciate. The idea is similar to what Paul de Man diagnosed as the blindness that both preconditions and enables insight and that only another observer can see. That observer, who operates from a different position, will distinguish between statement and meaning in the other's discourse – distinguish, that is, between what the speaker's words ostensibly say and what the observer construes as the unspoken preconceptions undergirding those words (Esposito 1996:600; de Man 1971:106). In the same vein Wolfgang Iser, drawing on the system theories of the biologists Humberto Maturana and Francisco Varela, notes the "descriptive complementarity" between operational and symbolic observation. The latter adopts a cognitive frame of reference that is different from that of the former. Symbolic observation can see what the operational observer cannot see (Iser 2000:109–112). Symbolic observation therefore constructs a different rationale for the actions observed by operational observation. Most causal explanations, for example, are of this kind.

Luhmann's term for this is second-order observation, which is the observation of observation. Observation is understood here in a broad sense, as the use of distinctions to gain information. Second-order observation observes not so much *what* others observe but *how* they observe. It is typically what critics and researchers do when they read cultural artefacts, social practices or individual behaviour as symptomatic of something larger and hidden. Karl Marx and Sigmund Freud are the towering models of this kind of symptomatic reading.

Translations observe the texts they represent. They engage in second-order observation when they comment on the work of other translators, not just in paratexts but through the form of their own translations. Second-order observation may then be understood as the active ingredient in that translation-specific intertextuality that enables translations to speak to and about each other. It sorts statement from meaning. What a translation says is one thing. Its meaning is something else. It is what another observer construes as the first translation's blindness, and the other observer may well be a translating translator who, while translating, comments on another translator by making differential choices. Second-order observation serves as a reminder of the contingency and the inevitable limitation of every viewing position.

We saw this kind of second-order observation at work on a micro-scale in Laureen Nussbaum's Anne Frank translation as it unpicked choices that may well have seemed self-evident to Mooyaart-Doubleday. For examples on a larger scale we might think of the tradition of orientalist translation, or what we now call gender bias in much historical translating. The bias, in both cases, is the second-order observer's construction: the first-order observers were only doing what came naturally to them.

The situation is epitomized in the story "Averroes' Search" by Jorge Luis Borges (1981). The story concerns the medieval Muslim philosopher Ibn Rushd (also known in the West as Averroes) who is engaged on a translation of Aristotle and, pondering Aristotle's *Poetics* and its section on dramatic forms, looks out of his window to see children play-acting in the yard. Nevertheless, lacking a concept of theatre in his own tradition, he remains incapable of grasping what (according to received wisdom in the Western tradition) Aristotle means by tragedy and ends up translating the term "tragedy", incongruously, as "panegyric", praise-poem. But note, again, that the incongruity is a construction of the second-order observer, who weighs Ibn Rushd's choice of a particular Arabic equivalent against the choices made by others in other linguistic and intellectual contexts. Ibn Rushd himself did not know he did not know: he interpreted Aristotle in the terms afforded by the world of which he was a part. Putting him right about tragedy, like Nussbaum lecturing Mooyaart-Doubleday, requires a viewpoint located in a different context, one that allows the conditioning of particular translation choices to be made visible. Second-order observation reminds the translation system that the criteria of what constitutes valid translation are subject to change. In this way the system reflects on itself. And as the Nussbaum example showed, this reflection can take the form of differential choices made in individual translations.

Let me round off this discussion of second-order observation by highlighting a recent and insightful demonstration of it in the field of the study of translation. Alexandra Lianeri's reappraisal of Schleiermacher's 1813 lecture "On the Different Methods of Translating" (Lianeri 2002) is concerned with Schleiermacher's problematization of translatability and his association of translation with the notion of culture. Among the essay's key points is that Schleiermacher's notion of translation is underwritten by a politics of culture. As Lianeri explains, she seeks

> to demonstrate [...] that Schleiermacher's theory of translation should not simply be grasped as a method of translation practice, but also as a means of creating a politically significant image of culture and society. Its historical importance, I suggest, lies not so much in the solutions it offered to the problem of untranslatability, as in the conception of translation as problem in the first place.
>
> (Lianeri 2002: 14)

There are three aspects of this reading of Schleiermacher that are of interest in the context of second-order observation.

1. Schleiermacher begins by separating commercial hackwork from what he regards as the properly intellectual pursuit of translation. As Lianeri shows, he then associates translation with a concept of culture that he describes, on the one hand, as being far removed from and unconstrained by the mundane realities of economic and sociopolitical life but that, on the other, he nonetheless envisions as a socially and politically unifying force. Schleiermacher, that is, appears to envisage culture as both above politics and as politically unifying, but he remains unaware of the contradiction. However, while he cannot see his own aporia, a modern observer who occupies a very different position and operates with different distinctions can see it.

2. Interestingly, Lianeri's investigation starts by remarking on the novelty of the Romantic preoccupation with translatability as a philosophical problem, and by wondering about the Romantics' insistence on associating translation with culture. She begins, that is, by closely observing how the Romantics observe translation and what distinctions they use to do so. Second-order observation is interested less in what another observer observes than in how the observer observes, that is, by means of what distinctions. And because it takes different distinctions to see how the Romantics distinguish, the exercise has a self-reflexive momentum.

3. To locate her own approach Lianeri invokes, not Luhmann or Iser, but Fredric Jameson and his idea of metacommentary, which aims to question the presuppositions of a cultural practice while remaining alert to the grounds on which this questioning itself takes place. Like Luhmann's second-order observation, Jameson's metacommentary (Jameson 1988/1971) seeks to read cultural practices for the distinctions that enabled them in the first place – it seeks, in other words, to separate statement from meaning so as to figure out the position from which statements are made. Like second-order observation, metacommentary rebounds on the observer. It leads Lianeri to describe Schleiermacher's concern with translation as part of his idealization of culture, an idealization which is itself a response to an increasingly riven social reality. That provides us with a view of Schleiermacher's viewing position, his own blind spot. But it also leads Lianeri to wonder about the indiscriminate use of "culture" in the humanities today, including today's translation studies. Although she does not pursue the matter in these terms, we may wonder: are we, as students of translation, perhaps as fond of "culture" as the Romantics were because, like them, we are politically powerless? If so, what about the much vaunted "cultural turn" in translation studies? Is it simply the mark, and the tacit admission, of political irrelevance?

These may be awkward questions at a time when the so-called cultural turn in translation studies is widely seen as beneficial. Raising them here will, I hope, show that the apparatus of social systems theory allows us not only to look into translation as socially and historically embedded, but to query our own observations about it.

References

Borges, Jorge Luis. 1981. *Labyrinths. Selected Stories and Other Writings.* D. A. Yates and J. E. Irby (eds). Harmondsworth: Penguin.

Chesterman, Andrew. 1996. "On Similarity". *Target* 8 (1): 159–64.

Clark, Herbert and Gerrig, Richard. 1990. "Quotations as Demonstrations". *Language* 66: 764–805.

Esposito, Elena. 1996. "Observing Interpretation: A Sociological View of Hermeneutics". *Modern Language Notes* 111: 593–619.

Gadamer, Hans-Georg. [2]1989. *Truth and Method.* Trans. Joel Weilsheimer and Donald G. Marshall. London: Sheed & Ward.

Genette, Gérard. 1979. *Introduction à l'architexte.* Paris: Seuil.

Gutt, Ernst-August. 1991. *Translation and Relevance. Cognition and Context.* Oxford: Blackwell.

Hill, Donna. 1977. *Joseph Smith, the First Mormon.* Garden City (NY): Doubleday.

Iser, Wolfgang. 2000. *The Range of Interpretation*. New York: Columbia University Press.

Jameson, Fredric. 1988/1971. "Metacommentary". In *The Ideology of Theory. Essays 1971–1986. Vol. 1: Situations of Theory*, F. Jameson. London and New York: Routledge. 3–16.

Lianeri, Alexandra. 2002. "Translation and the Ideology of Culture: Reappraising Schleiermacher's Theory of Translation". *Current Writing* 14 (2): 2–18.

Luhmann, Niklas. 1995. *Social Systems*. Trans. John Bednarz. Stanford: Stanford University Press.

Luhmann, Niklas. 1997. *Die Gesellschaft der Gesellschaft*. 2 vols. Frankfurt am Main: Suhrkamp.

Luhmann, Niklas. 2000. *Art as a Social System*. Trans. Eva Knodt. Stanford: Stanford University Press.

Luhmann, Niklas. 2002. *Theories of Distinction. Redescribing the Descriptions of Modernity*. W. Rasch (ed). Stanford: Stanford University Press.

Luhmann, Niklas. ²2004. *Einführung in die Systemtheorie*. D. Baecker (ed). Heidelberg: Carl Auer.

Man, Paul de. 1971. *Blindness and Insight. Essays in the Rhetoric of Contemporary Criticism*. New York: Oxford University Press.

Mossop, Brian. 1983. "The Translator as Rapporteur: A Concept for Training and Self-Improvement". *Meta* XXVIII (3): 244–278.

Mossop, Brian. 1998. "What is a Translating Translator Doing?". *Target* 10 (2): 231–266.

Nussbaum, Laureen. 1994. "Anne Frank". In *Women Writing in Dutch*, K. Aercke (ed). New York and London: Garland. 513–75.

Persuitte, David. 1985. *Joseph Smith and the Origins of the Book of Mormon*. Jefferson (BC) and London: McFarland.

Pym, Anthony. 2004. "Propositions on Cross-cultural Communication and Translation". *Target* 16 (1): 1–28.

Reuter, Paul. 1995. *Introduction to the Law of Treaties*. Trans. J. Mico and P. Haggermacher. London and New York: Kegan Paul International.

Robinson, Douglas. 2001. *Who Translates? Translator Subjectivities Beyond Reason*. Albany: State University of New York Press.

Venuti, Lawrence. 1995. *The Translator's Invisibility. A history of translation*. London and New York: Routledge.

PART II

Bourdieu's influence in conceptualising a sociology of translation

Objectivation, réflexivité et traduction

Pour une re-lecture bourdieusienne de la traduction

Jean-Marc Gouanvic
Université Concordia, Montréal, Canada

In translation studies, the major contribution of Bourdieu's theory resides, in my view, in the elaboration of the notions field, *habitus*, and *illusio*, in the definition of the symbolic capital and in its application to artistic products. In this paper, I will discuss how the notions of *habitus* and field can be applied to translation by analysing the *habitus* of three agents operating in the translation of US literature in France. *Illusio*, on the other hand, can be associated with texts classified in genres and types. Each genre is endowed with an *illusio* which conditions the taste of the reading public and makes the readers adhere to the game expressed in the texts. These reflections will be completed by associating them with the principle of "double reflexivity": first, the translation studies scholar analyses the translated texts and examines their determinations, second he/she makes an analysis on his/her translation studies position as a scholar and on what is at stake in his/her research field.

L'objet de cet article est de présenter certaines idées de Pierre Bourdieu appliquées à la traduction et de les discuter heuristiquement dans ce cadre. Pour nous mettre d'emblée dans la meilleure position possible, celle du traductologue, nous allons amorcer nos réflexions à partir de certaines positions d'Antoine Berman. Dans un petit article publié en 1989 dans la revue *Meta*, intitulé "La traduction et ses discours", Antoine Berman définissait la traductologie ainsi: "La traductologie est la réflexion de la traduction sur elle-même à partir de sa nature d'expérience" (Berman 1989:675). Et un peu plus loin: "La traductologie est [...] la reprise réflexive de l'expérience qu'est la traduction et non une théorie qui viendrait décrire, analyser et éventuellement régir celle-ci" (ibid.:676). Certes Berman attire les notions d'"expérience" et de "réflexion" nettement du côté du discours philosophique, en se référant à Kant, Fichte, Hegel, Husserl, Benjamin et Heidegger. Mais il semble également fasciné par une conception plus socioanalytique de la traduction, comme le montre la référence aux tâches 3, 4, 5 et 6 de sa nomenclature sur ce que doit être la traductologie. Dans ces tâches, l'historicité et la réflexion sur le traducteur comme agent occupent une place centrale.[1] Ces idées d'Antoine Berman sur la traductologie ont une parenté avec celles que propose Bourdieu. Ce que Berman nomme "expérience", Bourdieu l'appelle "pratique", et la "réflexion" bermanienne correspond à la réflexivité.[2] Cela étant dit, cette présentation comporte quatre parties: la première porte sur les conditions de l'objectivation en traductologie et sur les champs, puis, dans une deuxième section, nous verrons en quoi consiste l'*habitus* du traducteur en nous arrêtant sur trois cas (Maurice-Edgar Coindreau, Marcel Duhamel et Boris Vian), ensuite, troisièmement, nous examinerons en quoi consiste l'*illusio* et comment le traducteur se situe par rapport à cette *illusio*, enfin nous analyserons très brièvement sur quoi repose le capital symbolique du traducteur.

Les conditions de l'objectivation en traductologie

Quelles sont les conditions d'une réflexion sur la traduction en tant que pratique sociale? Dans *Méditations pascaliennes* (1997), Bourdieu consacre de nombreuses pages à analyser la posture intellectuelle du savant qui observe le monde social d'un point de vue détaché de la réalité, d'un point de vue "scolastique" (Bourdieu 1997:25) qui connaît un "temps libéré des occupations et des préoccupations pratiques" (ibid.). Ce temps est ce que Bourdieu nomme le temps de la "skholè". Le traductologue est susceptible, par l'arrêt sur image, par la suspension des phénomènes analysés dans laquelle est produite la réflexion sur ces phénomènes, de refouler la dimension sociale pratique de ce qui est analysé. L'objectivation pri-

---

1.   Berman écrit: "*La troisième tâche se rapporte à la temporalité et à l'historicité des actes de traduction*. Les traductions ont une temporalité propre, qui est liée à celle des œuvres, des langues et des cultures. [...]. *La quatrième tâche* consiste à analyser l'espace pluriel des traductions, sans confondre ce travail avec la constitution d'une 'typologie', aussi affinée qu'elle puisse être. [...]. *La cinquième tâche* de la traductologie consiste à développer une réflexion *sur le traducteur*. [...]. *La sixième tâche* consiste à analyser pourquoi, et de tout temps, la traduction a été une activité *occultée*, marginalisée, dévalorisée, qu'elle soit travail sur la lettre ou libre restitution du sens" (1989:677, italiques d'A.B.).

2.   Même si la théorie bermanienne est éloignée de la pensée sociologique (Bourdieu), elles se recoupent toutes deux en un certain sens dans la notion philosophique d'"expérience" telle que l'analyse toute la philosophie occidentale et dans la notion de "pratique" au sens où Bourdieu l'aborde notamment dans *le Sens pratique* (1980). Ainsi, par exemple, la manière dont Bourdieu définit l'*habitus* est centrée sur la pratique sociale dans les champs, les habitus fonctionnant "en tant que principes générateurs et organisateurs de pratiques et de représentations [...]" (1980:88). Notre perspective traductologique est fondée sur les mêmes hypothèses.

maire qu'opère le traductologue se situe ainsi en "apesanteur" sociale, celle que produit la posture scolastique. L'objectivation en traductologie ne peut s'arrêter en chemin si elle veut saisir la pratique de la traduction et sa logique propre. Pour cela, d'une part il y a lieu d'intégrer au modèle de pensée pratique les conditions économiques et sociales qui rendent possible la traduction, en particulier toutes ces pratiques qui prennent naissance dans les champs et qui font intervenir ce que l'on a coutume de nommer les institutions. D'autre part, il convient également d'intégrer au modèle les activités des agents qui s'efforcent de "construire leur représentation subjective d'eux-mêmes et du monde" (ibid.: 225), à savoir en tout premier lieu les traducteurs, mais également les auteurs du texte source (et leurs éditeurs), l'éditeur du texte cible et les autres agents d'édition du texte cible. Nous allons voir, en conclusion, qu'une autre objectivation s'impose en sociologie de la traduction, l'objectivation tournée vers le traductologue, ce que Bourdieu nomme la "double réflexivité".

Comment s'articulent la notion de champ et la traduction? Bourdieu définit un champ de la manière suivante:

> Un champ [...] se définit entre autres choses en définissant des enjeux et des intérêts spécifiques, qui sont irréductibles aux enjeux et aux intérêts propres à d'autres champs (on ne pourra pas faire courir un philosophe avec des enjeux de géographe) et qui ne sont pas perçus de quelqu'un qui n'a pas été construit pour entrer dans ce champ [...]. Pour qu'un champ marche, il faut qu'il y ait des enjeux et des gens prêts à jouer le jeu, dotés de l'habitus impliquant la connaissance et la reconnaissance des lois immanentes du jeu, des enjeux, etc.
>
> (Bourdieu 1984a: 113–114)

Tout d'abord, il convient de distinguer le champ de la traductologie, champ scientifique, et l'espace de la traduction des œuvres, champ littéraire dans les cas que nous allons examiner.[3]

Le champ de la traductologie est un champ au plein sens du terme. Il a émergé dans les années 1970 et au début des années 1980, et possède ses agents, ses institu-

---

3.   Il n'est pas impossible que la traduction soit construite comme un champ à certaines époques et dans certaines cultures (quoique nous n'en ayons pas d'exemple). Pour cela, il conviendrait que les productions traduites et reçues dans une culture soient dotées, d'une part, d'une autonomie qui les fassent reconnaître comme des produits spécifiques, distincts des productions indigènes et, d'autre part, qu'elles manifestent des enjeux qui ne valent essentiellement que pour elles. Si la première condition n'est pas trop difficile à remplir, la seconde paraît beaucoup plus problématique, car les genres littéraires (pour ne parler que de littérature) sont manifestement des configurations qui trouvent d'abord à se réaliser dans les cultures indigènes cible, les traductions ayant pour effet de contribuer fondamentalement à faire bouger les hiérarchies de goûts socio-esthétiques dans ces cultures.

tions, ses collections spécialisées et ses revues, ses associations, ses programmes universitaires de maîtrise et de doctorat, ses colloques, ses recherches, et ses enjeux propres. La traduction comme pratique ne constitue pas un champ pour la principale raison que les textes traduits appartiennent à de multiples configurations qui elles-mêmes sont rattachables à des champs spécifiques. Une traduction relèvera du champ auquel est lié le texte à traduire; par exemple, la traduction d'un texte scientifique demeure dans l'aire du champ scientifique auquel appartient le texte cible. Il en va de même pour un texte juridique, économique, informatique, littéraire, etc. Les enjeux que connaissent les traductions sont ceux de ces champs cibles, mais ce sont ceux aussi des champs sources, dont certains traits se communiquent aux champs cibles par la traduction. Le texte cible tire de sa double appartenance traductive des caractéristiques essentielles de la traduction. Cette double appartenance est également celle du traducteur, dont l'*habitus*, au moment de la traduction, est par nature bi-lingue et le résultat de la convergence de deux cultures. On va le voir dans les exemples que nous allons prendre dans un instant.

L'*habitus* du traducteur

Posons la question suivante: Qu'est-ce qui fait courir le traducteur? Ou, posée à la manière de Berman, d'où vient la "pulsion de traduire", et, façon Bourdieu, sur quoi repose la "*libido translatandi*"? Si Berman se borne à constater que les traductrices et les traducteurs sont mûs par une telle pulsion, Bourdieu, lui, construit sa théorie sociale spécialement sur le rôle de l'agent et répond que ce qui fait agir les agents dans la pratique (quelle qu'elle soit, traduction comprise), ce sont "inscrits dans le corps par les expériences passées", "ces systèmes de schèmes de perception, d'appréciation et d'action permett[a]nt d'opérer des actes de connaissance pratique [...]" (Bourdieu 1997: 166). En un mot, c'est leur *habitus* qui est à la source de leur mode d'appréhension pratique du réel. L'*habitus* peut être défini de la façon suivante:

> [S]ystème[s] de *dispositions* durables et transposables, structures structurées prédisposées à fonctionner comme structures structurantes, c'est-à-dire en tant que principes générateurs et organisateurs de pratiques et de représentations qui peuvent être objectivement adaptées à leur but sans supposer la visée consciente de fins et la maîtrise expresse des opérations nécessaires pour les atteindre [...].
> (Bourdieu 1980: 88, italiques de P.B.)

Plutôt que de commenter cette formulation de ce qu'est l'*habitus*, voyons comment peut être comprise la construction de l'*habitus* de traducteur à partir de la pratique.

Dans la pratique de la traduction, le traducteur accomplit sa tâche en mettant en œuvre dans l'opération deux processus (qui, on va le voir, se réduisent finalement à un seul). Par l'emploi des outils habituels du traducteur (dictionnaires généraux et spécialisés, banques et bases de données, logiciels d'aide à la traduction, *work benches*, etc.), il fait intervenir des processus interprétatifs fondés sur ces outils. Mais il existe une autre dimension de l'exercice professionnel de la traduction, les processus liés à l'acquisition intériorisée dans la vie individuelle et sociale de pratiques qui rendent possible l'opération de traduction; du point de vue du traducteur, les dispositions à traduire ne sont pas nécessairement des modes objectivés, délibérés et conscients, comme le dit Bourdieu à propos de l'*habitus*. Les productions linguistiques et culturelles bilingues sont le résultat d'une instrumentation objective et, pourrait-on dire, d'une pratique subjective, mais l'instrumentation objective tend à se subjectiver, de sorte que même cette instrumentation objective entre dans la catégorie des comportements subjectifs. C'est ce que l'on nomme couramment "expérience", "capacité", "faculté", "facilité", "compétence" de la traductrice et du traducteur. La capacité d'une traductrice ou d'un traducteur à traduire tel texte s'évalue à la facilité relative avec laquelle elle/il trouve des solutions de traduction comme en se jouant, sans délibérer, en trouvant dans son *habitus* des solutions ajustées à la situation; comme le dit Bourdieu (1987: 127), l'agent (ici le traducteur) "tombe sur" ces solutions, comme si le problème posé par la situation et sa solution s'imposaient en fin de compte d'elles-mêmes. Bien sûr, loin de moi l'idée que la traduction est toujours une activité facile qui s'accomplit sans souffrance intellectuelle ou matérielle. Les enquêtes effectuées par des chercheurs, telles que celle menée par Isabelle Kalinowski sur "la Vocation au travail de traduction" en France à l'heure actuelle (Kalinowski 2002: 47–54), montrent de façon patente que le métier de traduction de la littérature est tendanciellement précaire et déprimant, parce que les traductrices (surtout) et les traducteurs sont exploités économiquement et dominés symboliquement. Au Canada, la situation est bien pire en traduction littéraire, à en croire la seule traductrice littéraire professionnelle, Sheila Fischman, qui parvient à peine à vivre de ses traductions (français vers l'anglais).[4] Quant aux traducteurs qui travaillent dans les entreprises ou font du télétravail non littéraire, l'état du marché de la traduction est extrêmement différent. La traduction constitue un excellent métier, rémunérateur et reconnu par un Ordre professionnel, au moins au Québec, et à ce titre il jouit d'une considération sociale. Ces remarques prou-

---

4. La situation de la traduction littéraire n'est pas reluisante au Canada, ce qui est paradoxal dans un pays bilingue où l'on s'attendrait à ce que les traductions abondent entre les deux langues officielles. Les causes de cette situation sont multiples: exiguïté du marché, situation politique, etc. L'aide fédérale (subventions) vise à la contrebalancer (même si modestement).

vent que la traduction n'est pas un corps de métier homogène et qu'il est capital d'effectuer des distinctions entre les types de pratiques de traduction dont on parle dans les champs spécifiques. Elles prouvent également qu'on ne peut parler de l'*habitus* comme trajectoire sociale sans tenir compte de l'état des champs où les agents exercent leur pratique.

Voyons trois cas d'agents traducteurs, pris dans les champs littéraires français, ayant exercé leur pratique en traduction de l'anglo-américain vers le français au 20e siècle: Maurice-Edgar Coindreau, Marcel Duhamel et Boris Vian. Ces trois traducteurs sont dotés d'*habitus* spécifiques liés à leur trajectoire sociale particulière. Coindreau est un agrégé d'espagnol qui n'a qu'une connaissance livresque de l'anglo-américain. Il fait ses premières armes (son "apprentissage", Coindreau 1974: 37) en traduisant *Manhattan Transfer* de John Dos Passos en 1928 (c'est la date de publication du livre en français) aux États-Unis; car il a émigré aux États-Unis, où il est enseignant à l'Université Princeton. Après Dos Passos, et quelques autres (dont Hemingway), il traduit principalement Faulkner et les écrivains du Sud des États-Unis Flannery O'Connor et William Goyen, qu'il apprécie tout particulièrement. Pourquoi les écrivains du Sud ont-ils sa prédilection? Parce qu'il voit un parallélisme historique entre la situation des Chouans, ces contre-révolutionnaires vendéens vaincus auxquels il s'identifie profondément (il est originaire de Vendée), et les Sudistes également vaincus dont Faulkner, O'Connor et Goyen mettent en scène les descendants. Il n'a pas de mots trop durs pour les écrivains de la *Lost Generation*, les Hemingway, Scott Fitzgerald, etc., et il présente Hemingway comme un usurpateur, la vraie génération perdue étant celle de Faulkner. Pourquoi donc a-t-il traduit Hemingway? Parce que Gaston Gallimard le lui a demandé, et à Gaston Gallimard Coindreau ne peut rien refuser.[5] Ainsi il traduira *Of Mice and Men* de Steinbeck et *Tobacco Road* de Caldwell, un peu contre son gré, comme il l'explique dans *Mémoires d'un traducteur* (1974).

Marcel Duhamel, lui, a une connaissance pratique de l'anglais familier: il l'a appris à 15 ans pendant la Première Guerre mondiale à Manchester, où il avait accompagné sa sœur employée dans un hôtel dont l'un de ses oncles était le propriétaire. Duhamel est l'exact opposé de Coindreau: ayant à peine dépassé le niveau du certificat d'études primaires, sa connaissance de la langue anglaise est acquise sur le tas. À 16 ans, il parle anglais. De retour en France, après la Première Guerre

---

5.   Dans *Mémoires d'un traducteur* (1974), C. Giudicelli, qui l'interroge sur les raisons qui l'ont poussé à traduire les deux romans *le Soleil se lève aussi* et *l'Adieu aux armes* d'Hemingway dans lesquels il ne croyait pas, Coindreau répond: "Non [je n'aimais pas ces deux romans]. Mais j'aimais Gaston Gallimard qui avait accepté tout ce que je lui avais proposé auparavant. [...] Aussi, quand il m'écrivit: 'nous aimerions que vous traduisiez pour nous ces deux livres d'Hemingway', je n'allais pas faire la fine bouche et refuser" (ibid.: 46).

mondiale, il fait son service militaire en Turquie, où il rencontre Jacques Prévert et Yves Tanguy, avec lesquels il se lie d'une amitié qui durera toute leur vie. Mais, entre-temps, ils s'installent dans un petit appartement de la rue du Château dans les années 1920, et participent activement à l'émergence du mouvement surréaliste avec les Max Morise, Raymond Queneau, André Breton, Tristan Tzara... Dans les années 1930, il s'essaie à la traduction de Raoul Whitfield, Henry Miller, sans avoir d'éditeur, pour le plaisir. Mais il se fait connaître comme traducteur en publiant *Little Caesar* de Burnett dans *France-soir* et rentre dans une maison de doublage, la Tobis Klangfilm. En 1945, il fonde chez Gallimard la collection de la "Série Noire" et devient le bras droit de Gaston Gallimard pour la négociation des droits de traduction de la maison d'édition. Il effectue environ quatre-vingt traductions de Hemingway, Caldwell, Steinbeck, McCoy, etc., marqués par l'usage de la langue argotique et familière et par les vernaculaires (Duhamel 1972).

Boris Vian est l'introducteur de la science-fiction américaine en France dans les années 1950. Formé au métier d'ingénieur à l'école Centrale, il possède un *habitus* très particulier, qui allie le littéraire et le scientifique et fait de lui, avec Raymond Queneau, l'agent idéal pour promouvoir l'imaginaire mixte, littéraire et scientifique. De fait il écrit des articles sur la science-fiction dans *les Temps modernes, Arts, la Parisienne*, publie des adaptations des auteurs de *Galaxy Science Fiction* dans *France-Dimanche*, traduit pour *le Mercure de France* et pour la collection nouvellement fondée "Le Rayon Fantastique" des éditions Hachette-Gallimard. Dans cette collection, il publie deux traductions, *le Monde des non-A* et *les Joueurs du non-A*, où il découvre la sémantique générale de Korzybski. Il traduit le texte américain en le vernacularisant, en imposant au texte des formes familières françaises.[6]

Ces trois traducteurs, qui sont aussi les introducteurs talentueux de la littérature américaine dans la France des années 1930 à 1950 (le roman réaliste, le *detective novel* et la science-fiction), occupent des positions bien différentes dans les champs littéraires français: Coindreau, universitaire agrégé, se caractérise par un *habitus* qui le porte à apprécier la littérature sérieuse, celle dont les visées sont quasi-tragiques et qu'il va accentuer au détriment de la dimension comique, par exemple, chez Faulkner. L'*habitus* de Duhamel, lui, est plébéien et son trait principal est une conception eudémonique, ludique et jubilatoire, de la littérature, qui s'observe dans ses traductions-adaptations du *detective novel* américain. Son *habitus* est aux antipodes de celui de Coindreau. Quant à Boris Vian, son *habitus* est typiquement celui du *taupin* qui possède un réel talent littéraire.

---

6. Voir Gouanvic (1999: 96–97, notamment).

"L'habitus étant le social incorporé", écrit Bourdieu, "il est 'chez lui' dans le champ qu'il habite, qu'il perçoit immédiatement comme doté de sens et d'intérêt" (Bourdieu 1992: 103). Il n'en va pas exactement ainsi dans le cas du traducteur. L'*habitus* du traducteur, en effet, possède la particularité, on l'a déjà dit, de résulter de la convergence de deux cultures. Formé la plupart du temps à l'école avec l'apprentissage d'une seconde langue, l'*habitus* primaire ou originaire est une condition de l'acquisition de la pratique de la traduction, mais il ne fait pas le traducteur. L'*habitus* spécifique de traducteur se construit dans la rencontre de deux cultures, la culture indigène, française, dans les trois cas que nous avons examinés très brièvement, et la culture étrangère, que le traducteur a acquise la plupart du temps par un contact avec l'étranger ou par immersion. La culture indigène est celle de l'*habitus* primaire du traducteur, celle vers laquelle le traducteur traduit. (Entre parenthèses, cela est d'une importance capitale; lorsque le traducteur traduit vers sa seconde langue-culture son *habitus* peut plus volontiers le porter vers le champ source que vers le champ cible, et l'inciter à conserver dans la traduction les marques d'étrangèreté du texte source, dont il est plus proche par son *habitus*; autre cas de figure, l'interprète qui travaille vers sa deuxième ou même sa troisième langue. À chaque fois l'*habitus* est conditionné par la direction vers laquelle s'exerce le travail.) En général, c'est vers la langue-culture indigène cible que s'effectue la traduction. Le contact ou l'immersion est toujours plus ou moins une expatriation par rapport à la culture indigène. Le cas de Coindreau le montre bien. D'emblée il publie sa première traduction de l'américain, *Manhattan Transfer*, de Dos Passos en 1928, traduction faite à New York sous la supervision de Dos Passos lui-même. Son travail de traducteur est pris en charge par Gallimard, qui accepte sa manière de traduire,[7] et positionnera Coindreau dans les années suivantes comme traducteur attitré de la littérature américaine dans le champ littéraire français dominant. À l'inverse, Duhamel ne construit pas son *habitus* de traducteur dans la relation au champ littéraire français: il traduit dans les années 1930 au petit bonheur et pour le plaisir, sans trop espérer être édité dans le champ littéraire. La publication de *Little Caesar* dans *France Soir* le fait connaître, mais c'est dans le domaine du doublage cinématographique qu'il va commencer à faire carrière. Jusqu'en 1944, il sera confiné au doublage, sorte d'antichambre, pour Duhamel, de la traduction littéraire. Autant Coindreau se sera fait une position immédiatement dans le champ littéraire français, autant Duhamel aura dû attendre plus de dix ans pour qu'une place lui soit consentie chez Gallimard.

Ce qui vient d'être dit sur la relation de l'*habitus* des trois traducteurs Coindreau, Duhamel, Vian avec les champs en question (réaliste, policier, science-fic-

---

7. Cette manière de traduire penche nettement vers ce que Berman désigne comme une traduction "ethnocentrique" (Berman 1984).

tion) pourrait laisser croire que cette relation est directe et que la *vis* de l'*habitus* se communique aux champs de façon téléologique. Il n'en va pas exactement ainsi dans la réalité. L'énergie investie dans les *habitus* procède aussi par tâtonnements, un peu de façon stochastique, en cherchant à se réaliser dans des objets favorables à ce qu'ils sont. C'est selon une procédure semblable que sont choisis les textes à traduire, en amont de la traduction, par les agents (éditeurs, directeurs de collection). Si des stratégies interviennent alors, ces stratégies visant à faire accepter le texte choisi comme juste, bel et bon, c'est-à-dire à l'investir d'une légitimité optimale, les effets produits sont très variables dans la pratique. Il n'est pas dit que ce soit ce qu'on appelle les *bonnes* stratégies (*bonnes* parce qu'elles sont en apparence couronnées de succès) qui ont produit les résultats observés, la stratégie (par exemple une campagne publicitaire) ayant joué sur un certain sens de l'œuvre source, alors que ce sont probablement d'autres aspects de l'œuvre qui ont pu lui valoir la consécration. Dans ce cadre interviennent les traducteurs et la manière de traduire qui leur est jusqu'à un certain point propre (compte tenu bien entendu de l'œuvre source). Le rôle du traducteur et de son *habitus* est central dans le type de réception de l'œuvre traduite; le traducteur habité de son *habitus* introduit dans l'œuvre source tous ces signes infimes, souvent à son insu, parce qu'ils sont bien à leur place ainsi dans la traduction.

Illusio, champ et traduction

L'*habitus* spécifique des agents se constitue, s'exprime et se développe en relation avec les champs et leurs enjeux propres. Les agents s'investissent dans le jeu que leur offre le champ selon les dispositions ajustées à ce jeu, elles-mêmes acquises dans le champ. Leur investissement repose sur "l'inclination et l'aptitude à jouer le jeu, à prendre intérêt au jeu, à se prendre au jeu" (Bourdieu 1984a: 34–35). Le jeu que l'agent est prêt à jouer, ainsi que l'aptitude qu'il suppose, est dans le cas du traducteur la capacité à jouer le jeu dans le champ. Le traducteur s'efforce de "transporter" en quelque sorte les "traits" du texte source dans la culture cible. Or, ces traits sont producteurs de ce que Bourdieu nomme l'*illusio*:

> L'*illusio* littéraire, cette adhésion originaire au jeu littéraire qui fonde la croyance dans l'*importance* ou l'*intérêt* des fictions littéraires, est la condition, presque toujours inaperçue, du plaisir esthétique qui est toujours, pour une part, plaisir de jouer le jeu, de participer à la fiction, d'être en accord total avec les présupposés du jeu; la condition aussi de l'*illusion* littéraire et de l'effet de croyance [...] que le texte peut produire. (Bourdieu 1992: 455, italiques de P.B.)

L'illusio littéraire s'exprime dans chaque fiction; c'est une "willing[8] suspension of disbelief", comme le dit Coleridge (1907:6). Mais chaque texte a sa façon d'interpréter l'*illusio* littéraire, de lui donner corps, de sorte que cette *illusio* produise chez le lecteur cet effet de croyance spécifique à chaque texte, lesquels textes peuvent être regroupés selon des catégories génériques, réalisme, policier, science-fiction, fantastique, etc. Le travail du traducteur est dans ces conditions de trouver les moyens d'exprimer les traits génériques et discursifs du texte source de façon que le lecteur cible prenne part au type d'*illusio* littéraire qu'offre le texte. Car il y a dans l'*illusio* d'un texte l'image de l'*illusio* d'un champ: par exemple, l'*illusio* de *A Farewell to Arms* exprime l'*illusio* du champ du roman réaliste réinterprété selon les traits du roman d'Hemingway; celle de *Foundation* d'Asimov exprime l'*illusio* du champ de la science-fiction; celle de *The Lady in the Lake* de Chandler exprime l'*illusio* du champ du roman policier, etc. Ces traits sont les déterminants historicisés caractéristiques de ces textes et de l'état du genre et du champ à l'époque et dans le lieu où ont émergé les textes. Certes, les trois traducteurs de ces textes se sont acquittés de leur tâche en transportant homologiquement ces romans dans les champs correspondants de l'espace littéraire cible: *L'Adieu aux armes* traduit par Maurice-Edgar Coindreau et publié dans le champ réaliste cible français, *Fondation* traduit par Jean Rosenthal et publié dans le champ naissant de la science-fiction cible, *la Dame du lac* traduit par Michèle Léglise et Boris Vian et publié dans le champ du roman policier cible, la collection "Série Noire" de Marcel Duhamel.

Cependant, toute une série de problèmes peut se poser dans la traduction vue comme transport homologique – en terme de genres – d'un texte source dans le champ cible. Ces problèmes obligent à envisager la théorie bourdieusienne sous un jour complémentaire. Toute traduction est en effet régie par le principe du *décentrement*, concept proposé par Henri Meschonnic (1973:308), mais que nous employons dans un sens sociologique. Dans toute traduction il y a décentrement des enjeux, au sens de Bourdieu: les déterminants socio-historiques qui ont produit les œuvres et leurs enjeux dans l'espace littéraire source sont par nature coupés des enjeux du champ littéraire cible dans lequel prend place la traduction.[9]

---

8. La "*willing* suspension of disbelief" de Coleridge est proche de l'*illusio* de Bourdieu; elle s'en éloigne cependant dans la mesure où la "suspension of disbelief" procède chez Coleridge d'une décision volontaire ("*willing*"), alors que chez Bourdieu l'*illusio* n'opère pas au niveau de la conscience délibérante, mais au niveau de l'adhésion quasi réflexe.

9. Les productions étrangères importées dans les cultures indigènes par la traduction sont prises en compte, même si c'est à la marge, par Bourdieu. Cf. son article "Les Conditions sociales de la circulation internationale des idées" (1990). Pascale Casanova (1999), quant à elle, met en pratique la théorie bourdieusienne dans *La République mondiale des lettres*. L'auteure

Cette coupure est proprement une scotomisation, processus inconscient de réduction mentale par lequel le sujet nie l'existence d'une partie de la réalité ou de sa réalité. Le texte traduit est scotomisé du texte source et de ses déterminants source; il est et demeurera profondément étranger au texte source et de ses conditions d'émergence. Le traducteur déshistoricise d'abord le texte source, l'arrache à son lieu et à son époque, pour le réhistoriciser dans la culture ou le champ cible. Dés lors, si la traduction entretient un rapport d'homologie avec le texte source, cette homologie est relative, compte tenu du décentrement par scotomisation qu'opère la traduction. L'homologie est cependant d'autant plus grande que les traductions sont accomplies par des traducteurs dotés d'un *habitus* propre à négocier avec finesse des traits socio-historiques de la culture source, cette capacité à négocier étant l'une des principales caractéristiques de l'*habitus*.[10]

Capital de l'agent traducteur et légitimités transnationales

Comment s'évalue le capital de l'agent traducteur dans le champ littéraire? L'agent traducteur est assez souvent doté d'un très faible capital. Les traducteurs sont encore aujourd'hui cette armée des ombres qui sont pourtant d'une grande importance dans les relations entre les cultures. Les exemples sont innombrables de traducteurs tombés dans l'oubli et dont le style est présent, admiré même parfois, dans les œuvres traduites des champs littéraires. Lorsqu'émerge un traducteur au milieu de la masse des autres traducteurs inconnus, il fait figure d'exception, comme Coindreau, par exemple. Comment Coindreau a-t-il acquis son fort capital de traducteur/introducteur de la littérature américaine en France? Dans de nombreux cas, c'est l'auteur de la société source qui est porteur du capital reconnu dans le champ cible. Mais le traducteur est en collusion avec l'auteur source (on le voit bien avec Coindreau qui a une révérence absolue pour Faulkner: il l'aborde avec respect au contraire du journaliste qui veut forcer l'intimité de l'écrivain

---

analyse le cas de Paris, "ville-littérature", ville "dénationalisée et universelle de l'univers littéraire" (p. 55). Elle rappelle cependant que "le capital littéraire est national" (ibid.). Dans d'autres secteurs d'activités (que littéraire) où intervient la traduction, le capital (*stricto sensu* et capital symbolique) a cessé d'appartenir à des entités nationales, pour devenir la propriété de groupes d'intérêt transnationaux. Il faudrait sans doute voir si cela remet en question le modèle de P. Bourdieu.

10. On peut s'interroger sur l'effet de la diffusion "généralisée", "mondialisée", des biens culturels dans le contexte de la traduction. La mondialisation est-elle dotée du potentiel de "faire circuler" le sens sans entraves? Cela est possible. Il resterait à voir comment la traduction pourrait se penser autrement que comme *décentrement*.

américain). Le capital de l'auteur source peut rejaillir sur le traducteur – ou inversement –, lequel devient un agent actif qui travaille dans le même sens que l'écrivain. Agent créatif, dynamique, novateur, il s'inscrit dans la problématique de l'œuvre source, selon le principe de la communauté de destin des sociétés source et cible.

Mais les choses se compliquent, du fait que la traduction opère nécessairement un décentrement par scotomisation de certains déterminants du texte source, comme on vient de le voir. Il s'agit bien entendu d'analyser en traductologie quels sont les phénomènes qui sont à l'origine du décentrement. Cependant, globalement, on constate que l'échange est inégal dans la traduction (par exemple Casanova 2002). Dans les exemples que nous avons pris de la traduction de la littérature américaine en France de 1930 à 1960, le capital symbolique des États-Unis est dominant dans l'échange avec la France et c'est ce capital symbolique qui se transmet dans l'acte de traduction: Faulkner et Dos Passos (sans parler de Hemingway, Caldwell, Steinbeck) sont les écrivains qui, au 20ᵉ siècle, sont dotés du capital symbolique maximal dans le champ réaliste cible, comme le remarque Claude-Edmonde Magny dans *l'Âge du roman américain* (Magny 1948); et ils ne sont pas les seuls: l'hégémonie américaine s'exerce aussi en science-fiction après la Seconde Guerre mondiale et en *detective novel* également. Par comparaison, en littérature le capital symbolique de la France a été dominant jusqu'à la Première Guerre mondiale et c'était un honneur de se faire traduire en français jusqu'à ce que le champ littéraire français montre des signes de déclin, vers 1920. La traduction est donc marquée par des rapports de pouvoir entre les champs source et cible et ce qui est transmis dans les champs cible par la traduction, c'est la légitimité dont jouissent non seulement l'œuvre d'un écrivain, mais le champ national étranger dans le champ cible et aussi le champ source en tant que tel. Comme l'écrit Gore Vidal (cité par Malcolm Bradbury 1983: vi), "[W]riters in powerful countries often win far more attention than they deserve". En d'autres termes, la traduction d'une œuvre offre dans le champ cible une image de l'à-venir social en discussion dans l'œuvre, contribuant ainsi à universaliser les innovations esthétiques et politiques apparues dans les champs nationaux source, comme le montre de façon évidente le cas de la traduction de la science-fiction. Entre parenthèses, ces remarques prouvent, à notre avis, qu'il convient de rétablir et de réaffirmer la présence déterminante de l'œuvre source (et par-delà l'œuvre source, du champ littéraire et de l'espace social source) en traduction.

Conclusion

Bourdieu écrit: "Quelles que soient ses prétentions scientifiques, l'objectivation est vouée à rester *partielle*, donc fausse, aussi longtemps qu'elle ignore ou refuse de voir le point de vue à partir duquel elle s'énonce, donc le jeu dans son ensemble" (1982: 22, italiques de P.B.). Ces réflexions sur la traduction seraient donc incomplètes, si le traductologue ne faisait pas intervenir ce que Bourdieu nomme la "double réflexivité" dans la démarche sociologique. La double réflexivité en sociologie de la traduction consisterait *d'une part* dans la réflexivité appliquée à l'étude des traductions, c'est-à-dire à l'objectivation des déterminants des corpus de traduction que nous avons examinés brièvement, avec les notions de champs, *habitus*, capital symbolique, *illusio*; elle consisterait *d'autre part* dans la réflexivité tournée vers l'agent traductologue. Cette réflexivité tournée vers le traductologue vise à énoncer la position qu'il assume dans l'opération d'objectivation pour dégager l'enjeu des recherches qu'il a effectuées sur les traductions. Or, nous avons vu précédemment que les produits de la traduction ne constituent en aucun cas un champ, mais que la traductologie, elle, est bel et bien un champ scientifique; certes, le champ traductologique n'est pas doté d'une forte légitimité en ce début de 21ᵉ siècle, et les agents traductologues que nous sommes ont à pâtir d'un déficit de légitimité par rapport aux autres champs adjacents, champ linguistique, champ philologique, champ des études littéraires, champ comparatiste, de formation bien antérieure pour certaines disciplines. Mais on assiste à l'émergence d'institutions multiples, programmes, collections spécialisées, revues, colloques. Ainsi, les agents traductologues travaillent, selon le principe de la coopération conflictuelle, à construire la légitimité du champ de la traductologie à travers ces institutions et, tout particulièrement, à faire reconnaître la dimension sociale de la traduction, conformément en cela à ce qui a lieu dans les champs adjacents. Déterminé par le social, le traductologue est l'héritier interdisciplinaire de ces champs – et de bien d'autres. Pour ce qui nous concerne, nous avons emprunté à la pensée sociologique de Bourdieu certaines positions qui nous paraissent essentielles à une connaissance approfondie des enjeux de la traduction: premièrement, une théorie sociale qui prenne en compte les biens symboliques sans les réduire à des biens de consommation ordinaires, deuxièmement, la position centrale des agents traités autrement que comme des courroies de transmission de la structure et, troisièmement surtout, cette idée essentielle que la théorie de Bourdieu peut être retournée contre lui-même et qu'il n'est pas situé au-dessus de la mêlée. Comme le dit Bourdieu à propos du monde universitaire qu'il a analysé dans *Homo academicus* (1984b): "[...] je tombais nécessairement sous le coup de mes propres analyses, et [...] je livrais des instruments susceptibles d'être retournés contre moi: la comparaison de l'arroseur arrosé [...] désignant simplement une des formes, très efficace, de la réflexivité telle que je la conçois, c'est-à-dire comme une entreprise collective" (1997: 12). Réaffirmons donc les enjeux de ce que nous avons proposé: à savoir que la pratique sociale dont il est ici question fasse l'objet d'une recherche théorique, que soient mises en discussion traductologique, entre autres, les notions de champ, d'*habitus*, de capital symbolique, d'*illusio*, notions non conçues à l'origine pour des produits bi-culturels; et que nos discussions de traductologues débouchent sur une réflexivité collective qui fasse avancer la traductologie dans la connaissance scientifique.

Références

Berman, Antoine. 1984. "Traduction et ethnocentrique et traduction hypertextuelle". *L'Écrit du temps* 7: 109–123.

Berman, Antoine. 1989. "La traduction et ses discours". *Meta* XXXIV (4): 672–679.

Bourdieu, Pierre. 1980. *Le sens pratique*. Paris: Minuit.

Bourdieu, Pierre. 1982. *Leçon sur la leçon*. Paris: Minuit.

Bourdieu, Pierre. 1984a. *Questions de sociologie*. Paris: Minuit.

Bourdieu, Pierre. 1984b. *Homo academicus*. Paris: Minuit.

Bourdieu, Pierre. 1987. *Choses dites*. Paris: Minuit.

Bourdieu, Pierre. 1990. "Les Conditions sociales de la circulation internationale des idées". *Cahiers d'histoire des littératures romanes*. 14e année, 1–2: 1–10.

Bourdieu, Pierre. 1992. *Les Règles de l'art. Genèse et structure du champ littéraire*. Paris: Seuil.

Bourdieu, Pierre. 1997. *Méditations pascaliennes*. Paris: Seuil.

Bradbury, Malcolm. 1983. *The Modern American Novel*. Oxford and New York: Oxford University Press.

Casanova, Pascale. 1999. *La République mondiale des idées*. Paris: Seuil.

Casanova, Pascale. 2002. "Consécration et accumulation de capital littéraire. La traduction comme échange inégal". *Actes de la recherche en sciences sociales* 144: 7–20.

Coindreau, Maurice-Edgar. 1974. *Mémoires d'un traducteur*. Paris: Gallimard.

Coleridge, Samuel Taylor. 1907. *Biographia Literaria. Edited with his Aesthetical Essays, by J. Shawcross. 2 vol.* Oxford: The Clarendon Press.

Duhamel, Marcel. 1972. *Raconte pas ta vie*. Paris: Mercure de France.

Gouanvic, Jean-Marc. 1999. *Sociologie de la traduction. La science-fiction américaine dans l'espace culturel français des années 1950*. Arras: Artois Presses Université.

Kalinowski, Isabelle. 2002. "La Vocation au travail de traduction". *Actes de la recherche en sciences sociales* 144: 47–54.

Magny, Claude-Edmonde. 1948. *L'Âge du roman américain*. Paris: Seuil.

Meschonnic, Henri. 1973. *Pour une poétique II. Épistémologie de l'écriture. Poétique de la traduction*. Paris: Gallimard.

Outline for a sociology of translation*

Current issues and future prospects

Johan Heilbron and Gisèle Sapiro
CNRS, Centre de sociologie européenne, Paris, France /
ESSE (Pour un espace des sciences sociales européen)

If translations have to be understood as embedded in their specific social context three dimensions have to be taken into account:

1. As cross-national transfers, translations first imply the existence of a field of international relations of exchange.
2. At a more specific level of exchange, one must distinguish between political, economic and cultural dynamics.
3. Finally, the dynamics of translation depends on the structure of the space of reception and on the way in which relevant intermediaries (translators, critics, agents, publishers) shape social demand. Here the analysis focuses on the group of translators, its social profile and the stratification of their craft, as well as on the role of critics and academic specialists, which play a key role in literary translation.

Introduction

The sociology of translation practices, especially as it has developed recently in studies inspired by the work of Pierre Bourdieu, is at odds with both the interpretative approach to the text and the economic analysis of transnational exchanges.

The interpretative approach includes two opposite tendencies: the objectivist one arises from classic hermeneutics, which underlies most literary and philosophical studies of translation, whereas the subjectivist or relativist one has since the 1960s developed most notably within the framework of cultural studies. Within the classic hermeneutic problematic, the production of translations issues from an "art of understanding" (Gadamer 1960) which proceeds, just like interpreta-

---

* Translated from the French by Susan Emanuel. The translation was funded by the European network 'For a European Research Space in the Social Sciences' (ESSE).

tion itself, from a "hermeneutic movement" (Steiner 1975:296–303) that aims at gaining access to the "meaning" of the text and to its uniqueness. By contrast, cultural studies, in accordance with a relativist conception, insist on the various modes of appropriating texts, on the instability of their meaning, and on the mutual permeability of cultures. Both kinds of analyses, however, set aside the social conditions of the interpretative act, which amounts to ignoring the plurality of implicated agents, as well as the effective functions that translations might fulfil, both for the translator and for various mediators, as well as for the readerships in their historical and social spaces of reception.

The economic approach, more powerful socially but much less widespread within studies on translation, performs a reduction that is somewhat the contrary. In opposition to the obsession with a text's singularity and the uniqueness of its author, the economic approach assimilates translated books into the most general category of goods, identifying them as merchandise produced, distributed and consumed according to the logic of national and international markets. But to consider translated books as commodities like any other occults the specificity of cultural goods as well as the modalities specific to their production and marketing. The market of symbolic goods is a specific type of economy that functions according to its own criteria of valuation (Bourdieu 1977, 1993).

Breaking with both these reductive and opposite approaches, a proper sociological analysis embraces the whole set of social relations within which translations are produced and circulated. In this respect, it is closely affiliated to two related research areas developed by comparativists, historians of literature and specialists in cultural and intellectual history: translation studies, and studies of cultural transfer. Appearing in the 1970s in small and often multilingual countries (Israel, Belgium, Netherlands), translation studies managed to displace the problematic. Rather than analysing translation solely or principally in relation to an original, whether source-text or source-language, or inversely, encompassing them in the vague notion of cultural hybridization, as happens in Cultural Studies, this new research domain was interested in questions about the functioning of translations in their contexts of production and reception, that is to say, in the target culture (Holmes, Lambert and Lefevere 1978; Even-Zohar 1990; Toury 1995). The question of the relation between the contexts of production and reception also underpins the historical study of "cultural transfers", which investigates the role of the agents in these exchanges, both institutions and individuals, and their inscription in the political and cultural relations between the countries involved (Espagne and Werner 1990–1994). The development of comparative cultural history has given rise to reflection and debate on a suitable way of articulating a comparative approach with the analysis of transfers (Charle 1996; Espagne 1999:35–49).

Transcending a merely inter-textual problematic that is centered on the relation between an original and its translation leads to a series of specifically sociological questions about the stakes and functions of translations, their agencies and agents, the space in which they are situated and the constraints, both political and economic, that circumscribe them. A sociological approach to translation must therefore take into account several aspects of the conditions of transnational circulation of cultural goods: firstly, the structure of the field of international cultural exchanges; secondly, the type of constraints – political and economic – that influence these exchanges; and thirdly, the agents of intermediation and the processes of importing and receiving in the recipient country (Heilbron and Sapiro 2002a, 2002b).

The international field

Considered as a transnational transfer, translation first presupposes a space of international relations, this space being constituted by the existence of nation-states and linguistic groups linked to each other by relations of competition and rivalry. The sociology of translation can thus be inscribed more generally within the program proposed by Pierre Bourdieu (2002) on the social conditions of the international circulation of cultural goods. To understand the act of translating, one should in a first stage analyse it as embedded within the power relations among national states and their languages. These power relations are of three types – political, economic and cultural – the latter split into two aspects: the power relations between linguistic communities as assessed by the number of primary and secondary speakers (de Swaan 1993, 2001), and the symbolic capital accumulated by different countries within the relevant field of cultural production (Casanova 1999). In these power relations, the means of political, economic and cultural struggles are unequally distributed. Cultural exchanges are therefore unequal exchanges that express relations of domination. In accordance with these analyses, the flows of translations should then be re-situated in a transnational field characterized by the power relations among national states, their languages, and their literatures.

The global system of translations may be described as a set of highly hierarchized relations whose functioning demonstrates several general mechanisms (Heilbron 1999; Heilbron, de Nooy and Tichelaar 1995). Drawing on statistical data concerning the international market for translated books (acknowledging that the data suffer from various deficiencies; Pym 1998:72), the structure of these exchanges can be described in a general way. Crudely speaking, since half the books translated worldwide are translations from English, English occupies the most central position – even hyper-central. Well behind come German and French, which represent between 10 and 12% of the world market of translations. Eight languages have a semi-peripheral position, with a share that varies from 1 to 3% of the international market (Spanish and Italian, for example). The other languages all have a share of less than one percent of the international market, and might thus be considered as peripheral, despite the fact that certain of them (Chinese, Arabic or Japanese) represent linguistic groups that are among the most important in terms of number of speakers. This signifies, incidentally, that the number of primary speakers is not a very powerful explanatory factor in determining the hierarchy of "central languages" and "peripheral languages".

Before considering other criteria, several regularities may be derived from this structure. The first observation is that translation flows are highly uneven, flowing from the center toward the periphery rather than the reverse. A second is that communication among peripheral languages very often passes through the intermediary of a center. The more central a language is, the more it has the capacity to function as an intermediary or vehicular language. Thus, the English or French translation of a Norwegian or Korean work is quickly announced by its publisher, who foresees that translation into a central language will be immediately followed by a quite large wave of translations into other languages. A third property concerns the variety of works translated. The more central a language is in the world system of translation, the more numerous are the genres of books translated from this language.

The unequal share of translations in different countries also attests to these power relations. One of the most characteristic traits of the functioning of this international space concerns the relation between the degree of centrality of translation and their relative significance. In general, the more central a language is in the translation system, the lower the proportions of translations as compared to non translated texts. While the dominant countries "export" their cultural products widely and translate little into their languages, the dominated countries "export" little and "import" a lot of foreign books, principally by translation. Thus, in the beginning of the 1990s, the proportion of translated books represented, in England and the United States, less than 4% of the national production of books. In Germany and in France, this proportion hovered between 14 and 18%. In Italy and Spain it rose to 24% (Ganne and Minon 1992: 79; Jurt 1999). Similarly, in the Netherlands and in Sweden, a quarter of the books published are translations. In Portugal and in Greece this percentage reaches 35%, or even 45%.

The available data therefore seems to indicate an inverse relation between the degree of centrality of a language in the international system of translations and the proportion of translations in the national production of books. The more the cultural production of a country is central, the more it serves as a reference in other countries, but the less material is translated into this language. It is not by chance that translation studies has emerged in small countries (Netherlands, Belgium, Israel), or that translations are indeed more important there than in countries that are found at the system's center. Since the field of translation studies emerged in smaller countries with high translation ratios, it is possible that the cultural significance of translations has been somewhat overestimated.

Analysing the flows of translations in the light of the power relations among languages also allows us to better understand historical changes. A country's loss of prestige or power, and the resulting diminution of its language's status do have consequences for the level of translation activity. After the collapse of Socialist regimes, the international position of Russian underwent such an abrupt change: the number of translations from Russian dropped very sharply, and this drop was accompanied by a sharp rise in the number of foreign translations published in Russia. The relative decline of French has been similarly accompanied by a growth in the number of translations into this language. The size of the national market, which is sometimes considered as the most important factor in explaining the percentage of translations (de Swaan 2001: 41–59), has remained stable in both cases and cannot explain these changes.

The principles of differentiation in the dynamics of exchange

International cultural exchanges are differentiated according to three main factors: that of political relations between countries, that of economic relations (especially the international book market), and that of specifically cultural exchanges, within which literary exchanges may enjoy relative autonomy. The constraints upon the production and circulation of symbolic goods and upon international cultural exchanges can be located between two extremes: one with a high degree of politicization, the other with a high degree of commercialization (Sapiro 2003). The mode of circulation of texts will depend on these different logics, according to the structure of the fields of cultural production in the countries of origin and reception and the modalities of export and import, which partly determine the transfer circuit.

Thus, in countries where the economic field is subordinated to the political field and where the institutions governing cultural production as well as the organization of intellectual professions are state-run, as in fascist or communist countries, then the production and circulation of symbolic goods seem to be highly politicized from the outset. For example, this politicization conditioned the transfer of literary works from Eastern Europe during the Communist period, in both the legal and illegal circulation of works (Popa 2002, 2004).

At the opposite pole, certain transfers may be principally governed by the logic of the market. In cases of extreme liberalization of the book market, as in the United States, cultural goods appear primarily as commercial products that must obey the law of profitability: this is best illustrated by the process of manufacturing standardized worldwide bestsellers. Several studies have shown that the field of publishing is more and more dominated by large business enterprises that tend to impose criteria of profitability and modes of commercial operation to the detriment of the literary and cultural logic (Bourdieu 1999; Reynaud 1999; Schalke and Gerlach 1999; Schiffrin 1999). A study on the importing of Italian literature into France shows the growing impact of economic logic on the literary transfer (Bokobza 2004). This phenomenon is also observed in sectors that are in principle more protected, such as university publishing, as is attested by the deep crisis traversing university presses in the United States and Great Britain (Thompson 2005). But even the purely economic logic operating within publishing should be described and analysed by using more refined techniques than the standard models of *cultural economics*. Here, supply and demand are not simply given, but are social constructions made and maintained by specific groups. Non market forces, notably state institutions, are involved in these construction processes. Contrary to the economic definition of the economy, other dimensions (notably political and symbolic ones) are present and their specific effectiveness cannot be ignored if one wants to understand the functioning of cultural markets (Bourdieu 2000; Smelser and Swedberg 2005).

Between these two opposites, one finds a series of possible configurations in which the relative importance of political and economic factors varies according to the degree of protection of the national market and the degree to which culture fulfils an ideological purpose.

Historically, one observes an alternation between phases of strong regulation and those of free exchange. Thus, the tight control of monarchical regimes that still prevailed in the eighteenth century, which was a phase of expansion in the book market, was followed by a phase of liberalization in the period of industrialization of the book market at the start of the nineteenth century. The transnational circulation of symbolic goods, for the most part unregulated, then underwent a major expansion. At the end of the nineteenth century, policies of market regulation and exchanges were established to curb the effects of economic liberalism and to protect national markets. The transnational circulation of symbolically and ideologically valued cultural goods was incorporated within the diplomatic policies of many advanced nation-states. As a result of the gradual liberalization of exchanges and the unification of a world market for records, books, and cinema after the Second World War, specifically political constraints have weakened as compared to economic constraints. This process of liberalization developed after the Second World War within the framework of international negotiations that reflected the dominant position that the United States had acquired. It accelerated in the cultural domain after the GATT agreements of 1986, in the course of the Uruguay Round, which extended into service trades – and hence to immaterial or incorporeal goods and especially to cultural products – the liberalization of exchanges that had been previously restricted to trade in merchandise (Regourd 2002). This extension challenged the principle of the "cultural exception", that is to say, the status of exception granted to cultural goods, entitling them to be protected from purely mercantile mechanisms. This provoked a strong reaction in countries like France, and led the European Parliament to adopt in 1993 a resolution rallying member states to the principle of "cultural exceptionalism". This phase of liberalization (beginning in the second half of the 1980s) brought about a significant increase in international cultural exchanges, observable notably in the global increase in translation flows. In this respect, further investigations should examine the effects of international agreements like TRIPS (Trade Related Aspects of Intellectual Property Rights), adopted in 1994 within the framework of the WTO (World Trade Organization), upon the international circulation of books and translations.

However, this recent shift from political to more economic constraints has had the effect of weakening the supply-side and strengthening the demand-side, that is to say, diminishing, within the process of mediation, the preponderant role of agents of export (official bodies, translations institutes, cultural attachés, etc.), which are now increasingly obliged to take into account the space of reception and the activities of importing agents, specifically, the various agents in the book market: literary agents, translators, and most particularly, publishers.

The relative autonomy of cultural fields was conquered gradually against the influence of the state and the market, which continue to govern the production and circulation of symbolic goods. In fact, national cultures are themselves endowed with a symbolic capital that is relatively autonomous with respect to the economic and political power relations among countries or linguistic communities. From the standpoint of literary exchanges, transnational relations are above all relations of domination based on the unequal distribution of linguistic and literary capital (Casanova 1999). The dominated languages are those endowed with little literary capital and low international recognition. The dominant languages, due to their specific prestige, their antiquity, and the number of texts that are written in these languages and that are universally regarded as important, possess much literary capital. This differentiated accumulation of symbolic capital, which may vary from one creative domain to another, underlies the unequal power relations among national cultures, which has consequences for the reception of cultural goods as well as for their functions and uses: thus, for a national literary field in the course of being constructed, the translation of a canonic work of classic literature may serve to accumulate symbolic capital, whereas the translation of a text of a dominated literature into a dominant language like English or French constitutes a veritable consecration for the author (Casanova 2002).

With the unification of the world book market, the space of circulation of cultural goods is increasingly structured around the opposition between large-scale circulation and small-scale circulation (Bourdieu 1977). Whereas the making of global bestsellers favoured by the liberalization of exchanges illustrates the quest for profitability in the short run, a sizable share in the import process of foreign literatures arises from the specific cultural logic which prevails in the area of small-scale circulation seeking for peer recognition rather than commercial success, as witnessed by the modes of selection (often founded on criteria of literary or intellectual value rather than on chances of success with the public-at-large) and short print runs. The same split applies to the intermediary agents, who are also divided between large-scale and small-scale circulation, as we shall see.

This space of small-scale production most often relies on a system of subsidy in publishing and translation. In France, a system of assistance for translation into French of the literatures of small countries was established at the end of the 1980s. Inversely, a new subsidy program for the translation of French works in both literature and the social sciences was set up in 1990 by the Ministry of Foreign Affairs. Such subsidy systems spring from cultural policies that attempt to incorporate certain cultural goods into the national patrimony. Unlike fascist or communist regimes, in which cultural production is regulated in order to control its ideological orientation, state intervention in liberal democracy is designed in principle to curb the effects of economic constraints in a free trade economy, notably the risk of the standardization and homogenization among cultural productions aimed at the greatest number of consumers. This system of protection was created thanks to pressure from agents in the literary field and the book market (authors, publishers, booksellers). Though it varies from country to country, it attests to the recognition by states of a symbolic legitimacy resulting from the process by which the fields of cultural production gained autonomy. This is institutionalized in some cases in a legislative framework, as in fixed books prices and the ban on book advertising on French television – though these laws are nowadays threatened by the WTO's extension of the principles of free trade to services. One of the laws that have provoked the most opposition is the law on copyright. According to the French conception of the author's right, which strongly influenced the International Convention on Literary and Artistic Property (first adopted in Berne in 1886), so-called moral rights (the right to divulge, the right to respect, the right to correct) are inalienable: thus, for example, a work cannot be cut without the authorization of the writer or the heirs of his estate. This is what differentiates the author's right from American copyright legislation, which considers the book as a commercial good like any other. Having refused to sign the paragraph on moral rights in the international convention, the United States has still managed to impose its exclusion from the TRIPS agreements adopted within the WTO.

The agents of intermediation and the dynamics of reception

International cultural exchanges are organized by means of institutions and individual agents, each arising from different political, economic and cultural dynamics. The process of cultural construction of national identities (Thiesse 1999), closely linked to the formation of nation-states and to the competition among them within their spheres of influence, implied a regulation of diplomatic and cultural exchanges, which were delegated to a set of authorities (embassies, cultural institutes, translation institutes, journals launched to present a national literature abroad, etc.). The creation of law on authorship, the *droit d'auteur*, in the eighteenth century aimed to protect the French book market from foreign counterfeits. The industrialization of the book market, the growth in readership thanks to literacy, and the liberalization of cultural exchanges, all favored the emergence of groups of agents specialized in the trade in translated books: independent publishing houses with foreign rights departments, literary agents, international book fairs. The development of the market of cultural goods and the liberalization of exchanges in this latter period have marginalized state authorities, which have renounced their own export circuits in order to participate in the organization of commercial exchanges: national institutes supporting translation such as the Foundation for the Production and Translation of Dutch Literature (NLPVF) or the Institute for the Translation of Hebrew Literature increasingly behave like literary agents. Foreign policy representatives in charge with the promotion of national cultures abroad also work increasingly with agents in the market (publishers and literary agents), and local authorities may take part in the organization of book fairs, as is the case with the Jerusalem Fair. At the same time, official decision-making power is greatly reduced, and publishers do not hesitate to bypass these official intermediaries to take the advice of agents in the literary field of the country of origin, such as authors, critics or academics.

In fact, apart from these specialists of intermediation, literary exchanges also depend on a set of specific agents in the literary or scientific field (authors, translators, critics, academics, and scholars, for whom work founded on linguistic and social resources procures specific benefits). These interrelations would lend themselves to network analysis (Wasserman and Faust 1994). The conditions of importing US-American science fiction after the Second World War well illustrate these dynamics (Gouanvic 1997, 2002). Equally, the appearance of a group of importers and their specialization may favor the translation of the literary production of a small country into a central language, as is illustrated by the importing of Hebrew literature into France (Sapiro 2002).

Literary and academic translators are thus distinct in many ways, including economically, from the whole set of "technical" and professional translators, a split well illustrated by the fact that they are organized in France, for example, into two distinct professional associations. The professional organization of translators is relatively recent: in France, the *Société des traducteurs* (Society of Translators) was founded in 1947, and the *Association des traducteurs littéraires* (Association of Literary Translators) in 1973 (Heinich 1984). Performing an activity that was still weakly differentiated at the start of the twentieth century, the translator was often himself a writer, a commentator, a teacher and/or a critic (Wilfert 2002). The practice of literary translation underwent a process of specialization due to two principal factors: on the one hand, the development and institutionalization of language teaching that allowed the appearance of specialists with certified competence, and on the other, the growing demand of publishers in this area.

The professional development that began after this process of specialization has encountered obstacles, however. From the standpoint of the professional conditions, the world of literary translators is highly bifurcated between academic and professional translation, a division that cuts across other social cleavages, such as masculine/feminine (Kalinowski 2002). It is characterized by a strong individualism that results as much from the professional conditions as from the principle of vocational elitism and singularity that has been imported from the literary field. As in the literary field (Sapiro 2004), the divisions linked to heterogeneous professional conditions associated with this elitist individualism and with the logic of competition long posed an obstacle to the professional organization of these specialists in the countries of Western Europe, unlike in the communist regimes where intellectual occupations were organized within a strong statist framework.

These elements of division incite some scholars to approach the activity of translation as a field governed by a logic of competition for the monopoly of legitimacy founded on the accumulation of symbolic capital. This approach can be praised for breaking with the traditional sociology of professions and professionalization, whose limits have already been stressed (Chapoulie 1973; Heilbron 1986; Abbott 1988), but it encloses the risk of justifying the methodological autonomization of an object that is still weakly autonomized in reality.

Thus, to understand the dynamics of the circulation of foreign literatures through translation, one must relate it not only to the structure of the international space described above, but also to the structure of the space of reception. This particular space is also more or less governed by either market or political factors, and depends on the functioning of its institutions: controls over print publication, specialized book series, the editorial policy of each publishing company, the space of journals and periodicals, the modes of consecration (literary prizes and awards), etc.

In his article on the "social conditions of the international circulation of ideas", Pierre Bourdieu, taking up Marx's proposition, reminded us that "texts circulate without their context", a fact which often generates misunderstandings (Bourdieu 2002:4). Reception is in part determined by the representations of the culture of origin and by the status (majority or minority) of the language itself. Recipients reinterpret translated texts as a function of the stakes prevailing in the field of reception. Translated works may be appropriated in diverse and sometimes contradictory ways, as a function of the stakes proper to the intellectual field of reception (Pinto 1995; Kalinowski 1999).

In a more general way, translation has multiple functions: an instrument of mediation and exchange, it may also fulfil political or economic functions, and constitute a mode of legitimation, in which authors as much as mediators may be the beneficiaries. The value of translation does not depend only on the position of languages, but also on the positions of both translated authors and their translators, and each of them in both the national literary field and the global literary space (Casanova 2002). The translation into central languages constitutes a consecration that modifies the position of an author in his field of origin. Inversely, it is a mode of accumulation of literary capital for groups, such as German Romantics, and for national literatures in the course of being constituted, as is illustrated by the case of translations into Hebrew in the 1920s: these translations aimed to create "an organic readership" even though the community of Hebrew speakers was still very narrow and the great majority of them spoke another language (Shavit 2002).

One re-encounters this double function of translation at the level of bodies such as publishing houses and journals: while publishers endowed with significant literary capital have a power to consecrate authors whom they translate, the translation is a means of accumulating symbolic power for a publisher lacking economic and cultural capital (Serry 2002). The strategies of authors represent a large continuum of possibilities. Authors who are dominated in a dominant field, for example, may try to ameliorate their position by translating dominant authors of dominated fields. Beginners or authors who have a relatively marginal position, are often tempted to translate promising but still unknown authors: one thinks of Larbaud translating Joyce's *Ulysses,* to name one canonical example. At the level of mediators, too, the uses of translation vary from the consecration of the translated author to the self-consecration of the translator (Kalinowski 2001).

Finally, literary translation may play a role in the creation of collective identities. Literature, art, and music have played an important part in the creation of national identities in Europe (Thiesse 1999). We have already mentioned, with respect to translations into Hebrew in the 1920s, the role of translation in the constitution of national cultures. Brazil and Argentina built their national identities through competing cultural exchanges in which translations of Brazilian works into Argentinian Spanish played an important role throughout the twentieth century (Sora 2002, 2003). This use of symbolic goods can also be observed in the construction of social identities, of religious identity, genre identity, local identity (regionalism), and the identity of a social group (proletarian literature) (Thiesse 1991; Serry 2001). This work of construction is often all the more important when the group is a dominated one. The transnational reception of symbolic goods may thus have a function of maintaining the identity of communities of immigrants or religious minorities.

Unfortunately, we do not have room in this article to develop the issue of the norms and practices of translation, which are among the most explored domains of translation studies. But that level of analysis may evidently be linked to the others we have mentioned within the framework of a sociological approach to translation (see for example Kalinowski 1999). The *habitus* of the translator, the mode of acquisition of linguistic competence, the type of education and training, the publishing norms, the national tradition with respect to translation norms – all contribute to orienting linguistic and stylistic choices (Gouanvic 1997, 2002; Simeoni 1998; Sapiro forthcoming).

Conclusion

To understand translation as a social practice, it is necessary to bypass approaches that are purely textual and to reintegrate into the analysis all the agents – individuals and institutions – that participate in this practice. First and foremost, we must restore it to the international field of the circulation of texts, a hierarchized space with unequal exchanges. This hierarchy results from the structuring of power relations according to three principal dynamics – political, economic, and cultural. Bourdieu's sociological theory allows us to take into account the specificity of each of these logics and the different ways in which they interact in given historical conditions. These dynamics confer on the products of this activity their social and symbolic value and the diversity of its functions, from consecration to the accumulation of symbolic capital, or else the construction of collective identities. Each of these logics is enacted by a set of agents who are to greater or lesser degrees specialized in intermediation, who collaborate in the activity of translation while struggling to preserve or subvert the hierarchy of values within this space. Specialization and professionalization of the practice of translation is inscribed within the development of this space, with the boom in the cultural industries and the increase of international exchanges. This framework of analysis allows us to set up a program of comparative research that would study the historical sociology of the formation of an international space of circulation of translated texts and the agents in that field.

References

Abbott, Andrew. 1988. *The System of Professions: An Essay on the Division of Expert Labor.* Chicago and London: The University of Chicago Press.

Bokobza, Anaïs. 2004. *Translating Literature: From Romanticized Representations to the Dominance of a Commercial Logic: The Publication of Italian Novels in France (1982-2001).* PhD Thesis: European University Institute of Florence.

Bourdieu, Pierre. 1977. "La production de la croyance: contribution à une économie des biens symboliques". *Actes de la recherche en sciences sociales* 13: 3–43.

Bourdieu, Pierre. 1993. *The Field of Cultural Production.* Cambridge: Polity Press.

Bourdieu, Pierre. 1999. "Une révolution conservatrice dans l'édition". *Actes de la recherche en sciences sociales* 126/127: 3–28.

Bourdieu, Pierre. 2000. *Les Structures sociales de l'économie.* Paris: Seuil.

Bourdieu, Pierre. 2002. "Les conditions sociales de la circulation internationale des idées". *Actes de la recherche en sciences sociales* 145: 3–8.

Casanova, Pascale. 2002. "Consécration et accumulation de capital littéraire. La traduction comme échange inégal". *Actes de la recherche en sciences sociales* 144: 7–20.

Casanova, Pascale. 1999. *La République mondiale des lettres.* Paris: Seuil.

Chapoulie, Jean-Michel. 1973. "Sur l'analyse sociologique des groupes professionnels". *Revue française de sociologie* 14 (1): 86–114.

Charle, Christophe. 1996. *Les Intellectuels en Europe au XIXe siècle. Essai d'histoire comparée.* Paris: Seuil.

Espagne, Michel and Werner, Michael (eds). 1990–1994. *Philologiques.* Paris: Editions de la MSH, 3 vol.

Espagne, Michel. 1999. *Les transferts culturels franco-allemands.* Paris: Presses Universitaires de France.

Even-Zohar, Itamar. 1990. *Poetics Today* 11 (1). Special Issue "Polysystem Studies".

Gadamer, Hans-Georg. 1960. *Wahrheit und Methode. Grundzüge einer philosophischen Hermeneutik.* Tübingen: Mohr.

Ganne, Valérie and Minon, Marc. 1992. "Géographies de la traduction". In *Traduire l'Europe,* F. Barret-Ducrocq (ed). Paris: Payot. 55–95.

Gouanvic, Jean-Marc. 1997. "Translation and the Shape of Things to Come: The Emergence of American Science Fiction in Post-War France". *The Translator* 3 (2): 123–132.

Gouanvic, Jean-Marc. 2002. "The Stakes of Translation in Literary Fields". *Across Languages and Cultures* 3 (2): 159–168.

Heilbron, Johan. 1986. "La professionnalisation comme concept sociologique et comme stratégie des sociologues". In *Historiens et sociologues aujourd'hui.* Paris: Editions du CNRS. 61–73.

Heilbron, Johan. 1999. "Towards a Sociology of Translation. Book Translations as a Cultural World-System". *European Journal of Social Theory* 2(4): 429–444.

Heilbron, Johan, de Nooy, Wouter and Tichelaar, Wilma (eds). 1995. *Waarin een klein land. Nederlandse cultuur in internationaal verband.* Amsterdam: Prometheus.

Heilbron, Johan and Sapiro, Gisèle (eds). 2002a. *Actes de la recherche en sciences sociales* 144. "Les échanges littéraires internationaux".

Heilbron Johan and Sapiro, Gisèle (eds). 2002b. *Actes de la recherche en sciences sociales* 145. "La circulation internationale des idées".

Heinich, Nathalie. 1984. "Les traducteurs littéraires: l'Art et la profession". *Revue française de sociologie* 25: 264–280.

Holmes, James, Lambert, José and Lefevere, André (eds). 1978. *Literature and Translation: New Perspectives in Literary Studies.* Louvain: Université Catholique de Louvain.

Kalinowski, Isabelle. 1999. *Une histoire de la réception de Hölderlin en France.* Doctoral thesis. Paris: Université Paris XII.

Kalinowski, Isabelle. 2001. "Traduction n'est pas médiation". *Etudes de lettres* (Lausanne) 2: 29–49.

Kalinowski, Isabelle. 2002. "La vocation au travail de la traduction". *Actes de la recherche en sciences sociales* 144: 47–54.

Jurt, Joseph. 1999. "L'intraduction' de la littérature française en Allemagne". *Actes de la recherche en sciences sociales* 130: 86–89.

Pinto, Louis. 1995. *Les Neveux de Zarathoustra. La réception de Nietzsche en France.* Paris: Seuil.

Popa, Ioana. 2002. "Un transfert littéraire politisé: Circuits de traduction des littératures d'Europe de l'Est en France, 1947–1989". *Actes de la recherche en sciences sociales* 144: 55–69.

Popa, Ioana. 2004. *La Politique extérieure de la littérature. Une sociologie de la traduction des littératures d'Europe de l'Est (1947–1989).* Doctoral thesis. Paris: EHESS.

Pym, Anthony. 1998. *Method in Translation History.* Manchester: St Jerome Publishing.

Regourd, Serge. 2002. *L'Exception culturelle.* Paris: PUF.

Reynaud, Bénédicte. 1999. "L'emprise de groupes sur l'édition française au début des années 1980". *Actes de la recherche en sciences sociales* 130: 3–11.

Sapiro, Gisèle. 2002. "L'importation de la littérature hébraïque en France: Entre universalisme et communautarisme". *Actes de la recherche en sciences sociales* 144: 80–98.

Sapiro, Gisèle. 2003. "The Literary Field: between the State and the Market". *Poetics. Journal of Empirical Research on Culture, the Media and the Arts* 31 (5/6): 441–461.

Sapiro, Gisèle. 2004. "Entre individualisme et corporatisme: les écrivains dans la première moitié du XXe siècle". In *La France malade du corporatisme?*, S. Kaplan and P. Minard (eds). Paris: Belin. 279–314.

Sapiro, Gisèle (forthcoming). "Normes de traduction et contraintes sociales". In *Beyond Descriptive Translation Studies*, A. Pym (ed). Amsterdam and Philadelphia: John Benjamins.

Schalke, Claudia and Gerlach, Markus. 1999. "Le paysage éditorial allemand". *Actes de la recherche en sciences sociales* 130: 29–47.

Schiffrin, André. 1999. *L'édition sans éditeurs.* Paris: La Fabrique.

Serry, Hervé. 2001. "La littérature pour faire et défaire les groupes". *Sociétés contemporaines* 44: 5–14.

Serry, Hervé. 2002. "Constituer un catalogue littéraire". *Actes de la recherche en sciences sociales* 144: 70–79.

Shavit, Zohar. 2002. "Fabriquer une culture nationale". *Actes de la recherche en sciences sociales* 144: 21–33.

Simeoni, Daniel. 1998. "The Pivotal Status of the Translator's Habitus". *Target* 10 (1): 1–39.

Smelser, Neil J. and Swedberg, Richard (eds). ²2005. *The Handbook of Economic Sociology.* Princeton and Oxford (NY): Princeton UP/Russell Sage Foundation.

Sora, Gustavo. 2002. "Un échange dénié. La traduction d'auteurs brésiliens en Argentine". *Actes de la recherche en sciences sociales* 145: 61–70.

Sora, Gustavo. 2003. *Traducir el Brasil. Una antropologia de la circulacion internacional de ideas.* Buenos Aires: Libros del Zorzal.

Steiner, George. 1975. *After Babel: Aspects of Language and Translation.* Oxford: Oxford University Press.

Swaan, Abram de. 1993. "The Emergent World Language System". *International Political Science Review* 14 (3): 219–226.

Swaan, Abram de. 2001. *Words of the World: The Global Language System.* Cambridge: Polity Press.

Thiesse, Anne-Marie. 1991. *Ecrire la France. Le mouvement régionaliste de langue française entre la Belle Epoque et la Libération.* Paris: Presses Universitaires de France.

Thiesse, Anne-Marie. 1999. *La Création des identités nationales. Europe XVIIᵉ siècle-XXᵉ siècle.* Paris: Seuil.

Thompson, John. 2005. *Books in the Digital Age.* Cambridge: Polity Press.

Toury, Gideon. 1995. *Descriptive Translation Studies and beyond.* Amsterdam and Philadelphia: John Benjamins.

Wasserman, Stanley and Faust, Katherine. 1994. *Social Network Analysis.* Cambridge: Cambridge University Press.

Wilfert, Blaise. 2002. "Cosmopolis et l'homme invisible. Les importateurs de littérature étrangère en France, 1885–1914". *Actes de la recherche en sciences sociales* 144: 33–46.

The location of the "translation field"

Negotiating borderlines between Pierre Bourdieu and Homi Bhabha

Michaela Wolf
University of Graz, Austria

Pierre Bourdieu's theory of symbolic goods has been widely applied to the re-construction of various specific fields, such as the literary, the political or the media field. In the effort to re-enact the mediation processes between differ-ent fields – e.g. the translation procedure –, however, it becomes apparent that Bourdieu's analytical tools do not seem sufficient for the conceptualization of a "mediation space". This paper will attempt to further develop Bourdieu's field theory by means of Homi Bhabha's concept of the *Third Space*. This will enable us to trace the mechanisms underlying the enlacements between the various fields and to detect the processual character of the translation procedure, rather than the impact of its product(s).

Pierre Bourdieu was without doubt one of the most influential and productive thinkers of the last few decades. His theory of symbolic goods has been widely applied by both himself and by other scholars to the most diverse domains, lit-erary studies, history, media studies, political science, etc., resulting in the re-construction of specific social fields (see e.g. Bourdieu 1999; Jurt 1995; Bourdieu 1986; Bourdieu 2001). Yet it seems that Bourdieu's methodological devices are not entirely sufficient for the conceptualization of a "translation field", which takes into account the transfer operations between different fields. My contribu-tion will discuss the problems underlying this assertion and will try to identify the methodological deficiencies which hinder the modelling of a "translation field". Bourdieu's theory of cultural production will be enhanced utilising Homi Bhabha's theorem of the *Third Space*.[1]

---

1. Preliminary thoughts on this subject have been elaborated in Wolf (2005a).

Social fields and their functioning mechanisms

According to Bourdieu, four principles are at the basis of the social field's functioning: the constitution of the field as an autonomous field of practice, the order
in the field as a hierarchical structure, the struggle in the field as its self-dynamics,
and the reproduction of the field as a condition for its social endurance (Papilloud
2003: 59). A closer look at the transfer operations between various fields reveals
that Bourdieusian concepts can only partly shed light on the phenomenon of mediation. The space of mediation which generates the actions of the agents involved
in the translation enterprise seems to be driven only to a limited extent by the
functional mechanisms described above.

It is true that the mediation space evolves like any other social field – gradually, through the efforts and stakes of its agents and various relevant institutions.
Nevertheless, in the translation context, these efforts do not aim at durable relationships. Instead, due to the ephemeral character of their bonds they function
in relatively weak structures. This does not necessarily mean that the evolution
of this space is ahistorical. On the contrary; during its structuring, the agents
recur to elements and formations already existing in the "field". The agents' interests, which apparently show up only in specific situations and are constructed for
particular cases of mediation, grow and are activated in at least partially existing
networks. Another significant feature of the social field – its high degree of autonomy – does not suffice for mediation, despite the fact that every form of autonomy is the result of constructions. This might be due to the fact that for every sort
of transfer, the linkages and codifications fundamental to its occurrence are each
time established anew. In addition, they possibly follow other rules and standards
of value than those prevailing in the literary (religious, or other) field, into which
the transfer takes place. Bourdieu conceptualizes the configuration and establishment of the literary field on the basis of processes of codification and consecration
that effectively contribute to autonomizing the field. As will be shown, the consecration features relevant for the translation domain are very sparse and can only
moderately contribute to the conceptualization of a "translation field".

Conversely, the socializing principles relevant for the functioning of the mediation space are not only of an evanescent nature, but also subject to continuous
change, which of course is closely related to its transient character. This change is
conditioned both by the interests of the various agents and by the relatively small
degree of institutionalisation in the field.[2] Thus, the principles dominating the
mediation space up to a certain point contradict the logics of the literary field,

---

2. For the role of institutionalization in the field see particularly Bourdieu (1999: 408–410).

being subject to externally driven forces and consequently only admitting the creation of an autonomous status to a restricted extent.

Furthermore, the Bourdieusian principle of the hierarchical order in the field applies to translation contexts only to a limited extent. According to Bourdieu, the order of a field corresponds to the structure of the power relations between differentiated agents. In other words, a homology exists between the field's hierarchical structure and the agents' relationships in the field. Here we can distinguish between various types of power relations. First, each field can be viewed as a locus of permanent struggle between the two principles of hierarchization: the heteronomous principle, which acts as a base for those agents who dominate the field both politically and economically, and second, the autonomous principle (see "l'art pour l'art"), which defines itself by its independence from economic and political constraints. As a result, each field is characterized by competitive struggles striving for change or conservation of the power relationships. The field which Bourdieu explicitly denominated "field of power" is the space of power relations existing between agents and institutions who share the ability to dispose of the capital necessary to occupy dominant positions in the various fields (see Bourdieu 1999: 342). The agents participating in the process of mediation equally act in hierarchically organized power settings deployed through the stake of various types of capital. As a rule, the struggle for the movement of the various forms of capital is not founded on the establishment of the various agents' positions, as these positions are – at least partially – dissolved after concluding the act of mediation. As a result, unlike in the literary field, it cannot be claimed that the struggle for these positions is the driving force for the (relatively durable) existence of the field.

The third Bourdieusian principle is equally subject to the struggle for recognition in the field, which of course is also relevant for the transfer aspect. According to the logics of the field's autonomy it is the recognition through the agents and institutions in the field which is decisive rather than the external recognition through the market. As already mentioned, autonomy is not a fundamental principle in the space of mediation, for in the mediation context, recognition is only gained through the accumulation of various phases of recognition. The insufficient constitution of permanent relationships existing between the agents similarly contributes to the fact that the struggle for durable recognition is not part of the logics of the transfer procedures. This is also reflected in the codification of what, in the literary field, is called "author/writer": if in the literary field it is unquestionably possible to claim the "monopoly of literary legitimacy" and to determine (not only for oneself) who is entitled to be called "author/writer", but also, who ultimately is an "author/writer" (Bourdieu 1999: 354), this is not at all true for the role of mediators. Translators *qua* mediators, for instance, enjoy little prestige due to two major reasons: firstly, because many of them, especially in the literary branch, practise their activity more often as a "second profession", and secondly, because the description of their profession is not protected by law, which means that every individual who pursues the activity of translating can call him or herself a "translator" – regardless of his or her qualification or the translation's quality. This, of course, proves the relatively weak structuring of the mediation space.

The fourth Bourdieusian principle of the field's functioning rules is its reproduction as a precondition for its social endurance. Both the dynamics and the continued existence of the field are the result of a gradual substitution of dominant agents and institutions by those who previously had been dominated by them and who progressively occupy the dominant positions in the field. The reproduction of the field through the agents' struggle, therefore, does not result in the exact reproduction of its elements, but of its structure, and consequently of its order (see Papilloud 2003: 73). In this view, it seems appropriate to ask whether the principle of the field's reproduction can unconditionally be applied to the space of mediation or only to various aspects of it. Principally, the structure of the mediation space within which a transfer process is brought about, is dissolved, but this does not mean that all the space's elements disappear or become ineffective. They rather make up new space structures in different constellations and at different times. Newly formed mediation spaces always illustrate certain constant features and tradition lines, but these are constantly re-"mixed" and re-negotiated within the agents' stakes. As a consequence, the aspect of renewal as one of the conditions for the field's continued existence is primarily embodied in the positions of its agents and is inscribed into the space of mediation. The continuous substitution of agents is another feature fundamental to the existence of the mediation space. However, the changes characteristic for this space and conditioned through varying types of mediation create modes of relation between the agents which oppose the idea of struggle for the positioning of new agents in the field. What Bourdieu calls the "reproduction of the field" and its continuance in whatever form, is in the case of the space of mediation a permanent new configuration which seems constitutive for the – at least temporary – existence of this space.

In this context, how can the phenomenon of mediation and the moment of relational interlacing be explained in detail? If within cultural transfer processes our focus is on the moments of transitions, where the productive exchange between cultures takes place, we can observe that the Bourdieusian concepts are not entirely sufficient in order to convincingly represent the moment of mediation. It is therefore necessary for these concepts be enhanced. In what follows, I will proceed to such an enhancement with the help of Homi Bhabha's theorem of the *Third Space*.

Dynamizing Bourdieu's social fields

My hypothesis is that the theorem of the *Third Space*, as developed by Homi Bhabha, shows surprising analogies with what I have called "mediation space". Both the temporary character of the two concepts and their positioning in a space "in between", seem to underscore the following assumption: the *Third Space* results from the overlapping of cultures understood as "hybrid" and can be understood as a contact zone (Pratt 1992:6) between cultures and as the encounter of spaces, which now, as the product of "translation between cultures" can generate "borderline affects and identifications" (Bhabha 1993:167). Bhabha conceptualizes the hybrid as an active moment which challenges dominant power relations and transmits the zone of transition from a source of conflict into a productive element, opening the so-called *Third Space*:

> [W]e see that all forms of culture are continually in a process of hybridity. But for me the importance of hybridity is not to be able to trace two original moments from which the third emerges, rather hybridity to me is the "third space" which enables other positions to emerge.   (Bhabha 1990:211)

As an in-between space, the *Third Space* is an area of transition, which cannot be seen as a static, identity producing entity, but as a process: "A locus can be described, but its history has always to be written new" (Wägenbaur 1996:38, my translation).

The potential of tension resulting from the moment of encounter contributes to a great degree to the formation of new ascriptions of meaning. In the *Third Space*, the relationships of those who possess different claims and requirements clash, resulting in power struggles which entail negotiation. It is in this *Third Space* where varying life worlds and life styles superimpose upon each other with all their contradictions, which within the *Third Space* produces social interaction. This interaction causes the principle of negotiation to become the fundamental prerequisite for the space's existence. According to Bhabha, a simple act of communication between the "I" and the "You" is not sufficient for the production of meaning as usually occurs in any transfer; it seems rather necessary to mobilize this "I" and this "You" "in the passage through a Third Space" (Bhabha 1994:36).

In this encounter, which entails the transformation of all agents involved and brings about new positions that do not allow the recurrence of already existing structures and formations, the temporary character of the agents' activities is revealed. These agents emerge only for a short time, as "informants" or mediators qua translators in the narrower sense of the word, whose main characteristic is not to struggle for enduring positions, but to abandon the field after concluding the interaction and to look for other areas of activity, occasionally at the intersection with other fields. In addition to its location in a zone of transition and its temporary character, other features necessary for the conceptualization of the mediation process on the basis of the notion of *Third Space* can be identified in the processual nature of the two theorems. As has been shown, processuality is one of the main traits of the Bourdieusian field, but, as has also been illustrated, it is not – or at least insufficiently – inscribed in the moment of transfer.

Interactive encounters in the *Third Space* result in a continuum of transfers evoking the new contextualisaton of signs, and are vice versa determined by these signs. Furthermore, these transfers involve the agents participating in the joint space of action in a process of negotiation. The concept of negotiation, however, should not be associated with the claim to limitless productivity or to a never end-ing inventiveness, and its room for manoeuvre should not be over-estimated (see Bachmann-Medick 1999: 535). It is rather in the actions of the central mediation figures in this process of negotiation that the informative value of the theorem of the space of mediation can clearly be identified. These figures meet in order to "translate" each other, and as hybrid subjects they are positioned at cultural points of intersection which presuppose and simultaneously leave open the process of exchange of the elements resulting from these intersections. As protagonists of the "negotiation" they are also crucial for initiating certain changes in their envi-ronment, and hence in the fields that are contingent to their activities inside the space of mediation.

The (dis)location of the translation field

As a heuristic concept, the space of mediation is located, similarly to the *Third Space*, in the "in-between", and interacts with its surrounding fields.[3] As such, it definitely challenges the notion of the "translation field". Translation studies scholars have repeatedly discussed the possibility of conceptualizing a "transla-tion field", translators being mediators *par excellence* between different fields. This section will present the main arguments offered by several of these scholars.

The functioning rules of the social field developed by Bourdieu are, as already illustrated, inadequate for sketching cultural transfers. Even if Daniel Simeoni, in the context of his analysis of the translatorial *habitus*, does not explicitly discuss the transfer aspect inscribed in the act of translation, he asserts that the formation of a "translation field" is only possible under certain conditions. The reasons for

---

3.   For the postcolonial context of this issue see Wolf (2000).

these restraints lie in the translators' submissive behaviour[4] and the consequent difficulty of positioning the translators in the field: "The pseudo- or would-be field of translation is much less organized than the literary field, being far more heteronomous for reasons having much to do with the ingrained subservience of the translator [...]" (Simeoni 1998: 19). Without proceeding to outline such a "pseudo-field of translation", the author continues:

> As long as this assumption holds, it will be difficult to envisage actual products of translation as anything more than the results of diversely distributed social habituses or, specific habituses governed by the rules pertaining to the field in which the translation takes place.   (ibid.)

Thus, according to Simeoni, the translation process, determined by various *habitus* forms, takes place in different fields that are subject to the respective changes: "The translator may [...] want to move to another field. The field will also change under different circumstances" (ibid.: 31). The temporary character of the "(translation) field" implicitly touched upon here, is also focused on by Jean-Marc Gouanvic. Comparably to Simeoni, Gouanvic points to the various fields in which translations can be carried out (literary field, scientific field, administrative field, etc.), and subsequently claims that these fields do not necessarily exist within the target culture at the moment when the translation is performed (Gouanvic 2001: 36). Gouanvic, however, does not intend to say that the agents' fundamental decision to embark on a translation or to carry out this decision takes place in a "translation field", however this might be conceptualized. He rather suggests that through the translation of certain texts, a new field can be created which will be structured according to the Bourdieusian conditions of social fields. The conceptualization of an independent "translation field" is not envisaged by Gouanvic:

> Admittedly, Bourdieu does not include translated texts in this theory of fields. There is, among others, a very simple reason for this. Far from constituting a field of their own, translated texts are submitted to the same objective logic as the indigenous texts of the target space.   (Gouanvic 2002: 160)

This "logic", to which originals as well as translations are submitted and which in this quotation seems to be the essential argument for the absence of a "translation field", is relativized by Gouanvic when he differentiates between the various legitimizing mechanisms responsible for the formation of a cultural product (original or translation). Additionally, he comprehensively elaborates the differences between the commercially oriented profit expected by publishers from the market-

---

4. The submissive behaviour is also associated with the translator's traditionally low social prestige and his or her "invisibility" in society.

ing of translated products (if, for instance, the authors had already some success in his home country), and the intellectual satisfaction of discovering new and interesting forms which result from the translation activity (if, for instance, a new literary form has been introduced through translation) (Gouanvic 1997a: 127). This, however, cannot delude us as to Gouanvic's claim – that the field in which the translation is performed and from which it is "distributed" is equated with the respective "genre field" (e.g., the literary field) pertinent to the translation's genre or text type.[5]

The ambiguity of the idea of a "translation field", stressed particularly by Simeoni, is recalled to our mind by Rakefet Sela-Sheffy, who points to the marginality of the translator's profession and its subsequent lack of institutionalisation. As a semi-professional group, translators operate in a field with blurred boundaries. Sela-Sheffy attentively investigates the translator's profession, underscoring the lack of unified professional ethics and formal obligatory training frameworks, and additionally attributes the resulting low social status of translators to the fact that translation is not fully recognized as an "art trade" (Sela-Sheffy 2005: 10). According to the author, the existence of a "(literary) translation field" is proven by means of the dynamics which keep a social space moving, that is mainly through the specific capital invested by those who play the "game of translation". Within this framework, Sela-Sheffy argues that there is no need to distinguish between a literary field, in which the translator operates, and a separate translation field – "both perspectives are right". She views the translation field and the literary field equally structured, the translation field being regulated by its own internal hierarchies, professional ethos and self-images and the struggles over the determining of the agents' stakes. The field's autonomy is primarily associated with the symbolic capital, a main feature in the effort to resist subservience. Accordingly, the translators' increasing attempts to transcend their current image and to strive for more professional recognition are a sign of the field's gradual autonomization. However, the author does not take into account the principles underlying the field's functioning. The literary field's operational devices as developed by Bourdieu are embraced too quickly, and a "translation field's" specificities are not taken into account. The concentration on the features making up the translator's symbolic capital – even if these are convincingly presented using the example of

---

5.   For this question, see also Gouanvic (1997b: 35). In his contribution to this volume Gouanvic returns to discuss the issue and once again stresses the main reason for the lack of an independent "translation field" when he claims that translated texts are inscribed by various configurations which make them belong to different specific fields, such as the economic, judicial or any other field.

the Israeli literary translators' situation – conceals the overall context of the field's structure and the potential for changes in the field.

As has already been outlined in the first two chapters of this essay, the equation of the space, where the transfer qua translation takes place, with a specific field (literary, political, religious) is not legitimate. In his study on the conceptualization of a "comics field", Klaus Kaindl claims that until now an independent "translation field" with distinct structures has not existed. One of the prerequisites for such a field is the field's autonomous status. Kaindl argues that:

> While for instance the literary field can by all means be considered an autonomous social space [...], the translation field is not recognizable as an independent entity, neither with respect to the positions of its agents, nor regarding the values which are at stake in the field.   (Kaindl 2004: 133, my translation)

Kaindl identifies the reasons for the non formation of a translation field – analogously to Simeoni – in the weak positions of the various agents and in the generally dissatisfactory image of translation as a secondary activity. Consequently, he asserts that translations are negotiated or fabricated in the (genre-)specific field, from where they then will be distributed for consumption (ibid.: 178).[6]

Most of the authors who engage more intensely in the question whether a "translation field" exists and if so, how it is structured, generally doubt that it exists at all. They do not go further and take steps to develop an alternative or completing theoretical model which enables the integration of the transfer process into the conceptualization of Bourdieu's field theory. As has been shown, such a conceptualization could prove productive for the comprehensive understanding of the translation process not only from the perspective of social aspects.

Conclusion

What has been described in this article as "mediation space", is of course not a space which disappears without leaving a trace, once a cultural product has

---

6. It seems worth noting that, despite their repeatedly postulated equation of "translation field" with "literary field", none of the authors dealt with in this section recur to Bourdieu's suggestion to conceptualize a "sub-field" for the location of translations. According to Bourdieu, a sub-field is formed through the specialization of those agents who develop specific interests for the struggle of new stakes in the field. An example is the "field of art" autonomizing itself in the course of the nineteenth century. This entailed the formation of sub-fields such as painting or sculpture (see Papilloud 2003: 60). In light of my arguments in this essay, it seems evident, however, that these sub-fields also do not correspond to the transfer necessities of the translation procedure and its involvements.

been – more or less successfully – introduced into a field. A mediation space, which is built up through new connections, and in which the agents are subject to continuous re-interpretations, tends to question existing orders and leaves open the potential for multiple contextualisations. This space also displays numerous continuities or tradition lines, for instance stable self images, references to well known locations or stereotyped ascriptions, which can undoubtedly be inscribed into the construction of new interlaces between agents and their stakes.[7] The social interactions taking place in a mediation space open the door for negotiation. Negotiation is performed in light of the various experiences of the agents participating in the production and reception processes of translation who virtually meet here in order to "translate each other". Thus, these agents can be viewed as hybrid subjects which are the (preliminary) result of cultural overlappings in the "in-between" space, the (preliminary) product of intersection of permanent transfer processes. It must also not be forgotten that through the process of mediation and the act of negotiation, the cultural products to be negotiated – texts, signs, and others – become intricate and ambiguous; they are "thickened" through the multiple voices of all the agents involved (Scherpe 2001). The hypothetically harmonious character of these moments of transfer is ruled out by the moments of conflict inherent in the agents' positioning and crucial for the reconstruction of a field in Bourdieu's sense – this is one of the main points where the concepts merge and which bears the potential for a more comprehensive understanding of the functioning of social interactions in the process of mediating between cultures.

References

Bachmann-Medick, Doris. 1999. "1 + 1 = 3? Interkulturelle Beziehungen als 'dritter Raum'". *Weimarer Beiträge* 4: 518–531.

Bhabha, Homi K. 1993. "Culture's in between". *Artforum International* September 1993: 167–168, 211–212.

Bhabha, Homi K. 1994. *The Location of Culture*. London and New York: Routledge.

Bourdieu, Pierre. 1986. "La force du droit. Éléments pour une sociologie du champ juridique". *Actes de la Recherche en Sciences Sociales* 64: 3–19.

Bourdieu, Pierre. 1999. *Die Regeln der Kunst. Genese und Struktur des literarischen Feldes*. Trans. Bernd Schwibs and Achim Russer. Frankfurt am Main: Suhrkamp.

Bourdieu, Pierre. 2001. *Das politische Feld. Zur Kritik der politischen Vernunft*. Trans. Roswitha Schmid. Konstanz: UVK Verlagsgesellschaft.

7.   Some of these considerations have been developed in the context of the "mediation space" relevant for the translation activity in the late Habsburg Monarchy and have been empirically proved by adopting them to a vast corpus of translations from Italian into German for the period between 1848–1918 (see Wolf 2005b).

Gouanvic, Jean-Marc. 1997a. "Translation and the Shape of Things to Come. The Emergence of American Science Fiction in Post-War France". *The Translator* 3 (2): 125–152.

Gouanvic, Jean-Marc. 1997b. "Pour une sociologie de la traduction: le cas de la littérature américaine traduite en France après la Seconde Guerre mondiale (1945–1960)". In *Translation as Intercultural Communication. Selected Papers from the EST Congress Prague 1995*, M. Snell-Hornby, Z. Jettmarová and K. Kaindl (eds). Amsterdam and Philadelphia: John Benjamins. 33–44.

Gouanvic, Jean-Marc. 2001. "Ethos, éthique et traduction: vers une communauté de destin dans les cultures". *TTR* XIV (2): 31–47.

Gouanvic, Jean-Marc. 2002. "The Stakes of Translation in Literary Fields". *Across Languages and Cultures* 3 (2): 159–168.

Kaindl, Klaus. 2004. *Übersetzungswissenschaft im interdisziplinären Dialog. Am Beispiel der Comicübersetzung*. Tübingen: Stauffenburg.

Papilloud, Christian. 2003. *Bourdieu lesen. Einführung in eine Soziologie des Unterschieds. Mit einem Nachwort von Loïc Wacquant*. Bielefeld: transcript Verlag.

Pratt, Mary Louise. 1992. *Imperial Eyes. Travel Writing and Transculturation*. London and New York: Routledge.

Scherpe, Klaus. 2001. "Auf dem Papier sind Indianer weiß, im Ritual sind die Weißen farbig. Fremdheitsforschung in der Literaturwissenschaft". http://www.kakanien.ac.at/beitr/theorie/KScherpe1.pdf. Visited May 2007.

Sela-Sheffy, Rakefet. 2005. "How to be a (recognized) translator. Rethinking habitus, norms, and the field of translation". *Target* 17 (1): 1–26.

Simeoni, Daniel. 1998. "The Pivotal Status of the Translator's Habitus". *Target* 10 (1): 1–39.

Wägenbaur, Thomas. 1996. "Hybride Hybridität: Der Kulturkonflikt im Text der Kulturtheorie". *Arcadia* 31 (1/2): 27–38.

Wolf, Michaela. 2000. "The 'Third Space' in Postcolonial Representation". In *Changing the Terms. Translating in the Postcolonial Era*, S. Simon and P. St-Pierre (eds). Ottawa: University of Ottawa Press. 127–145.

Wolf, Michaela. 2005a. "'Der Kritiker muß ein Verwandlungsmensch sein, ein ... Schlangenmensch des Geistes'. Ein Beitrag zur Dynamisierung der Feldtheorie von Pierre Bourdieu am Beispiel von Hermann Bahr". In *Entgrenzte Räume. Kulturelle Transfers um 1900 und in der Gegenwart*, H. Mitterbauer and K. Scherke (eds). Wien: Passagen. 157–171.

Wolf, Michaela. 2005b. *Die vielsprachige Seele Kakaniens. Translation als soziale und kulturelle Praxis in der Habsburgermonarchie 1848 bis 1918*. Graz: Habilitationsschrift.

PART III

Mapping the field

Issues of method and translation practice

Locating systems and individuals in translation studies

Mirella Agorni
Università Cattolica del Sacro Cuore di Milano, Sede di Brescia, Italia

In this article a number of approaches to translation studies are taken into consideration, in order to explore the possibility of developing a model which could bring together the socio-cultural and the individual aspects of translation. The author demonstrates that the dichotomy between descriptive and explanatory models can be superseded by adopting a methodology that concentrates on the local dimension of translation. By bringing together the various facets of translation phenomena (i.e. the social, linguistic, cultural aspects), and focusing on their material specificity, localism projects a limited but comprehensive image of translation and its social environment. Such an image stands for the original in a metonymic way: working via connection, this model produces multiple meanings, instead of striving for unique solutions.

Descriptive vs. explanatory approaches in translation studies

This article will attempt to carry out an analysis of current research methodology in translation studies, and explore the possibility of developing an approach encompassing both the socio-cultural and the individual dimension of translation, capable of bringing effectively together systems and individuals.

Research methodology in translation studies has come under scrutiny in recent years: it came prominently to the fore just a few years ago, when it was taken as the subject of a major conference held in Manchester in the year 2000 (the title was "Research Models in TS"). One of the recurrent themes of this conference was the opposition between conventionality and creativity in translation, a dilemma often discussed in the papers presented by several scholars, who investigated it from several points of view (for example psycholinguistic analyses, use of corpora in translation pedagogy, translation theory).[1] This dilemma can be

---

1. Some of these works have been published in Olohan (2000) and Hermans (2002).

"translated" in methodological terms by referring to the opposition between what can be broadly described as quantitative or descriptive models (focusing on patterns or regularities) and qualitative or explanatory approaches (focusing on the contingent dimension of translation and the creativity of the human translator) (see Crisafulli 2002).

It is essential not to confuse the distinction between descriptive and explanatory models with the well-known polemics opposing linguistic vs. cultural/literary approaches to translation studies, so often discussed by scholars such as Mona Baker (1996, 2001) and Lawrence Venuti (1998), for example. The dichotomy explored by this article (descriptive vs. explanatory approaches) is not so much theoretical as methodological, and in some cases it can be found within one and the same theory of translation. It is the case of Gideon Toury's theoretical model, which is concerned, on the one hand, with the definition of translation norms and laws (here the emphasis is obviously on the discovery of regularities), while, on the other, it aims at formulating explanatory hypothesis, in order to investigate the cultural role of translation (1995:53).

From a strictly methodological point of view, however, it seems possible to draw a distinction between descriptive translation approaches that emphasise neutrality and objectivity in research (see for example Baker's work on the universals of translation 1993 and 1995, or Toury's insistence on norms 1995), as opposed to those highlighting issues such as translators' agency and choices, and questions of power and ideology (Bassnett and Lefevere 1998; Venuti 1995; Calzada Pérez 2003; Tymoczko and Gentzler 2002; etc.).

In a paper that aims at a reassessment of the descriptive paradigm in translation studies, Edoardo Crisafulli (2002) argues that the opposition amongst the kind of approaches which have just been described corresponds to a basic distinction between empirical and hermeneutic research methods. In his opinion, however, such a distinction is more apparent than real, as all descriptive frameworks necessarily depend on acts of interpretation.

Even in the case of one of the most explicit empirical models of research in translation, based on quantitative linguistic methods, that is the corpus-based approach to translation, it is impossible to draw a clear-cut distinction between description and interpretation. Dorothy Kenny has amply demonstrated that the very design of corpora is to be considered as an act of interpretation. As she puts it, the criteria governing the compilation of a corpus "will inevitably affect what the observer will notice" (Kenny 2001:70).

And yet the corpus-based model has something to say to all those interested in the dilemma between quantitative or descriptive models and qualitative or explanatory approaches to translation. Kenny herself is working on such an issue as creativity by using tools which would seem more appropriate for the investigation of routine patterns in translators' behaviour. But she argues her case in a very convincing way: the ability of Corpus Translation Studies to identify what is "central" and "typical" in translators' behaviour has the "side-effect" of highlighting cases which go beyond routine patterns. When she describes Corpus Linguistics she writes: "creative uses of language are brought into greater relief when one sees them against a backdrop of what is typical for a language" (ibid.: 32). This can be applied to translation too: creative uses of translation are brought into greater relief when one sees them against a backdrop of what is typical in translation; such creativities need to be projected against the rules.

It seems to me that this has a strong bearing on the discipline of translation studies as a whole, among other disciplines. Maria Tymoczko is one of those scholars whose research interests lie outside the field of Corpus Translation Studies, and yet she makes the most of the insights that can be inferred from this model (1998). She points out that most approaches to translation are based on comparative methods, but these are usually applied in a rather "limited" way: in fact, not only Tymoczko herself, but a large number of scholars have noticed and criticised a tendency to focus on relations of likeness, rather than difference, in translation research (see Johnston 1992; Venuti 1995, 1998; Cronin 2000; Kenny 2001). This means that scholars end up by constructing frameworks of analysis which privilege sameness and similarity, to the detriment of what lies outside it – all the discrepant or "indeterminate" cases.

According to Tymoczko, corpus-based approaches to translation are more likely than other models to avoid that tendency, and "remain open to difference, differentiation, and particularity" (Tymoczko 1998: 4), because they focus on the "infinite variety" of language use. Such a variety is a guarantee for the inclusion of difference: the odd cases will be represented side by side with what is more "regular" and "normal", and instead of being neglected as a result of their lack of conformity, they would stand out more clearly.

As a result, it seems high time translation studies employ research models committed to register both stability and change, both norm and norm-breaking. If translation researchers keep on focusing only on rules which are to the detriment of strategies – that is the different, idiosyncratic ways in which rules are materially applied – they are often going to miss the specificity of translation activities, together with all those irregular, contradictory features of translation which are hardly subject to regulation.

Thus the relationship between patterned translation behaviour and the translator's distinct choices, that is the social and individual aspects of translation, could be of special interest for researchers in the field: instead of considering them as two opposing poles, their mutual dependence and modes of interaction could be productively investigated. In order to do this, both quantitative (descriptive, empirical and corpus-based research models), and qualitative methods (critical/interpretative, research on translator's agency and ideology) should better be linked, in order to blend trans-individual and individual concerns – so that the singular, marginal case would no longer be perceived as contradictory vis-à-vis the general, but rather could be seen as a "structural variant" of it.

System theory revisited

Rather than considering the opposition between descriptive/quantitative and explanatory/qualitative research methods as an automatic premise, a simple change of perspective could make the difference, and reconcile the two poles: instead of seeing them in a binary logic, one excluding the other, they can be considered as points on a continuum, linked by a relation of mutual dependency. For example, a methodology such as localism (which will be illustrated in the next section) aims at taking account of the complexity of the dynamics of translation that present themselves in specific contexts by accommodating historical, cultural, linguistic and sociological analysis, together with a special attention to individual translators' behaviour – thus reducing the distance between descriptive and explanatory approaches.

Although the so-called "cultural turn" in translation studies has apparently addressed similar issues since the early '90s (cf. Bassnett and Lefevere 1990), as it began to bring attention to the large cultural context which housed translation activities, yet research produced under that label generally focused on aspects of literary production or reception in an unmistakable textual perspective. In this perspective "culture" represents the environment of translations, providing data to be used in order to shed light on translated texts or translating processes. Hence, the large majority of scholars subscribing to the cultural turn failed to notice the powerful connection amongst translation activities and ended up drawing fascinating, yet in a way incomplete, pictures of distinct translation practices (Bassnett and Lefevere 1998).

Even before the emergence of the "cultural turn", however, polysystem theory provided a more comprehensive scenario, one in which translation is viewed in dynamic connection with large social and cultural developments (Even-Zohar 1978, 1990). Rather than using "culture" in order to analyse and explain translation practices, translation practices are used to investigate entire cultural developments. As we know, in this model translation is inserted into a complex and dynamic network of systems (each of them representing an aspect of a large socio-cultural framework), influencing and, in turn, being influenced by the relations amongst them. The methodology provided by such an approach has proved to be extremely fruitful in the last two decades,[2] and yet polysystem theory, together with other systemic methods,[3] have been criticised by many scholars (Niranjana 1992; Hermans 1999), for what seems to be a mechanical conceptualisation of the forces at play in translation practices.

Hermans is probably the scholar who has gone furthest of contemporary systemic approaches, and has become particularly aware of their limitations: the weakest point of several systemic models have been meticulously illustrated as early as 1999 (Hermans 1999). According to Hermans, system theory does not seem to take into proper account the social and political interests (involving producers and consumers of translations as well as institutions) linked to translation practices. It is the material, social milieu of translation which is somehow overlooked: for example, questions of power and ideology, issues of primary concern for researchers and practitioners alike, run the risk of appearing obscure and ineffectual if they are not linked to the actual people involved in translation activities.

Hermans also stresses the fact that translation phenomena should be analysed without loosing sight of their complexity: it is not enough for system theory to postulate that translation is both produced by and in turn helps to produce the environment which houses it, if the model does not appear to be fully capable of accounting for the manifold aspects of the process. The level of analysis envisaged by many systemic models may appear too simplistic in this respect, as it is built around a series of binary oppositions (centre vs. periphery, innovative vs. conservative cultural practices, etc.) which make it impossible for researchers to investigate those ambivalent and hybrid cases, which cannot be given a clear-cut definition (Hermans 1999: 118, 119).

This kind of critique led several scholars to work out "correctives" to the more deterministic aspects of systemic models – such as research on the degree of agency of individual translators (a topic which has been accompanied by a flourishing debate on ethics, see Pym 1998, 2001) or study of the function of power and ideology. The latter subject was initially developed by Lefevere, who as early as 1992 called attention to social and individualized control factors on translation activities (namely, patronage and ideology on the one hand, and poetics on the other). The task of these elements is to regulate the interdependence between translation practices and their socio-cultural context (Lefevere 1992). This task has been more recently taken over by other control factors, that is norms (Toury

---

2. See the following works, for example: Vanderauwera (1985); Lefevere (1992); Lambert (1997); Bassnett and Lefevere (1998); Tymoczko (1999).

3. Cf. for ex. norm theory or the early descriptive paradigm, particularly in Toury (1995).

1995; Hermans 1996; Chesterman 1997), a concept which gives prominence to the social environment of translation.

Generally used to map socially acceptable behaviour, norm theory envisages translation as a socially patterned type of linguistic communication. Norms are to be understood as codes employed to "decipher" translators' strategies and choices. Not only do they play a fundamental role at the production pole, but they are also of vital importance at the reception end/pole, where they establish "what a particular community will accept as a translation" (Hermans 1999:77–78).

No longer focusing merely on their apparent prescriptive nature, scholars progressively have stressed the productive aspect of norms (Toury 1998).[4] By presenting a regulated choice of behaviour, norms do not impinge on translators' agency; on the contrary, they assist translators in their process of decision-making. Translators' room for manoeuvre also appears to be guaranteed by the diachronic flexibility of norms: since they are produced by social and historically-specific communities, they are subject to change over time.

The strength of norm theory lies in its capacity of bringing together social and individual features of translation, as they ultimately offer the practitioner a socially acceptable repertoire, from which s/he can select their choices. However, there is an important aspect which has to be clarified: as has been pointed out, the definition of norms depends on social groups and institutions, conventionally named "communities". Communities are socially-culturally- and historically-specific, and can be visualised in systemic terms.[5] In order to integrate norm theory into a methodology capable of dealing with the complexity of translation phenomena, we still need some theoretical instruments which would enable us to tackle the materialist specificity (i.e. the contingent social and historical nature) of the forces at play in translation.

---

4. In this article (Toury 1998), which deals at length with the social nature of the norms concept, Toury lays special emphasis on those aspects of norms, which are produced by social and historically-specific communities in order to regulate (and facilitate) translators' processes of decision-making.

5. Rakefet Sela-Sheffy has provided a very useful description of the complex forces involved with translation practices: "editors, publishing houses or commercial companies, and their policy of encouraging or discouraging translation, translation criticism, prizes and grants, translators' associations and clubs" etc. (2000:353). The author stresses the fact that these heterogeneous forces are hierarchically ordered, in a state of dynamic interaction. Side-by-side with this materialist description of the forces at play in translation, we should not forget another interpretation of "community", the "imagined communities" seminally described by the historian Benedict Anderson (1983). In spite of their fictitious character, "imagined communities" brought about very concrete effects, such as the rise of a sense of national identity in certain historical periods (such as the eighteenth century).

Mediating between systems and individuals: Localism

The contingent nature of the various agencies and institutions involved in translation practices can be investigated with the help of the notion of localism. I have derived the concept of localism from the work of Tymoczko (1999: 31–32), and developed it in my own book on eighteenth-century women and translation (Agorni 2002),[6] as a complement of the systemic approach I employed. According to Tymoczko, "localized" research into specific translation phenomena (providing a careful and detailed reconstruction of their social, linguistic, historical, and cultural contexts) allows individual case studies to avoid the danger of generalisation. In this perspective case studies are definitely brought to the fore: their role is no longer perceived as marginal, but rather acquires a fundamental significance in their role as a testing-ground for the discovery (and implementation) of general patterns of translation behaviour. The fact that case studies provide the vital setting that makes translation activities "real" may appear obvious, and yet their primary function is neglected by those approaches which create a rigid dichotomy between the metaphorical and practical dimensions of translation phenomena.[7] Rather than reinforcing old divergences in translation studies, it would seem more productive to consider translation as a set of symbolic *and* materialist practices, each side of the coin giving substance and weight to the other, and both united in the effort of performing a fundamental cultural activity.

Localism is a concept which focuses on the local, circumscribed aspects of cultural phenomena, and aims at mapping the details of the historical, social and linguistic contexts of translation activities. This approach works effectively by

---

6. The notion of localism has been used in my research as a theoretical basis for a minute and detailed historical analysis of the cultural production of eighteenth-century British women (Agorni 2002). A distinctive focus on the local allowed translation activities to display their specificity (for example by means of a close textual analysis, see Chapter 3) and, at the same time, provided the details for an accurate socio-cultural contextualization (see the long discussion on the social and cultural position of eighteenth-century women and the effects of this on translation in Chapter 1 and 2). On methodological terms, localism is committed to register every act of translation, irrespective of its significance, without forcing it into a coherent, meaningful pattern. My work attempts to demonstrate that even apparently unimportant translation minutiae, such as the eighteenth-century translation of an Italian handbook on Newton's theory of light and colours, may acquire a fundamental role once appropriately contextualized against the broad backdrop of intercultural activities in the period concerned.

7. Michael Cronin has argued that some poststructuralist approaches do not take into proper consideration the materialist side (i.e. linguistic nature, in his examples) of translation phenomena (2000: 103). However, the increasing sophistication of poststructuralist criticism is effectively working to reduce such a risk (for a discussion on this topic see Agorni 2002: 90–91).

grounding translation in its environment, and, at the same time, stressing its connections with other translation or translation-like phenomena.[8] For example, Tymoczko has demonstrated that a large variety of translation forms were adopted in her detailed reconstruction of the role of the Irish translation movement in the shaping of the Irish struggle for independence (1999). The extreme flexibility of strategies employed by these translators was what best enabled them to cope with the shifting social and political context of Ireland's transition from postcolonialism to autonomy. Tymockzo offers us a series of "localized", minute pictures that represent various instances of interaction between translation and the Irish struggle of independence – yet, her representation is not meant as a full historical reconstruction of two centuries of history, but as a thorough contextualization of a series of events, that, brought together, generate a pluralistic image of a complex social and historical experience.

By means of its effort at the reconstruction of both text and context, that is both the individual dimension and the trans-individual or social dimensions of translation, localism "locates", i.e. gives substance to, the broad cultural function of translation. Such an approach appears to work against the mechanical tendency implicit in system thinking: it is a qualitative, explanatory model, and represents a corrective to more schematic, quantitative methods.

From a methodological perspective, the function of localism has been described as metonymical, in Tymoczko's own words (1999: 42–57). Unlike metaphorical processes of representation, which work towards a faithful reproduction of the original by aiming at an ideal, albeit impracticable equivalence, metonymical processes produce well-defined but "provisional" images, based on relations of contiguity and combination. Rather than striving for a "perfect" correspondence with their original, metonymical processes of translation work via connections, producing complex contextualizations open to variation and specificity, which eventually create multiple meanings, instead of a single, exemplary solution.

This is extremely important from a methodological point of view: it means that researchers will not favour any translation practice (there will be nothing like a correct vs. a faulty, or a dominant vs. resistant practice), but they will attempt to accommodate the peculiarity of specific activities by locating their social and historical milieu. In order to do that, this approach will necessarily tackle questions of representation and linguistic description. Ethnographic techniques of "transcription" appear to be particularly fruitful in this respect, as they have dealt at length with the thorny issues of observers' partiality and instability of

---

8. In the case of my work, the connection between eighteenth-century translation activities and another translation-like phenomenon such as travel writing has been dealt with at length. On the same subject see also Cronin (2000) and Polezzi (2001).

representations. As we know, a "thick description" (Geertz 1973) methodology has already been applied to translation, resulting in an attempt at designing a type of "translation that seeks with its annotations and its accompanying glosses to *locate* the text in a rich cultural and linguistic context" (Appiah 2000/1993: 427; my emphasis). The result will necessarily be a partial picture of translation and its setting, but objectivity is not the point of this approach: localism has learnt from ethnography to acknowledge its historical and discoursive contingency.

According to this model, researchers will attempt a thick, "located"[9] trans-lation by producing rich, elaborate contextualizations of translation processes: the contingent social and historical specificity of translation will be (re)produced both by means of techniques of description and explanation. Localism will end up by proliferating meaning, instead of reducing it into coherent, but often artificial, patterns (Agorni 2002: 34). Rather than moving along the beaten track, scholars will be committed to follow the loose threads which stem from the idiosyncratic behaviour of human and institutional agencies. The complex pictures resulting from this practice will provide case studies with a "thick", materialist specificity that will allow them to become exemplary for the theory of translation as a whole. Localism, in fact, stands in a metonymical relation to translation theory: the logic of the same, at the basis of the concept of equivalence, will be discarded in favour of a more creative logic, which works via association and connection in order to produce specific, but contingent, approaches to translation. Such a perspective will therefore favour the development of a coherent plurality of theoretical mod-els in translation studies, each of them concentrating on a specific field.

Theo Hermans has presented a series of arguments that challenge the neat separation between the theoretical and descriptive branches of translation studies (Hermans 1999: 160). Localism points in this direction: it seems to be able to pro-duce the "self-reflexive, provisional theorizing which is prepared to be awkward and experimental" (ibid.), a fruitful novelty for the study of translation phenom-ena.

On similar premises, Keith Harvey has recently been using an exemplary mixture of what have so far been called descriptive and explanatory research tools in his work. He aims at sketching an "interactional-interventionist" picture of "lo-cated" systems and individuals in translation studies, a picture which "allows for contradictory behaviours, unforeseen effects and small acts of resistance which are not just seen as departures from established norms [...] but rather as deployments of a capacity for translational agency" (Harvey 2003: 48). Translation is conceived as an "event" which is not merely the product of socio-cultural constraints, but it

---

9. I have used the word "located" rather than "localized" to avoid any reference to localization practices (cf. Agorni 2002: 39–40).

also displays a certain potential for "action".[10] Hence, translation "acts" in a partial and relational (i.e. dialectical) kind of autonomy (Agorni 2002:2): it is subject to socio-systemic pressures, and yet, at the same time, it is also capable of creating new cultural meanings and social relations and/or transforming existing ones.

Conclusion

This article has attempted to draw a broad methodological picture, capable of bringing together theoretical aspects of translation that have too often been seen as worlds apart. The idea that the growth of a discipline focusing on translation phenomena has been held back by the inhibiting force of binary thinking is an old story, yet new, increasingly sophisticated dichotomies continue to appear. A few of them have been discussed in the course of this article – such as descriptive vs. explanatory approaches to translation, quantitative vs. qualitative models, norms vs. strategies, and above all (social) systems vs. individuals. The basic function of such a prolific binary logic appears that of dealing with a profound anxiety against all those ambiguous and overlapping areas of translation that resist clear-cut classification. Yet, several scholars have pointed out that it is precisely in places like "contact zones" or "intercultures" (Pratt 1992; Pym 1998) that the complex, materialist character of translation phenomena can be best observed.

Localism stands for mediation at a methodological level, as I have attempted to explain, and appears particularly suited to address such a hybrid practice as translation. Although the risk of incurring into a pervasive relativism is always close at hand, yet the strength of this approach lies in its commitment to depict the experiential, materialist side of the forces at play in translation. In fact, localism is at its best in historical and sociological analysis of translation phenomena, a kind of research in which attention is not restricted merely to the end products of the process of translation (that is translated texts), but is more productively directed towards the dialogic relations between products themselves and those complex social factors or agencies (individuals, institutions, communities, the market of translation, etc.) which make up the broad scenario of translation.

References

Agorni, Mirella. 2002. *Translating Italy for the Eighteenth Centure. British Women, Translation and Travel Writing.* Manchester: St Jerome Publishing.

---

10. For "action" Harvey means a potential for ideological innovation (Harvey 2003:46).

Anderson, Benedict. 1983. *Imagined Communities. Reflections on the Origins and Spread of Nationalism.* London and New York: Verso.

Appiah, Kwame Anthony. 2000/1993. "Thick Translation". In *The Translation Studies Reader*, L. Venuti (ed). London and New York: Routledge. 417–429.

Baker, Mona. 1993. "Corpus Linguistics and Translation Studies. Implications and Applications". In *Text and Technology: In Honour of John Sinclair*, M. Baker, J. Francis and E. Tognini-Bonelli (eds). Amsterdam and Philadelphia: John Benjamins. 233–250.

Baker, Mona. 1995. "Corpora in Translation Studies: An Overview and Some Suggestions for Future Research". *Target* 7 (2), 223–243.

Baker, Mona. 1996. "Linguistics and Cultural Studies: Complementary or Competing Paradigms in Translation Studies?". In *Übersetzungswissenschaft im Umbruch. Festschrift für Wolfram Wills zum 70. Geburtstag*, A. Lauer, H. Gerzymisch-Arbogast, J. Haller and E. Steiner (eds). Tübingen: Narr. 9–19.

Baker, Mona. 2001. "The Pragmatics of Cross-Cultural Contact and Some False Dichotomies in Translation Studies". In *CTIS Occasional Papers 1*, M. Olohan (ed). Manchester: UMIST. 7–20.

Bassnett, Susan and Lefevere, André (eds). 1990. *Translation, History and Culture.* London and New York: Pinter.

Bassnett, Susan and Lefevere, André. 1998. *Constructing Cultures. Essays on Literary Translation.* Clevedon and Philadelphia etc.: Multilingual Matters.

Calzada Pérez, María (ed). 2003. *Apropos of Ideology.* Manchester: St Jerome Publishing.

Chesterman, Andrew. 1997. *Memes of Translation. The Spread of Ideas in Translation Theory.* Amsterdam and Philadelphia: John Benjamins.

Crisafulli, Edoardo. 2002. "The Quest for an Eclectic Methodology of Translation Description". In *Crosscultural Transgressions. Research Models in Translation Studies II. Historical and Ideological Issues*, T. Hermans (ed). Manchester: St Jerome Publishing. 26–43.

Cronin, Michael. 2000. *Translating Travel. Translation, Languages, Cultures.* Cork: Cork University Press.

Even-Zohar, Itamar. 1978. *Papers in Historical Poetics.* Tel Aviv: The Porter Institute for Poetics and Semiotics.

Even-Zohar, Itamar. 1990. *Poetics Today* 11 (1). Special Issue "Polysystem Studies".

Geertz, Clifford. 1973. *The Interpretation of Cultures: Selected Essays.* New York: Basic Books.

Harvey, Keith. 2003. "Events and 'Horizons'. Reading Ideology in the 'Bindings' of Translations". In *Apropos of Ideology*, M. Calzada Pérez (ed). Manchester: St Jerome Publishing. 43–69.

Hermans, Theo. 1996. "Norms and the Determination of Translation. A Theoretical Framework". In *Translation, Power, Subversion*, R. Álvarez and M. C.-Á.Vidal (eds). Clevedon and Philadelphia etc.: Multilingual Matters. 25–51.

Hermans, Theo. 1999. *Translation in Systems. Descriptive and System-oriented Approaches Explained.* Manchester: St Jerome Publishing.

Hermans, Theo (ed). 2002. *Crosscultural Transgressions. Research Models in Translation Studies II. Historical and Ideological Issues.* Manchester: St Jerome Publishing.

Johnston, John. 1992. "Translation as Simulacrum". In *Rethinking Translation. Discourse, Subjectivity, Ideology*, L. Venuti (ed). London and New York: Routledge. 42–56.

Kenny, Dorothy. 2001. *Lexis and Creativity in Translation. A Corpus-Based Study.* Manchester: St Jerome Publishing.

Lambert, José. 1997. "Itamar Even-Zohar's Polysystem Study. An Interdisciplinary Perspective on Culture Research". *Canadian Revue of Comparative Literature* 24: 7–14.

Lefevere, André. 1992. *Translation, Rewriting and the Manipulation of Literary Fame*. London and New York: Routledge.

Niranjana, Tejaswini. 1992. *Siting Translation. History, Post-Structuralism, and the Colonial Context*. Berkeley and Los Angeles etc.: University of California Press.

Olohan, Maeve (ed). 2000. *Intercultural Faultlines. Research Models in Translation Studies I. Textual and Cognitive Aspects*. Manchester: St Jerome Publishing.

Polezzi, Loredana. 2001. *Translating Travel. Contemporary Italian Travel Writing in English Translation*. Aldershot: Ashgate.

Pratt, Mary Louise. 1992. *Imperial Eyes. Travel Writing and Transculturation*. London and New York: Routledge.

Pym, Anthony. 1998. *Method in Translation History*. Manchester: St Jerome Publishing.

Pym, Anthony (ed). 2001. *The Translator* 7 (2). Special Issue "The Return to Ethics".

Sela-Sheffy, Rakefet. 2000. "The Suspended Potential of Culture Research in TS". *Target* 12 (2): 345–355.

Toury, Gideon. 1995. *Descriptive Translation Studies and beyond*. Amsterdam and Philadelphia: John Benjamins.

Toury, Gideon. 1998. "A Handful of Paragraphs on Translation and Norms". In *Translation and Norms*, C. Schäffner (ed). Clevedon and Philadelphia etc.: Multilingual Matters. 10–32.

Tymoczko, Maria. 1998. "Computerized Corpora and the Future of Translation Studies". *Meta* XLIV (4): 1–6.

Tymoczko, Maria. 1999. *Translation in a Postcolonial Context*. Manchester: St Jerome Publishing.

Tymoczko, Maria and Gentzler, Edwin (eds). 2002. *Translation and Power*. Amherst and Boston: University of Massachusetts Press.

Vanderauwera, Ria. 1985. *Dutch Novels Translated into English. The Transformation of a "Minority" Literature*. Amsterdam and Atlanta: Rodopi.

Venuti, Lawrence. 1995. *The Translator's Invisibility. A history of translation*. London and New York: Routledge.

Venuti, Lawrence. 1998. *The Scandals of Translation. Towards an ethics of difference*. London and New York: Routledge.

Translations "in the making"[*]

Hélène Buzelin
Université de Montréal, Canada

Based on the presentation of an ongoing research program inspired by the works of the French philosopher and anthropologist Bruno Latour – a program that consists of following translation projects "in the making" in three Montréal-based independent publishing houses – this article discusses the benefits and implications of designing a sociology of translation that would focus on the production end rather than the reception end, looking at translation from the viewpoint of its manufacture within publishing houses and integrating ethnography among the research methodologies used. Drawing more particularly upon the observations and analyses deriving from the fieldwork conducted so far in Montréal, this essay suggests how Latour's "sociology of translation" could help overcome the limits of the polysystemic model.

What we today understand as "the sociology of translation" has been, in part, inspired by the work of the Louvain and Tel Aviv Schools. This scientific movement has been renewed by scholars attempting to circumvent the limits of its initial model, the polysystemic model designed by Itamar Even Zohar and further developed by Gideon Toury (e.g. Hermans 1999), and, additionally, by scholars who have borrowed certain concepts from or, more generally speaking, drawn upon the work of Pierre Bourdieu (Simeoni 1995, 1998; Gouanvic 1999; Wolf 1999; Heilbron and Sapiro 2002a; Inghilleri 2003, 2005) and, to a lesser degree, that of Niklas Luhmann (Hermans 1999 and in this volume). Curiously, the thinking of anthropologist and philosopher Bruno Latour, one of the authors of the actor-network theory and an intellectual adversary of Bourdieu, seems never to have particularly interested translation scholars. And yet, since the early 1980s,

[*] This essay could not have been written without the assistance of a number of persons I wish to thank: Jean-Sébastien Marcoux, who introduced me to the works of Bruno Latour, research assistant Éric Plourde who did meticulous bibliographical work, Judith Lavoie who provided judicious comments regarding a preliminary version of this text, Peter Vranckx who translated it into English and, above all, the informants who have participated in the research.

this theory, whose key concept is that of *translation* – understood in the sense of the transformation of an object during the course of an innovative process (Latour 1989: 172–194) – has found numerous fields of application. While originally conceived to account for the way that science "is done" (Latour and Woolgar 1988: 19), it has since been adapted to the study of numerous spheres of production and power (other than those of knowledge) – from the functioning of private businesses to the operation of financial markets and courts of law. I have already explored, in a previous article, Latour's potential contribution to translation studies (Buzelin 2005).[1] At that stage, my argument was strictly theoretical. This essay pursues on a more concrete and applied level my reflections on this subject. Drawing upon the fieldwork I have been conducting for two years among three Montréal-based independent publishers, I seek to better establish the originality and limits of Latour's thinking with regard to translation studies. More specifically, my aim is to demonstrate the interest and implications of a "sociology of translation" that would – not only, but also – take as its object of study a translation's *production* process and integrate ethnography into its research methodologies.

On Bruno Latour's "sociology of translation"

Bruno Latour's theoretical work reflects two distinct phenomena that marked the social sciences during the same period – the 1970s: the repatriation of anthropology within so-called "modern" societies and the study of the relationships between knowledge and power. Interested in the sociology of sciences, Latour was among the first persons to cast an anthropological eye upon scientific practices, to study the processes of scientific and technical innovation in the field – what he calls "la science en action" (1989). Why study science "being done" (Latour and Woolgar 1988: 19), rather than its breakthroughs, its institutions, its great figures or its history? Quite simply, to better understand its mechanisms and social underpinnings, to avoid adopting visions that are too idealized or deterministic and, above all, to demonstrate to what extent "[cette] science ne se produit pas de façon plus scientifique que la technique de manière technique" (Latour 1997: 157).

Latour's approach proceeds from a two-part criticism of his contemporaries sketched out in his first publications and stated more fully in his "Essai d'anthropologie symétrique" entitled *Nous n'avons jamais été modernes* (1997/1991). In his view, modernity is a mere illusion resting upon two complementary practices: the production/multiplication of hybrids, or "quasi-objects" –

---

1.   This contribution can be epistemological, methodological or theoretical in nature, depending upon how Latour is interpreted and appropriated.

what he calls a process of "traduction" – and a work of purification masking the process of production of these hybrids: "L'erreur des modernes sur eux-mêmes est assez facile à comprendre une fois que l'on rétablit la symétrie et que l'on prend en compte à la fois le travail de purification et le travail de traduction. Ils ont confondu les produits et les procédés" (Latour 1997: 156). In his opinion, in order to re-establish symmetry and correct the mistake, it is necessary to analyse these translation processes, abandoning Cartesian dichotomies such as body/spirit, human/machine and nature/culture that have long delimited research objects and methods. Latour replaces the study of traditional science with that of the world of research in order to better grasp where these "hybrids" – scientific facts, theories or products of technological innovation – originate and what they are made of. From this perspective, his two favoured fields of study are science laboratories and scientific controversies. Starting from these fields and together with fellow researchers (who include Michel Callon, John Law and Andrew Rip), he developed the actor-network theory.

This theory, which thus first attempts to understand innovative processes, draws upon two key concepts: *translation* and *network*. In this framework, *translation* designates a process of mediation, of the interpretation of objectives expressed in the "languages" of different intermediaries engaged in an innovative project/process – intermediaries whose viewpoints and interests are not, initially, necessarily the same. This concept, in sum, refers to the strategies by which objectives change and move among the intermediaries, ensuring these persons' participation, the pursuit of the project and the concomitant generation of a demand for the product that will result.[2] For its part, *network* is defined as a set of routes and connections. The concept that lent its name to this theory concerns neither a social network (since it includes humans and machines alike) nor a technological one (since, contrary to such a network, it does not involve a rigid structure). These two concepts – *translation* and *network* – presuppose and underline the creative dimension and, to a certain extent, the unpredictable aspect of the processes under study, as well as the difficulty in reifying them and, thus, the need to study them from within by turning to, among other things, ethnomethodology.

Beyond metaphors: Actor-network theory and translation studies

Latour's work, like that of Pierre Bourdieu, has had applications well beyond the object with which it was initially concerned, in spheres rather far removed from

---

2. This theory is presented in more detail in Buzelin (2005).

science such as courts of law (Latour 2002) and financial markets (Knorr-Cetina and Preda 2005). However, contrary to Bourdieu's work, Latour's remains largely unknown in translation studies. Without necessarily endorsing his model in its entirety, would it not be in the interests of translation theoreticians to appropriate its concepts – indeed, to take inspiration from this approach? Interpreted from a translation studies perspective, Latour's writings raise a number of questions. While Latour is clearly not interested in interlinguistic transfer processes, his definition of translation – synonymous with transformation, movement – is close to the one now proposed by post-structuralist translation scholars who would like to see their field of research expand to include the study of processes of intersemiotic transformation. Is this a matter of a simple terminological coincidence? The concept of hybridity can be looked at similarly. Increasing numbers of translation scholars are considering translation from the standpoint of *métissage* (Nouss and Laplantine 1997) and hybridity (Simon 1999; Wolf 2000). Does the epistemology of these researchers overlap Latour's? If so, how might his thinking contribute to their reflections? Or are we dealing, as might be the case with *translation*, with assorted floating polysemic signifiers used – based upon very different acceptations – within various research areas that in fact are little connected to one another?

On another level, we can also take an interest in the usefulness of concepts such as that of actor-networks in understanding translation scholars' primary object of study: interlinguistic transfer. Increasingly, *networks* are present in translation studies literature.[3] Apart from its current acceptance in semantics and lexicology, the network metaphor often concerns technology – at times a set of relations and, less frequently, interest groups and professional or cultural communities. With a few exceptions (e.g. Pym 1998), the term is rarely defined precisely, however, and it is used even less often as an operational concept in the study of translation practices. Should it be? And if so, is the meaning it has in actor-network theory relevant and appropriate? Lastly, in an even more immediate respect, by simple analogy, Latour's work reminds us just how little we indeed know about how translations commissioned by commercial publishers are produced.

The possible lines of inquiry, as noted by Chesterman (2006), are numerous. The one I have chosen to follow is the most empirical. It consists of closely studying the "making" of various literary translations hosted by commercial publishing houses – from the negotiations pertaining to the purchase of the translation rights to the marketing of the finished product. The context of this four-year program

---

3.   See the contributions in Buzelin and Folaron (2007).

(2004–2007)[4] is provided by the following Montréal-based companies: Fides, Boréal and Les Allusifs. Created in 1937 with an originally religious focus, Fides is one of Québec's oldest book publishers. Nowadays, it has a more generalist orientation and has released approximately 80 titles per year over the past ten years, including essays, fiction, children's literature, coffee-table books and reference works. Translations account for 11% of the titles published. Founded in the early sixties, Les éditions du Boréal is another well-established Québec literary publishing house. It has a team of some 10 full-time employees (as well as three persons working as subcontractors on sales and promotion) and releases around 70 titles per year. Initially specializing in Québec literature and historical writing, Boréal released its first translation in the late 1970s but only started to produce a number of translations – on a modest but more regular basis – in the 1990s. Since then, most of the translations produced under this imprint (an average of five per year until 2005, when 15 foreign titles were released) have been works by Canadian authors in the form of fiction and essays. Les Allusifs is a much smaller and more recently created (2001) company releasing around 10 titles per year. Its catalogue is composed mainly of translations (around 75% of the titles released so far) and authors from Africa, South America and Eastern and Western Europe writing in many different languages. The editorial line favours short novels (novellas) by authors who enjoy literary recognition in their domestic market and who write, in a studied and polished literary style, stories dealing with usually dark issues (e.g. dictatorship, colonization, death).

In studying one particular translation project in each of the three publishing houses, I am working with three types of data. The first is the discursive type. These data consist of comments collected during interviews with the actors participating in the translation project: the managing director, editor-in-chief, translator(s), reviser(s), press officer(s), representative, etc. To analyse – over and above the discourse – the practices themselves, I also collected two kinds of written data: (1) different versions of the translation corresponding to the distinct phases of its development; (2) materials pertaining to management of the translation project (contractual documents, correspondence between the participants, limited-distribution promotional brochures). In short, it is a matter of gathering the traces of the text in the act of becoming and of the paratext prior to publication. Lastly, the third type of data involves the research notes taken throughout the process: fol-

---

4. This program, entitled *Traductologie in the making* and funded by the *Social Sciences and Humanities Research Council of Canada*, is linked to another three-year program, entitled "Traduction et réseaux: le rôle des intermédiaires dans le processus de fabrication d'une traduction en contexte éditorial" and funded by the *Fonds québécois de la recherche sur la société et la culture*.

lowing interviews or during instances of participant observation, when attending private meeting (such as the work session between translators and their editor after the initial submission of the translation) semi-private ones (such as events organized by the publishing house in connection with the translation promotion) as well as when accompanying or meeting some of these publishers on book fairs.

Though the process of analysis and writing up of the results is ongoing, the work accomplished to date has allowed me to better assess – beyond my initial intuition – to what extent both the viewpoint and methodology suggested by Latour could be valuable to translation studies. The two following sections are aimed at developing these ideas. The final and longest section provides more illustrations based on the data collected.

Studying the manufacture of literary translations

The principal originality of Latour's work is, I believe, the viewpoint from which he approaches the object: its manufacture. Following the genesis of a literary translation in the publishing context allows for more specifically documenting from within two interdependent realities: the selection and promotion of foreign texts (this selection and promotion comes under editorial practice, but sometimes also involves the translators) and the work of translation and editing strictly speaking, i.e. from the translator's initial drafts through to the marketed version. In the first case, working in close collaboration with the publishers enables us to better understand their choices and both the constraints and the strategies underlying these choices. In this respect, one may distinguish between different types of publishers, depending on the position that translation occupies with respect to their editorial line. Some (such as Les Allusifs) are clearly oriented towards foreign literatures, while others have a more "domestic" orientation, as was, for example, initially the case with Le Boréal and Fides. The choice between these orientations may depend on the publisher's life path, his/her tastes and position in the literary field in which he/she operates. As it expands and enriches its catalogue, though, each publishing house will tend to open and widen its editorial line. This means that without losing their identity, most publishers are likely – at some point – to act as both exporters and importers of literature, engaged in the search both for foreign outlets for the original texts they publish and for promising new foreign titles that could be published in translation in their domestic market. These two activities often take place at the same time, mainly at book fairs. In relatively small structures (which is often the case with independent publishers), they are also carried out by the same person, but are increasingly mediated by international networks of literary agents. As exporters of domestic texts, publishers (who, in this position, have everything to gain) attempt to create interest among their foreign counterparts, talking up their titles with as many of the right people as possible. This promotional work takes time and the outcome is always uncertain. At the opposite end of things, as importers of literature, publishers need to keep their ears wide open and to be attentive and receptive to the buzz surrounding a title before this buzz gets too loud and before negotiations regarding the title's sale turn ferocious. And they must be all the more receptive (and willing to take a risk) when they operate within a small market and mainstream language.

In an address at the joint conference of the ATTLC and the ATLA (the Canadian and American Associations of Literary Translators) in October 2005, André Vanasse, vice-president of Montréal-based publishing house *XYZ*, insisted that publishers could no longer hope to have their "home" writers known and translated if they themselves (the publishers) did not show an interest in foreign literatures. Obviously, publishers do not simply choose foreign titles among publishers who are likely to buy theirs. Such an idea would be extremely reductive and basically inaccurate. The reasons underlying the selection of foreign titles are much more complex and convoluted but, as Vanasse's statement suggests, they do pertain to an overall and long-term logic of exchange and, as such, ought to be analysed from that perspective. Indeed, if this research has revealed anything up until now, it is that *literary* translation in the strictest sense (i.e. translation of fiction or essays) and in the very context of study, is often risky, costly, or at least usually perceived as such, and not always profitable (even when subsidized). Nevertheless, most publishers are committed to promoting it in large part because it is one of the primary generators of symbolic capital (Casanova 2002). It also provides an opportunity to enhance a catalogue while strengthening ties abroad and to acquire, in the long run, greater visibility in order to create a (small) niche within the world literary market.

Similarly, analysing the process of translation from the viewpoint of a work's manufacture allows for documenting the editorial and revision work done on the manuscript delivered by the translators and thereby better understanding the role of actors who participate in the making of the text but whose actions and practices have so far received little attention. Indeed, contrary to creative (artistic and scientific) processes that have been amply documented,[5] the process of "making" a literary translation has not, to my knowledge, been the subject of any in-depth field study. This is perhaps due to translators' legendary invisibility, to the perceived secondary status of the texts they produce or quite simply to the fact that, compared with dissemination and reception, this aspect of the process

---

5. Thanks to textual genetics, sociology and literary anthropology studies or authors' biographies, as well as to the work of Latour and his collaborators.

of translation/publication falls partly within the private sphere of the publishing house and is thus less easily studied. But perhaps the absence of such a study is also explained, to quote Venuti (1998), by the fact that the work of translation, revision, rereading, correction, etc., which involves the presence of actors who are united in the same project but whose viewpoints might diverge, could be the source of conflicts ... and sometimes "scandals"? Whatever the reasons, this near-absence of field studies on the genesis of literary translations in publishing houses is particularly paradoxical and regrettable given that translations (in the process of becoming), by their perceived derivative and secondary nature, are – more than any other types of texts – subject to manipulation, fine-tuning and revision by third parties. Following a translation project in the making offers such a way of accounting for the multiple subjectivities involved in the making of the text and the logic underlying stylistic choices, as well as for the way each participant – translator, reviser or editor – negotiates his/her own manoeuvring room. And this kind of data may provide us with powerful illustrations of the way translation norms get formed and transformed.

In summary, I believe that the Latourian perspective's principal appeal lies in the fact that it responds to the call for a more process-oriented kind of research while avoiding the pitfalls of the main research paradigms within which this process has thus far been studied. The first paradigm is represented by hermeneutically or psychologically inspired analyses[6] that examine the literary translation process but tend to remove it from its professional or social context. With respect to avoiding a second pitfall, Latour's viewpoint also stands apart from heretofore-dominant sociological studies of literary translation. Indeed, while first-generation polysystemic studies were inclined to depersonalize the translation by frequently restricting themselves to the study of a text corpus (a restriction noted by Theo Hermans 1999), Bourdieusian sociologists of translation tend, on the contrary, to neglect the study of the work performed on the text (translation, revision, proofreading, etc.) to explore instead the agents and institutions participating in the circulation of cultural products within or between literary fields.[7] Tak-

---

6. Here I refer, for instance, to the research tradition initiated by people like Antoine Berman (1984) and Barbara Folkart (1991) on the hermeneutic side, or by Paul Kußmaul (1995) and Gyde Hansen (1999) on the cognitivist side.

7. This criticism primarily concerns the contributions published in Heilbron and Sapiro (2002a). In fact, reading this issue, we can ask ourselves if the refusal of "l'obsession pour la singularité textuelle" (Heilbron and Sapiro 2002b: 3) from which this sociology of translation proceeds, in part, does not translate in reality, at least to this point, into a more outright refusal to acknowledge textual singularity in itself, in other words, a refusal to see the text, its form and its transformations as worthy of analysis.

ing the manufacturing process as the object of study, Latour's approach allows for documenting the practices that sociologists have sought to understand in order to identify the norms governing them (the logic of selection and modes of writing), while avoiding the determinism of the polysystems model. This is done by way of a research methodology that is relatively marginal, though gaining in popularity among translation scholars – ethnography.

On the use of ethnography

Since the time that anthropologists "returned home", ethnography has been applied to research objects of varying natures within neighbouring disciplines that are sometimes rather far removed from anthropology. Considering that today there exist ethnographies of writing (Fabre 1993, 1997) and of communication, among others, can we not envisage one or more ethnographies of translation? In a certain way, each time they have attempted to reflect upon and theorize about translation on the basis of their own practice, translation scholars and translators have acted as ethnographers. Thus, while not presented as such, contributions like those of Suzanne Jill Levine (1993), Françoise Massardey-Kenney (1994) and Gillian Lane-Mercier (1998, 2001) could participate in the construction of an ethnography of translation. Research that claims to be rooted in this approach is more recent.[8] Ethnography, as it is understood, proceeds before all else from work in the field that presupposes an exchange (and, thus, close collaboration) between the actors engaged in the phenomena under study and the researcher. Combining interviews, observations and, in the present case, the analysis of written documents, it also seeks to confront the discourse and practices in question. It rests, ultimately, upon an epistemology that is essentially inductive in nature, viewing the object in such a way as to allow the emergence of new questions and new categories that exceed pre-constructed oppositions. All this makes the approach a delicate and costly one, for it is only in the long run, after multiple interviews, in-field observations and the reading of manuscripts that recurring themes and significant data begin to stand out, and the whole effort becomes meaningful.

Other difficulties relate to the very nature of the object of study: i.e. a moving object under construction. Taking a production process such as the making of a translation as an object of study radically alters the nature of the field, which no longer corresponds to a circumscribed location but, rather, to a network (Latour

---

8.   See, among others, the writings of Michaela Wolf (2002), Kate Sturge (1997, 1998) and Kaisa Koskinen (2000, 2006), as well as the doctoral research being conducted by Kristiina Abdallah (University of Tampere) and Éric Plourde (Université de Montréal).

and Woolgar 1988: 29) – a network whose different components will sometimes be situated thousands of kilometres apart. This approach is complicated by the fact that while the initial phase of the process (the selection of the original text) may be long and slow, once the rights are acquired, the pace quickens and the process's different stages tend to overlap. For example, the translators' work may begin prior to the signing of the contract and the press team moves into action well before the translation is delivered. This obliges the researcher to track several activities at once, with a significant portion of these activities occurring away from the publishing house. Therein, in part, lies the interest in also collecting written documents that will aid in reconstructing the thread of the story – movements and exchanges that the researcher cannot witness.

Beyond these questions of method lie other issues related to ethics and subjectivity. When planning to undertake the research, I usually received two kinds of negative comments and questions: How to get people agree to take part in this kind of study? How to handle and disseminate the information collected? The first question was quickly answered. It seems that the literary field (at least in Montréal) is not as closed a world as is often thought. For all the above reasons, data collection was not always easy. However, to my surprise, I realized that the professionals met along the way were more often than not willing "to play the game", to talk about their practice and to take some time to reflect on them. This might have to do with the fact that I was dealing with independent publishing houses and with professions that may suffer from a lack of visibility and recognition (here, I am obviously not speaking about publishers, but translators, editors or even literary agents). Things might have been more complicated if the research had involved more structured and integrated publishing groups, though this assumption (like the one implied by the first question) relies on a presupposition that future research could very well deny.

The second question is more complex. Looking at things "from the actor's viewpoint" should not mean being complacent nor loosing critical distance once and for all. In that respect, the very fact of dealing with different professionals (publisher, translator, editor, agents etc.) whose roles are complementary but whose viewpoint and power with regard to the same object (the translation in becoming) are neither the same nor equal, was the first way to get contrasted views and to reach a balance. Similarly, dealing with three different publishing houses (each with its own editorial line) and different teams also ensured more relativity when interpreting one's particular position. Also, being at once researcher, translation teacher and someone who has been practicing pragmatic as well as literary translation, meant that my own position and attitude with regards to informants was not fixed, but could change so as to generate more or less distance. These changes were not always conscious nor even always chosen,[9] but they could help, I think, to trigger more discussions, free dialogue and, above all, to avoid as much as possible stereotypical or fake attitudes.

Another important question has to do with the researcher's intrusion into a more or less private sphere. The correspondence examined, the contracts and the preliminary versions of the translation constitute personal and sometimes confidential documents that the authors are not accustomed to sharing with others. Likewise, part of the information exchanged during interviews with publishers may lie behind a so-called "corporate veil", by which I mean data that tend to be regarded as confidential, sometimes more owing to a tradition within the industry than owing to what may be considered their truly compromising nature – for example, figures relating to the number and size of copy runs, sales, costs, etc. So the work of collecting data presupposes a relationship of confidence. This confidence is never a given but, rather, must be established and sometimes redefined as the research continues. Though the modalities of each researcher/informant exchange were set on an individual basis, they were underlined by the same ethical line aimed at ensuring that the collaboration would allow to reach a balanced and critical account without jeopardizing informants' work and working relationships.[10] In all cases, participation was based on the following agreement: on the one hand, the publishers, their employees and the translators accepted to give me access to information; on the other hand, I committed myself to let them read what I would write before it would be published, so that they could ensure it is not detrimental to their interests. So far, this arrangement has worked pretty well. As I explained elsewhere (Buzelin 2006b), what was initially a constraint that I had accepted as a prerequisite to data collection finally proved a good opportunity to fine-tune my account and to develop particular points.

As far as dissemination is concerned, the main implication of this approach has to do with confidentiality (or its absence). This was discussed and negotiated with each publisher on an individual basis. Two had no objections to revealing

---

9. The translators and publishers I met seemed to hold very different presuppositions (when they had some) about what a "translation scholar" does. While translators seemed to initially perceive this kind of researcher as "someone who usually criticize translations", publishers, on the opposite, looked more inclined to believe that this scholar endorses a viewpoint rather similar to (and in defence of) that of translators.

10. In writing up, I therefore avoided reporting any direct comments (whether positive or less positive) informants might have made about their partners. I tried to stick as much as possible to the facts, placing importance on those that directly related to my research objectives and that I intuitively felt to be relevant, and paid close attention to the informants' perceptions of these facts rather than to their general opinions about broader issues.

the title of the books under study, while one preferred to leave things implicit, to avoid proper names. Though this publisher was fully aware that I could not easily guarantee confidentiality, inasmuch as the translation process was presented in detail, he was more comfortable with this writing strategy. As this request did not prevent me from reaching my research objectives, I complied with it.

These methodological and ethical issues are, in fact, those involved with any qualitative-type method based on fieldwork. Without minimizing them, these limits must be assessed with regard to the approach's potential contribution. This approach has at least two strengths that make it especially adapted to today's challenges in translation studies. The first characteristic – fieldwork based on exchanges – provides an effective response to the need to consider translation from the standpoint of agents, a need demonstrated by Simeoni (1995), reiterated by Heilbron and Sapiro (2002b) and evoked anew by Andrew Chesterman (in this volume), among others, as though the efforts (and considerable work) in this regard over the past ten years had not sufficed. The line – or cleavage – between theory and practice is one of the discipline's recurrent themes and constitutes a challenge that training programs are still struggling to take up. Because our undertaking places the researcher literally within the field occupied by the agents in question – not only the translators themselves but all those participating in the production of translated texts – and because it seeks to understand the object of study from these persons' viewpoint and to better identify their working methods as well as the perceptions and the objective constraints underlying them, it offers one way (among others) to minimize the cleavage.

Beyond this aspect, it is the method's flexibility and inductive nature that provide it with all its value for translation studies. Indeed, the re-centring of the agent discussed above constitutes the most concrete expression of a recent calling into question of the structuralist ascendancy models in human and social sciences. According to Douglas Robinson (1998), "we need to deconstruct and demystify the old knowledge [about translation]". Thus, replacing the conventional ways of conceiving of translation as a linear operation consisting of seeking equivalents wherein the meaning of a source text (in language A) is transferred to a target text (in language B), we are seeing new conceptualizations that highlight the creative, disruptive and unpredictable nature of translation at the crossroads of multiple practices. This vision of translation is not shared by everyone, however, and therefore has not disrupted the project that involves establishing general laws. In an environment cohabitated by such divergent presuppositions and theoretical discourses, it may be prudent to remain flexible in approaching the object under study and thereby avoid imposing upon it an overly weighty framework, without making over-assumptions. Similarly, while the actors (publishers, agents, translators, authors, representatives, etc.) are themselves increasingly inclined to underline and to criticize – sometimes cynically – the hold that economic and market-logic factors exercise on their own practices, it seems wise not to overly presuppose with regard to the degree of specificity of the (cultural) goods they produce and cause to circulate. At least, given the profound changes that are affecting the publishing industry worldwide, it seems reasonable to assume that the ways translations are produced are also changing and the changes ought to be documented. The following section tries to illustrate this assumption with examples from the fieldwork carried out so far.

Making literary translations in Montréal: Preliminary conclusions

As noted above, three analyses of particular translation projects were conducted – one in each company. All three consisted of documenting the process, *in situ* and as it developed, as precisely as possible and writing a thick description (see Geertz 1973) of it, paying particular attention to the relation between the various actors involved and the links between linguistic, stylistic, editorial and commercial decisions. Inasmuch as these companies do not publish all that many translations per year (from five to ten titles), I did not have to select between different projects. I simply picked the one that met the two following criteria: (1) the rights had not yet been acquired when data collection started (i.e. the translation was still a "project" in the most wishful sense);[11] (2) this author was a "new" author, i.e. no other text from this person had been translated and published by the company. A detailed ethnographic account of the study conducted with Boréal has already been published (Buzelin 2006b). Data collection for the other two has just been completed and the writing-up of the results is in progress. The following pages briefly present these case studies together with the principal observations and preliminary conclusions deriving from them.

A few words on the Québec book industry

The Québec book industry established itself in the 1960s and consolidated its position in the 1970s (Ménard 2001). It was only during that decade that liter-

---

11. As negotiations are not always successful, there were some instances of "false starts" – cases where I started to collect data on negotiations concerning a title for which the company would finally not acquire the translation rights. Inasmuch as they are indicative of the way translation licenses are acquired/sold, these data were taken into account in the analysis.

ary translation activity really started up.[12] According to Bibliothèque nationale du Québec statistics,[13] the number of translations submitted – a very small one, amounting from 60 to 90 titles per year until 1970 – quadrupled during the '70s and doubled again during the 1980s. Two systemic features have helped to shape this industry, as well as the place and role of literary translation in it.

First, being established in Québec and Canada, local publishers can count on subsidies such as the Book Publishing Industry Development Program (at the federal level), as well as financial assistance or funding from the book sector of Québec's SODEC (*Société de développement des entreprises culturelles*) along with tax reductions. These public subsidies have regularly increased over the years and now account for roughly 10% of publishers' revenue. With regard to translation, the only substantial source of funding is provided by the Canada Council for the Arts' translation program, whose mission is to promote literary exchanges between English and French Canada. As such, this program "provides financial assistance for the first translation of literary works written by Canadian authors. Translation must be into French, English or an Aboriginal language for publication in Canada".[14] This also means that publishers wishing to undertake the translation of non-Canadian titles must do this at their own expenses or find funding elsewhere.

Second, as French-speaking North Americans, Québec publishers have close, though sometimes difficult, relationships with other parts of the French-speaking world, starting with French publishers, who are often seen both as a "natural" but difficult outlet when exporting domestic production and as "unfair competitors" in the rush for good translation opportunities. Indeed, being about ten times smaller than France's, Québec's book market is *a priori* not a very attractive one to

---

12. The *Canada Council for the Arts*' translation assistance program began in 1972, the Literary Translators Association of Canada (LTAC) was founded in 1975 and Montréal-Contact, a Québec literary agency that handles many transactions between major English- and French-Canadian publishers, was created in 1980.

13. To be interpreted cautiously since, in addition to new titles, these statistics indiscriminately include re-editions and brochures and group together all categories of works. Data from 1968 to 1982 were taken from Allard et al. (1984). From 1983 to 1998, data were compiled through consultation of all the brochures published yearly under the title *Statistiques de l'édition au Québec en ...* by the Bibliothèque nationale du Québec (1983–1997). For data from 1998 to 2005 see Bibliothèque nationale du Québec (1998–2005).

14. See Canada Council for the Arts 2006a. To be eligible, the book must be translated by a Canadian citizen or permanent resident The more recent program, created in 1985, "provides assistance to foreign publishers for the translation of literary works by Canadian authors, into languages other than French or English, for publication abroad" (Canada Council for the Arts 2006b). In both cases, the application is made by the publisher of the translation.

foreign agents in search of a French-language publisher. This, in addition to this field's recent development, explains why part of the national literary canon and best-selling authors such as Leonard Cohen, Mordecai Richler, Margaret Atwood and Michael Ondaatje have generally been translated and published in France, though this trend has been changing over the past ten years. Throughout the past forty years, translations have accounted for a limited but increasing percentage of the overall number of made-in-Québec publications, up from 7% in 1968 to 16,2% in 2005 – or more than 20% if we consider commercial publishing only, which seems to have been the principal motor of this activity.[15]

On the whole, in polysystemic terms, Québec appears as a hybrid context that is at once weak (in terms of size) and strong, or at least mainstream (in terms of language). It has its own literary institutions (hence, it constitutes a proper literary field in the Bourdieusian sense), as well as all the agents and economic channels required for a sustainable book industry (from literary agencies to literary magazines to publishers, distributors, bookstores, etc.). As such, Québec cannot be seen simply as a parcel of the French and Canadian book industries. Rather, it is a specific market/industry operating primarily at the crossroads of, and informed by, the European French and English-Canadian ones.

On a per capita basis, this industry, which developed quickly and recently, now compares with its counterpart in France regarding the diversity of titles offered. Since 1994, however, it has gone through a period of stagnation. According to a report by the *Observatoire de la culture et des communications au Québec* published in 2004, the market attained saturation (demonstrating difficulty in absorbing new titles), and the situation in the publishing sector has been declining for the past ten years as companies have posted reduced sales, revenues and profit margins. The report concluded that in such a context, governmental support was more necessary than ever (p. 117), while mentioning that the publishing-assistance policy also reached its limits.[16] In terms of structure, the level of (horizontal) concentration among publishers compared, in 2004, to that prevailing in France in 1998, before the acquisition of Vivendi Universal by Lagardère: i.e. the top

---

15. Indeed, whereas in 1975 only 10% of published translations were produced by commercial editors, today the figure is close to 95%, while commercial publishing accounts for only a slightly increased percentage with regard to editorial activity as a whole.

16. An analysis of Québec publishers' financial reports revealed a positive relationship between "la croissance des subventions et celles des ventes de livres, [ce qui] signifie que les fonds injectés dans l'édition de livres permettent effectivement aux éditeurs de faire connaître les auteurs... Toutefois, le taux de croissance des ventes de livres étant plus faible que celui des subventions [...] il semble que ce modèle de développement ait atteint les limites de ses possibilités" (Observatoire 2004: 107).

three publishers (excluding educational publishers), accounted for 48% of overall sales and the top ten for nearly 80%. However, the landscape has changed drastically since October 2005, when Sogides (a publishing group representing eleven Québec publishing companies) was acquired by Quebecor Inc.[17] The merger, which was scrutinized and finally accepted by the Competition Bureau Canada, put pressure on independent publishers, leading them to react by joining forces too. In October 2006, four of the leading independent publishers (Boréal, Fides, Hurtubise HMH, Québec Amérique) decided to create RELI (*le Regroupement des Éditeurs Littéraires Indépendants*), an association whose first initiative was the shared publication of a common seasonal catalogue to be inserted twice yearly in local newspapers. The back cover of this catalogue's second edition, released in Spring 2007, contains a text titled "L'avenir de la littérature québécoise: non à l'apathie! [The future of Québec literature: fighting against apathy]" in which the four publishers state their concern about the future of the book industry or, rather, its diversity. More specifically, they complain about the "appalling indifference" of local media that no longer support literature but, instead, strictly promote best sellers and "entertainment books", criticize the government's "apathy" and "inactivity" and its lack of a "consistent cultural policy" and, lastly, appeal to the Québec culture minister to act quickly in support of Québec literature".[18]

Yet, crying for help and making public statements are obviously not the only steps independent publishers have taken to save their situation. The above-mentioned changes were foreseeable and, as such, publishers may also have taken less visible, more-subtle day-to-day actions with respect to their publication choices and how they handle their projects. In any case, in such a "gloomy" context, where even the future of local literature is (supposedly) threatened, one may wonder about the place and role (already rather limited) of literary translation. Does insecurity lead these publishers to domestic withdrawal, to change attitudes in the way they choose "foreign" titles or in the way they produce them? This is the range of questions I had in mind when undertaking the research program presented below.

---

17. "[A] communications company with operations in North America, Europe, Latin American and Asia [with] two operating subsidiaries: Quebecor World Inc, one of the largest commercial print media services companies in the world and Quebecor Media Inc, one of Canada's largest media companies" (Quebecor Inc. 2004).

18. These comments echoed a portrait contained in a special issue of the Québec literary journal *Liberté* published in 2006, the year UNESCO named Montréal the "World Book Capital City". Including contributions from many actors in Montréal literary life (publishers, booksellers, critics, associations, etc.), this portrait was a rather dark, even cynical one, calling into question the "prestigious" nomination and highlighting many "problems" such as overproduction, cultural institutions' parochialism, media convergence, concentration within the industry and "best-sellerization" – issues obviously not specific to the Québec market.

An affair of state: translating an "outrageous portrait" of a prime minister

As explained above, Québec publishers wishing to release translations traditionally have had to deal with two sets of constraints: a nationalist subsidy policy (only
literary translations from Canadian authors are subsidized) and competition with
French publishers. As such, the translation of essays by Canadian writers, more
particularly, those dealing with national issues (in the field of politics, sociology,
history or cultural studies) and targeting a general but domestic audience appears
to be a safe niche for Québec publishers: such texts fall into the category eligible
for the translation grant program and are unlikely to be of much interest to a
French-speaking foreign publisher. Besides the fact that "faction" (at least topical
books) is usually easier to promote than "fiction" (at least formal experimenta-
tion), the author (and subject) being Canadian may make promotional work easier and help arouse interest. This may explain why, during two years of fieldwork
interviewing Québec publishers and accompanying some at book fairs, I have
never seen these publishers compete against one another to acquire the rights for
a title by a Canadian poet. But I have often seen them fight, using various strategies from intimidation to seduction, to get their hands on a topical (Canadian)
title and fight all the more fiercely when the topic was a sensitive and catchy one
or the author a national figure. The following title that I tracked at Fides though,
was an exception to the rule.

The Secret Mulroney Tapes by Peter C. Newman, "an outrageous and intimate
portrait of a Canadian prime minister, as told in his own words",[19] would have
probably interested many Québec publishers, if Random House Canada, the original publisher, had not decided to have this book prepared in the utmost secrecy.
This strategy implied that no publisher would be approached or even informed
about this title before the general public – something quite exceptional. The
strategy worked. In the weeks following its release in fall 2005, the book was the
subject of intensive media hype and spotlighted even on radio, as well as on TV
news throughout the country, including in Québec. But this exceptional coverage
was double-sided: it revealed the book's power while infringing on the reception
space a French translation of it might get. Given the book's length (more than 400
pages), by the time the French translation was ready for publication, the media
would have probably turned to something else. Not to mention that interested
Québec readers capable to read in English would have had the opportunity to
buy the original version. This is why this time, there was no mad competition to
acquire the translation rights when Random House (through its Québec agent)
started to present this title to Québec publishers in October 2005 at the Frankfurt

---

19. Blurb on the front jacket.

Book Fair. Publisher Fides did, however, show interest. There were pros and cons, but the editorial board finally decided that the risk was worth taking provided the translation could be released within a short timeframe, ideally less than three months, in order to take advantage of the buzz. The 120,000-word original was split into 40,000-word blocks among three experienced translators, three translation contracts were prepared and an application for a translation subsidy was sent to the Council for the Arts. Each translator submitted ten pages to the editor within two weeks; recurring translation difficulties were spotted and discussed with the editor, who set general guidelines in terms of style and lexical choices so as to avoid, or at least limit, disparities. Then, each translator worked on his own and handed in his text within two months.

But as the translation was about to be revised, the project was suddenly interrupted. The former prime minister, outraged by author Newman's portrait of him, had taken him to court and Random House kindly requested Fides to put the project on hold, at least until things were settled, and refunded the expenses incurred. More than six months later, the trial was over and things could go ahead. However, the reception context had changed and a new contract, with different terms, was required. Each party negotiated its position with conviction, but at length, a deal was reached. Eleven months after the initial agreement, a new contract was signed, with no cash advance upon signing (the first contract involved a $6,500 advance) and a revised royalty rate. As Fides's general director commented, the context was no longer favourable to this title, and no other French-speaking publisher would have been interested in acquiring it anyway. Though still believing in the quality and usefulness of Newman's book, this publisher had lost much of his initial enthusiasm and knew that he would neither make nor lose much money out of it. In his view, resuming the project was mostly a means of saving a business relationship, of reconnecting with an English-Canadian publisher who could become a partner again in the future – a kind of long-term investment. At this stage, the title was no longer a priority and went through regular channels. The editor and reviser acknowledged that splitting the text among three translators had complicated their task: one had to first check the uniformity and homogeneity of style, lexical choices and references (which were numerous), while the other had to compare and consider the different ways the translators had handled identical translation units (such as recurring "colourful" expressions used by Mulroney, subtitles or surnames, etc.). Furthermore, as each translator had his own strengths and weaknesses, setting the right standard involved some surprises and more difficulties.

The publisher went ahead with an initial copy run of 3,000, a slightly optimistic estimation in his view. The representatives surpassed expectations by managing to place more than three quarters of these copies in stores. Since *Mulroney: les enregistrements secrets* was released only in late February 2007 (sixteen months after the original), it remains to be seen whether these placements will turn into true sales or returns to the distributor. Though highlighted by the main retailers, the translation didn't make much waves. But that was expected. As already mentioned, the title had received nationwide media coverage upon its initial release in English, so that the press officer knew it felt like an old story to Québec journalists. And in any case, the author was not present for its promotion.

This case study is not explicitly representative of Fides's way of producing translations. The sensitive subject and nature of the book and the legal action undertaken make this project quite an exceptional one. Besides, Fides has a very wide editorial line, so it would be difficult to select one title as representative of the company. However, this case provides a good illustration of the institutional role of translation in Canada, where historically this practice has not been so much a means of "introducing the foreign" as it has been a way of "breaking the two solitudes", of enhancing exchanges between French- and English-speaking Canadians. Since Canada became an officially bilingual country in 1969, translation, more specifically English/French translation, has become a public and legal affair – a commitment. And the policy of the *Canada Council for the Arts* is the expression, in the field of culture, of this commitment.

The Secret Mulroney Tapes story falls perfectly into this domestic agenda. At the same time, the way this project was conducted is also indicative of the relationship (and power differentials) between English- and French-Canadian publishers, as well as the intertwined nature of their respective markets. As explained above, this project would have been much more interesting to any Québec publisher if he or she could have cooperated with the English-Canadian publisher in order for the French and English versions to be released at the same time. Yet, the French North American market (which is four times smaller than the English-Canadian one) obviously did not weigh much in the English Canadian publisher's decision. This might have to do with the sensitive, even explosive nature of the book. Indeed, a number of essays of "national interest" are now released simultaneously, in French and English, to maximize media impact and/or save on promotional costs. However, in speaking with some Québec publishers who worked in partnership with their English-Canadian counterparts, it was clear that cooperation is not always simple and often involved a speeding-up of the translation process to keep as close as possible to the original publisher's initial schedule. Cooperation becomes easier, in a way, as both parties clearly benefit from it. In this respect, one may differentiate between "straight" black-and-white non-illustrated books that entail low production costs and coffee-table illustrated coloured works that are much more expensive to produce. In the latter case, English and French versions are likely to be not only released at the same time, but also co-produced to save on printing costs.[20] Such projects are usually planned years in advance to give enough time to find different partners who will release their version in their own market. Fides has been involved in a number of such projects over the past ten years and has even undertaken to produce, on its own, multilingual versions of coffee-table books (supervising the writing of the original and preparation of the translations) and to sell these versions directly under its own name or via other publishers. Whether they have dealt with hockey (the national sport) or else exhibitions or shows that have toured the country and abroad, these co-productions have usually been success stories, "the kind of translation projects we would like to do more often" in the managing director's words.

Translating English-Canadian fiction in "mid-Atlantic" French

Like Fides and others, Boréal often publishes translations of English Canadian essays targeting a national (domestic) audience. However, more recently, the company has also tried to obtain English-Canadian titles with international potential, with fictional works more likely to look promising in this regard. That was the case with the translation project I documented. This project involved a 250-page English Canadian novel published by Random House Canada and covered a period of ten months (from the time rights were negotiated to the translation's launch). The title was suggested to the publisher by one of his translators, who, around the same time, was offered a position as "title-hunter", more precisely, "English-Canadian title-hunter" for this company. At the time translation rights were negotiated the title had already been spotted as a potential international best-seller. So for a cash advance of around $3,000 and a royalty rate of 8%, the company acquired French rights strictly for North America; translation rights for francophone Europe would be sold, eight months later, to a Parisian publishing house (approached by Boréal's managing director), which acquired the translation produced in Montréal and released it a year later. This translation was also subsidized by the Canada Council for the Arts and done by two persons who, unlike Fides' translators, acted as a single legal entity. The original, which had been a best-selling summertime read, won Canada's most prestigious literary awards that fall. So when the translation reached the editor's desk in December, he decided it would be revised twice – by himself and by his closest colleague, the chief reviser. The translators said that this text had not raised, in itself, major translation

---

20. Co-production also has direct implications on the translator's work in the sense that, working within a strict and ready-made graphic layout, they will have very little freedom in terms of translation length and interpretation.

difficulties; the most recurring source of concern and discussions among them and their editor was the need to translate the book using a variety of French that would suit both a Québec readership and a Parisian publisher – a "mid-Atlantic" French as they called it, an abstract entity located halfway between France and Québec. While the original text remained a bestseller for two years in English-Canada, where it sold more than 200,000 copies, and rights sold to about ten different countries as well as to Channel 4 for a screen adaptation, the transla-tion (with an initial 3,300 copy run) had sold more than 2,000 copies a year after its release in Québec. The whole project had generated a meager profit of $1000 (though the translation was subsidized and the production costs were shared with the French co-publisher). Yet, Boréal's general director considered this result "a bit better than usual", i.e. slightly better than how his publishing house usually fared when introducing a new novelist in translation.

Compared to the others, this case study could be regarded as an intermediary scenario, where translation appears as a way of consolidating one's position nation-ally[21] ("one" referring to both the publisher and the translators), hence contribut-ing to the ideal of "breaking the two solitudes", while making alliances internation-ally, mainly through co-publishing efforts with Parisian publishers. Thus, Boréal managing director's challenge is to secure these titles before these French publish-ers show interest (hence the need to recruit people who closely follow the English-Canadian market) while singing to these same publishers the virtues of coopera-tion and territory sharing. For the translators, this basically "translates" into the following objective: producing a text that will suit everybody, North American and European readers alike. The goal will be all the more difficult to reach than the cul-tural realities depicted in the book are North American, or even more specifically Canadian, ones – and Boréal focuses primarily on Canadian writing –; i.e. realities that French Canadians are likely to have named in a specific way.

In all cases, the challenge is to do away with preconceptions and imperial-ist attitudes by demonstrating to French publishers that good translations can be produced at a reasonable cost in Montréal and that selling these translations under one's own name, in Québec and in France, makes it possible to sell more copies. The cooperation works both ways. In trying to find French partners for its own translation projects, Boréal has also been editing and promoting, under its own name, in Québec, an increasing number of translations initially produced and released in France. In one way, the company consolidates its position as pub-lisher of the national literary canon – and being co-published in Europe may still

---

21. Boréal has made the most of its reputation as a publisher of contemporary Québec (hence Canadian) literature, more particularly novelists, so that releasing translations of English-Ca-nadian authors remains in line with its initial positioning.

be for Canadian writers a way of being "validated" (to cite Robert Lepage), a way to be held in greater esteem by their fellow countrymen. In another way, it adds foreign (mainly British or American) writers to its catalogue. As both an exporter of Montréal-made translations or an importer of Paris-made ones, the company positions itself on the world literary market without taking too great a risk. As I have argued elsewhere (Buzelin 2006a), cases of French/Québec co-editions such as the one documented here are far from exceptional, both in this company and among other Québec publishers, including Fides. Consequently, the dilemma of writing in "mid-Atlantic French" faced by Boréal's translators cannot be dismissed as anecdotic. In fact, for these translators (who had completed more than 15 contracts for various Québec publishers at the time I conducted the research), writing for both markets at once had become a kind of routine imposing many compromises and sometimes a sort of self-censorship. One could assume that, in the long run, this practice also generates its own translation norm – a norm that will be neither target- nor source-oriented but, rather, "middle-ground-oriented", designed for nobody in particular and for the francophone community at large.

To conclude, this case study reflects an attempt at expanding one's manoeuvring room and one's visibility by endorsing the domestic agenda and by targeting a local audience first, while going beyond, following rather traditional routes and rules. Operating within existing structures, primarily the English/French-Canadian connection and the France/Québec connection, this strategy appears as a double-sided one. In the long run, it could very well help change from within (in day-to-day negotiations concerning a title or in choices between different translation options) the nature of these structures (and the power relationships underlying them), or it could equally well reinforce them.

Publishing world fiction, delocalizing translation

The third and final case study, conducted with Les Allusifs, concerns *Neighbours*, a 131-page novel by Mozambican writer Lilia Momple, originally published in Portuguese in 1995 and released in English by Heinemann in 2001 as *Neighbours – The Story of a Murder* in the "African Writers" Series, with the translation by Richard Bartlett and Isaura de Oliveira. Behind the misleading "murder mystery plot" surface suggested by the English title,[22] the novel is actually a political novel, portraying the country or more specifically its exploitation by colonial Portugal and, more recently, by South Africa. This title was brought to the attention of

---

22. The original Portuguese title was simply *Neighbours*. This was also the title used in the French edition.

the Montréal publisher by one of her translators, a Portuguese-French translator living and working in Paris who had met Lilia Momple during a literary conference in the French capital city and discovered her books on that occasion. A few years before, on a trip to Brazil, this same translator had met a Brazilian writer, read her books, and decided to translate them for pleasure with her Portuguese teacher and friend. She had then decided to send her translation to Les Allusifs, feeling that it might be suitable with respect to the editorial line of this recently formed company, with which she had no connection at all. Her instinct was right: the publisher liked the text, released it as well as others, and this Brazilian writer became one of the company's leading authors. History sometimes repeats itself and the translator succeeded in convincing her publisher to undertake this new project (though she sent only a short portion of her translation this time). This was seen as an opportunity to strengthen the Portuguese line while opening up to African writing, particularly to writing by African women – a genre that, as the translator commented, is underrepresented in France. The French rights were bought (after rather tough negotiations) from Harcourt Education, which held world rights for this title, for a cash advance of 864 euros. This translation was also a team effort, but involved work dynamics that differed from those characterizing the Boréal translators' collaboration.

Because Les Allusifs sells about 80% of its production in France, this Brazilian-French translation team did not face the dilemma of using "mid-Atlantic French". The sensitivity of the French-Canadian readership was not an issue, especially since the original was not a Canadian title. The difficulty had rather to do with its "exotic" character. Indeed, with the text written in a linguistic variety the publisher did not master, this translation process did not involve the usual binary move from language A to language B. Instead, it was a three-part production involving the Portuguese original, the target French version and the English one by Heinemann used as a kind of "pivot" translation by the publisher and the reviser. The intrusion of English complicated the process: it caused some confusion and misunderstanding in the initial stages, led the publisher to question her translators' choices and prompted the translators to go back to this English version and to critically analyse it in order to defend their translation. The translators soon concluded that this version was not reliable, but they had to prove it to their publisher. This problem resurfaced, though to a lesser extent, in the revision phase, as the reviser could not easily go back to the original to check the accuracy (or lack of it) of fuzzy passages. Another difficulty concerned the difference between Brazilian Portuguese (the variety known by the translators) and the variety spoken in Mozambique. This was a concern to the publisher more than to the translators, who acknowledged, however, that they had to do research regarding the original context and the specific language used in order to translate this text. Most discussions on linguistic variation related to passages written in a Portuguese variety that had been rendered as broken English in Heinemann's version and, initially, as a kind of similar broken French by the French translators. The publisher was uncomfortable with this choice, feeling that it resembled "petit-nègre", a stigmatizing form reminiscent of the most reactionary representations of French Creole. Thus, the translation of these dialogues was revised and a more standard variety was adopted.

Another feature distinguishing this case study from the previous ones is the search for funding. Unlike those published by Fides and Boréal, this translation was not eligible for the national translation subsidy program. Yet, as the publisher confessed, a grant covering at least part of the translators' fees had to be found. In her estimations, this might allow, at least, to reach the breakeven point; otherwise it would be a financial disaster. The translators learned of a program offered by the *Institut portugais du livre* in France, but the deadline had passed. So the publisher, as with all her non-Canadian titles, submitted a subsidy application to the *Centre national du livre* in Paris (the main source of funding for literary translation in France). The application (consisting of the original text, 20% of the translation and a text justifying the project's literary importance) was successful, though the jury pointed out a number of changes that would have to be made to the translation. Though the translators disagreed with some of them, they complied, at the publisher's request, since not doing so might have jeopardized the success of future applications. This translation was revised and edited in Montréal. Once ready, the text was sent by email to a printer in the south of France near the distributor's offices. Some 2500 copies were printed: 100 were sent to the press office in Paris, a quarter to the Montréal distributor and the rest to the French distributor.

This translation project is quite representative of Les Allusifs' editorial line. Born out of overt discontent about a literary field perceived as too parochial (Bouchard 2006), this publishing house is not concerned about "breaking the two solitudes". Rather, it is committed to the recognition and promotion of world fiction, more particularly, that of "minor" literatures. The few Canadian authors who are part of its catalogue are generally migrant writers, living in Québec but from abroad, from Eastern Europe to the Caribbean; most of the other titles are selected from very diverse regions (from Latin America to Europe to North America) and, so far, among eleven different languages, including Catalan, Serbo-Croatian, Dutch and Polish. Most of the titles are sold abroad in the French market (which is quite unusual for a Québec-based publisher, the French book industry being usually perceived and experienced by Québec publishers as a rather protectionist one). With such an international catalogue and a target readership located 4,000 miles away from its head office, Les Allusifs appears as an original and high-risk business, resting on the shoulders of a publisher who is not afraid of looking in different directions, of developing new connections off the beaten track, following new migratory routes that reflect this publisher's life path, that of her family, or that of people she has met along the way.[23]

Of course, freedom and detachment have some implications. First, the publisher has to call on a network of close collaborators to build her catalogue, a network where translators take on an important role. Secondly, in its day-to-day functioning, the company has to show a high degree of flexibility, almost to the point of dislocation. The publisher now spends most of the year abroad, at international literary fairs as well as in France, and relies on a team consisting of one full-time employee (assisted by trainee) responsible for supervising the production process in Montréal, a part-time accountant also based in Montréal, and a part-time press officer based in Paris.[24] The company deals with two regular distributors (the main one in France, the second in Montréal) and three printers – one in Québec, a second in Italy and a third in France – the choice between the three depending on the title's specificities and the estimated target market.[25] Translators are selected in France and Montréal alike, while revisers are chosen among former colleagues and friends, as well as among the French-speaking authors most closely connected with the company. Thirdly, the editorial line chosen involves little financial security. Hence, this publisher and her translators spend much time looking for and applying to all possible translation aid programs around the world.

As the case study revealed, Les Allusifs' editorial choices are closely linked to translation in the strictest sense and to the type of difficulties encountered during the process. Some of the most interesting of these links consist of the use of a pivot language (such as English) and the high involvement of the translators at all stages, from book selection to promotion, including the search for funding. In fact, the role played by translators in this company appears to be a central and

---

23. Some of these connections may result from the publisher's previous experiences in the book industry, notably her participation in the Frankfurt Book Fair Fellowship program, as well as her continuous presence at this and other fairs. Interestingly, for the first time in 2006, the company leased a stand in Frankfurt neither in the Anglo-Saxon nor the francophone hall, as 99% of Canadian publishers do, but in the southern European one, sharing it with three other small publishing houses from Spain and Italy.

24. The company hires the services of a Montréal communications firm on a case-by-case basis for particular titles.

25. Canadian titles are usually printed in Québec as this is required to receive public funding here; the others (which comprise the majority) are published in the south of France to save on shipping costs.

valued one, as the publisher often includes these professionals – even relies on them – in her decision-making.

Since Les Allusifs is a young company that has grown quickly, its editorial line is still in the making. While it dismantles cultural and national boundaries, it seems to have operated so far within clearly defined sociological ones, targeting demanding highbrow French-speaking readers, without regard with their citizenship. Within Pierre Bourdieu's framework, it could be said that the company has positioned itself on the "restricted sphere" or elitist side of the literary field – a side that generates much symbolic capital but less financial capital. Perhaps this publisher will have to diversify its catalogue to achieve more balance between high- and low-return books, move its head office to Paris (although regarding book production, particularly nowadays, there may be some advantages in being based in Montréal rather than Paris) or join a larger publishing group. But whatever its future choices, this company has already proved itself to a certain extent during the past six years. It has shown that it may be possible to follow a literary agenda that is original, that is less driven by domestic concerns and national politics - following an agenda in line neither with the institutional pattern of literary translation in Québec (and the patterns of literary exchanges between this market and neighbouring or foreign ones) nor with the logic of best-sellarization. Lastly, like any other, the book industry is subject to delocalization. This is already common knowledge and practice in the field of printing. Les Allusifs' example suggests that the trend may also apply, in a different way, to the publishing sector – even the most literary one.

Beyond differences: Finding new allies, redefining roles and boundaries

Each of these translation stories is much more complex and intricate than the above outlines suggest. Each is, by definition, unique and at the same time, each points towards realities that may, I believe, have a broader relevance. One could draw from these three case studies a sort of continuum, ranging from the most domestic-oriented project (targeting a general but local audience) undertaken by one of Québec's oldest publishing companies, through a second project involving an English Canadian work with international potential (a project targeting a local readership first while trying to reach a wider audience abroad) conducted by a company that grew out of Québec's Quiet Revolution, to the most delocalized project (targeting a highbrow audience across different cultural boundaries) undertaken by one of the most recently formed companies. Are these initiatives coincidences or the sign of a change in the way literary translation is perceived and practiced in Québec? It is difficult to say, though one thing is certain: fifty years ago, probably no French publisher would have bought a translation made in Québec (as was the case with Boréal), and a publishing house such as Les Allusifs could not have come into being, if only because this company simply couldn't function without the continuous use of communication channels and technologies unavailable (or less affordable) at the time. These case studies show above all that there is no direct and obvious relationship between where a translation is produced, the publisher's location and the location of its target readership. In other words, they show us that literary translation (as a business) is, to varying degrees and like any business, subject to delocalization, which has two direct consequences, one for translators and their collaborators, the other for translation scholars: (1) translation choices – made by editors, translators and revisers when they do work –, are not necessarily driven by domestic concerns. Put differently, translators do not always translate for their fellow countrymen; (2) from this perspective, the definition and understanding of preliminary and operational translation norms is not impossible, but becomes extremely complex.

Literary translation generates considerable symbolic capital, but does not easily produce financial capital, especially if the title is produced by an independent publisher, the author is a foreigner (and not involved in promotion) or unknown, the content is fictional rather than factual, and the target market is a small one. In an industry marked by overproduction, concentration and best-sellarization, the rush for translation rights for promising titles appears to be fiercer than ever (all three acquisitions had involved rather harsh negotiations with the original publisher/agent) and promotion has become an essential factor in a book's future life. So, as independent publishers fear for their future but have committed themselves to continue "promoting diversity", they know that they must develop strategies to keep on producing translations (which are an important source of such diversity), but that they need to do this in an efficient way, at least one that limits losses. One of the oldest ways to become stronger is to recruit new allies and stick together, and one of the most recurring features of all three case studies, beyond their differences, was the importance of cooperation.

Cooperation may be "horizontal", between actors who have the same role, actors who may also sometimes be in competition with one another. Let's start with publishers. Cooperation often involves publishers operating in different markets, i.e. French/English-Canadian ones, as is often the case with the translation of Canadian titles of national interest, and North American/European French ones, as shown in the second case study. Likewise, English-Canadian publishers may team up with British or American ones when producing translations or even original texts. These publishing alliances can take different forms, with varying degrees of complexity and commitment. They may be national or international, monolingual or multilingual, and involve co-printing or not. The logic underlying these alliances is likely to reflect each constituent's political history, although other routes based on social rather than political distinctions may also develop, as suggested by Les Allusifs' case study. The benefits of these alliances are basically two-fold: achieving economies of scale and/or obtaining more visibility locally or abroad. Cooperation may also take place among translators as they share their projects with partners. This work sharing may originate with the translators themselves (as in the second and third cases) or the publisher (the first study). As such, co-translation may also take very different forms, the most obvious benefits of which are the compressing of translation deadlines and/or attaining of better quality standards.

Cooperation may also prevail between actors taking on different roles in the translation and publication process: for example between publishers and translators. Translation scholars have traditionally emphasized the power relations between translators and their clients or employers, in this case publishers and editors. Power differentials were also visible in the cases recorded. But these were somewhat overshadowed by other types of relations that involved a partial redefinition of roles. In two of the three cases, translators (at least one member of the team) also acted as "title-hunter" for the publisher. This, in itself, is not necessarily new. Many literary translators have surely played a similar role in the past. What may be more interesting, though, is that in both cases, this function was officialized (hence recognized and valued) by the publisher. One translator became a member of the editorial board while the other became the author's official agent in French. This recognition was felt, by both translators, as a way to compensate, symbolically and financially, for the low status of their profession: as a way to get more power over the selection process (hence over the very nature of titles they would translate) and/to get some royalties (something generally not included in the translation contract). One may regard these cases as anecdotic ones, though in the current publishing context marked by overproduction and insecurity for independent publishers, translators are likely to become extremely useful allies to publishers, at least those who operate in the more restricted sphere of literature and who have agreed to keep on promoting diversity.[26]

At first view, all these cooperation practices may appear to be marginal practices – marginal in the sense that they have received very little attention from translation scholars. But one may wonder how marginal they are in nature. During the compiling of additional data on the catalogue of the three publishing houses that are part of this research and looking more generally at the titles recently translated and published in Québec, it appeared that these practices are far from

---

26. Also, it is worth noting that all three publishers occasionally hire their domestic authors as translators or revisers, or otherwise offer translation projects to their revisers etc.

exceptional.[27] Therefore, the dilemma of writing in an invented "mid-Atlantic" French faced by Boréal's translators, the need to coordinate a project split among three different translators to save time and to "standardize" the resulting text faced by Fides's reviser and editor, and the need to use a pivot language faced by Les Allusifs' team should not be dismissed as anecdotal or trivial issues. Instead, they seem rather symptomatic of the challenges of publishing literary translations today and, as such, are indicative of the type of skills that may be required of professional literary translators. Interestingly, these practices and skills bring us closer to the world of pragmatic translation where work sharing, linguistic standardization, delocalization, outsourcing and the use of a pivot language are quite common. Analyses of translation processes (conducted by publishing houses or translation agencies) or workplace studies might therefore be highly valuable from a pedagogical viewpoint. They might even be an opportunity to reconnect Descriptive Translation Studies with the concerns and goals of translation training. Thus, the first step is to document these practices in the most precise way, so as to contribute to understanding their complexity and their implications with regard to the translator's work. It is in this perspective that I have undertaken to write a thick description of each case study.

Now comes the question of generalization and theorization. Beyond the production of case studies, it is necessary to enquire about the frequency of the practices observed in order to assess to what degree they are representative and revealing of the way translations are produced, as well as differentiate between the different forms these practices may take. This can be done by use of other methods such as the analyses of existing bibliographical databases or the making of new ones, as well as the production of more targeted and structured interviews with key actors. As far as co-translation is concerned, this type of analysis seems possible using existing tools. Regarding co-production and co-edition, the challenge is more difficult. Indeed, mapping the trajectory of literary translations, for example – from their initial publication to the various markets in which they are distributed – requires information that rarely appears in existing bibliographical databases. One has to look at the books themselves or to examine different databases. Also adding to the difficulty is the fact that a concept such as "co-edition" is seen as polysemic. When I began bibliographical research on co-edition in Québec, for example, I soon realized that Québec librarians, i.e. people who compile bibliographic databases, define a co-edition as "a book on which two publishers' names appear". This definition seemed reductive and far from that of all the publishers and agents I met, for whom co-edition means a practice in

---

27. See Buzelin (2006b) for more details.

which several publishers, usually operating in different markets, cooperate on a particular project. Thus, compiling wider-scale data on the practice observed is, in itself, a challenge – but not an impossible one.

Beyond their objective (reducing costs, getting more visibility) and their echo in the field of pragmatic translation, practices of cooperation such as those recorded here share another feature: they are not easy to formalize. This was already noted by Dollerup and Orel-Kos (2001) with regard to co-printing. The authors highlighted how much co-printing is looked upon, criticized, and largely dismissed by scholars, as the latter often believe that this practice produces low-quality books. One could also add that it was neglected because it generally involves paraliterature (i.e. genres less prestigious than fiction, poetry or essay writing). Yet, as the authors pointed out, co-printing has been regularly increasing over the years. As far as illustrated books are concerned, it may have indeed become the norm. Though this genre may be less prestigious, it is the most dynamic one in the book industry. In any case, the fieldwork done in Montréal has shown that co-printing and co-edition is *not* restricted to how-to titles or children's literature. As such, translation scholars have much to lose, I think, in ignoring these practices. Yet, since the publication of Dollerup and Orel-Kos's article, little has been done, to my knowledge. Co-edition and co-production pose a challenge for translation theorists for two principal reasons. First, they can only be understood from within, hence, they require the collaboration of those who practice it. Second, and more interestingly, these practices rest upon flexibility and tend to make the production processes more complex and more volatile, though this volatility depends on the nature of the alliance. Alliances based on weak but multiple ties will open more opportunities, but also more volatility and insecurity; on the opposite, those resting on strong ties may allow to save new negotiations and provide more security, while potentially involving (on the dangerous side) a loss of editorial freedom, particularly if there is a significant power differential between the publishers involved.[28] Co-production and co-edition do not constitute a random

---

28. Two Québec literary publishers – Leméac and Boréal – provide interesting illustrations of each strategy. While Leméac relies on an exclusive partnership with a particular French publisher (Actes Sud), Boréal has co-edited titles with ten different French publishing houses (but, with one exception, rarely more than five titles with the same one). In Boréal's case, which seems to be the type of strategy most frequently used, each translation project requires a search for a new co-editor, hence, new negotiations and perhaps new compromises. Even with the same partner, the terms of exchange will differ from one title to another. There is no guarantee. Boréal's managing director may convince a French colleague to co-edit and have a title translated in Montréal. But if the next title by this author happens to be much more popular, as was the case with Michael Ondaatje's novel *The English Patient*, this publisher may not succeed in translating the title or even obtain North American translation rights. On the opposite,

activity, however. Rather, they constitute a practice that, at all levels, may be quite revealing as to how power relationships are played out between different publishers and between different literary markets. As such, it is not impossible to analyse, it only requires to develop methodologies that are somewhat different from those that have been traditionally used (so far) in translation studies.

A final word

The purpose of this essay has been to propose research ideas and avenues, rather than provide a firm conclusion – and even less so present a ready-made model. At this stage, however, a few certainties are seen. As I have argued elsewhere (Buzelin 2005), Latour's thinking can be interpreted in a "strong" form (as a "theory" of social chaos, though its underlying assumptions call into question the very possibility of drawing theories) or in a weaker one – as a research methodology that allows us to view our object from a different perspective. In the field of translation studies, this means, for example, looking at translation as a production process and trying to highlight the link between linguistic/stylistic decisions and those pertaining to the product's features and its mode of dissemination. Though I started this project with the "strongest" version in mind – and thus did not exhaustively research the Québec literary field or its book industry before undertaking fieldwork – two years of data collection have led me to readjust my agenda. Having studied the genesis and trajectory of literary translations produced by three different publishers, I now find it extremely difficult to go along with Latour's claim that there is no pre-existing structure, there are simply networks and actors that develop and change (hence, the introductory section on "the Québec book industry"). The case studies presented above revealed that nations (here, Canada) and literary institutions/fields (here, Québec) still play a strong role in shaping international literary exchanges (hence, translation) but they obviously do so along with economic considerations – more precisely, market and market-sharing considerations. In other words, the systemic constraints Québec independent publishers, translators and editors must contend with are real and evident, though there are tangible signs that the systems in question are changing in scope and nature, as international literary exchanges intensify according to the dictates of a global and market-driven economy. And this is where network analysis may be relevant to a sociology of translation.

Leméac's catalogue contains many more titles and many more translations from international best-selling authors, though one can wonder the part played by its general director in the acquisition of these titles.

Network analysis is nothing new to sociologists and may take on highly diverse forms. Looking at literary translation from a very localized but dynamic viewpoint – taking a publishing house (or translation agency) as a "reference point" and letting the context emerge as the translation project unfolds along with the process – is one such form of analysis. This particular approach is not a panacea, but it can have at least one advantage: it allows for unveiling, so to speak, practices that have received little attention from translation scholars, simply because they seem to transcend ready-made and traditional categories. Producing thick descriptions of ongoing translation processes provides illustrations of the type of questions the professionals involved in this process may face on a daily basis, hence, of the skills that may be required of future professionals (this is the pedagogical side). But as I have tried to suggest, these case studies may also tell us something about relationships between more abstract entities, such as literary markets and move legal ones, such as translation "territories". For it may well be within micro-phenomena (negotiations regarding the purchase of a title's translation rights, the search for a translation partner or co-publisher, discussions or conflicts concerning the choice of a given term, or exchanges between publishers and translators in the search for translation opportunities) that broader relationships are being played out. It is also at this very local level that one can appreciate how, more than ever, the actors are torn between the quest for symbolic capital and the need to comply with economic imperatives, position themselves and play their game well without selling their soul to the devil.

Now, the observations drawn from these case studies immediately call for other questions: how widespread are the practices observed? To what extent do they reproduce or change traditional roles, working patterns, international exchanges and the power relations underlying them? What impact do they have on the establishment of translation norms? etc. – questions that other types of network analysis, resting on more formal or quantitative methodologies, may help to answer. The agenda underlying these questions is somewhat different from that of polysystemic studies and field/institutional analyses. Whether they are undertaken on a small scale (based on the analysis of the genesis of a particular translation) or on a wider one (aimed at drawing a map of the international trajectories followed by literary translations as they pass through different markets), network analyses may not tell us much about the cultural functions of literary translation. But they will help us to better understand the relationships underlying the way literary translations are produced, hence to understand why these translations (as products) are as they are. As such, network analyses could offer a contribution to a "sociology of the translation process" as suggested by Chesterman (2006), while providing data that may be valuable to translation scholars interested in rethinking the very notion of translation norm.

Data collected so far showed that independent literary publishers, with very distinct editorial lines but operating in the same context – a context that appears at first sight both politically and economically not too favourable to the development of literary translation – are willing and able to keep on releasing translations. Surprisingly, the number of translations released yearly by the three companies that are part of this research did not decrease. It increased, in some cases even quite drastically, over the past ten years. This suggests that the growing insecurity felt by these publishers does not lead to domestic withdrawal, at least in the short run. Indeed, might the opposite be true, with translation increasingly being seen as a way to create links, to build new alliances and connections in order to strengthen one's position? Given this, and the fact that the publishers in question and their collaborators readily admit, in a half-concerned half-resigned tone, that the production and international circulation of books is more intensive than ever, it might be time to address no longer functionalist questions only (why do these people keep on producing translations?) but also to look more closely at pragmatic ones: how do they do it?

References

Allard, Pierre, Lépine, Pierre, Tessier, Louise and Brault, Jean-Rémi. 1984. *Réflexions sur l'édition au Québec*. Montréal: Ministère des affaires culturelles, Bibliothèque nationale du Québec.

Berman, Antoine. 1984. *L'épreuve de l'étranger*. Paris: Gallimard.

Bibliothèque nationale du Québec (ed). 1983–1997. *Statistiques de l'édition au Québec*. Québec.

Bibliothèque nationale du Québec (ed). 1998–2005. *Statistiques de l'édition au Québec*. http:// www.banq.qc.ca/portal/dt/a_propos_banq/nos_publications/nos_publications_a_z/ t0258. jsp?bnq_resolution=mode_800. Visited May 2007.

Bouchard, Brigitte. 2006. "Montréal, capitale mondiale". *Liberté* 271 (48): 20–22.

Buzelin, Hélène. 2005. "Unexpected Allies. How Latour's Network Theory Could Complement Bourdieusian Analyses in Translation Studies". *The Translator* 11 (2): 193–218.

Buzelin, Hélène. 2006a. "Traduire pour le Groenland, en Mid-Atlantic French". *Les contradictions de la globalisation éditoriale*. International symposium organized by *Le centre de sociologie européenne* and the *ESSE network*, May 23, 2006.

Buzelin, Hélène. 2006b. "Independent Publisher in the Networks of Translation". *TTR* 19 (1): 135–169.

Buzelin, Hélène and Folaron, Deborah (eds). 2007. Forthcoming. *Meta* (special issue "Translation and network theories") LII (4).

Canada Council for the Arts. 2006a. http://www.conseildesarts.ca/grants/writing/ ex127227344686875000.htm. Visited May 2007.

Canada Council for the Arts. 2006b. http://www.conseildesarts.ca/grants/writing/ wr127227348212968750.htm. Visited May 2007.

Casanova, Pascale. 2002. "Consécration et accumulation de capital littéraire". *Actes de la recherche en sciences sociales* 144: 7–20.

Chesterman, Andrew. 2006. "Questions in the sociology of translation". In *Translation Studies at the Interface of Disciplines*, J. Ferreira Duarte, A. Assis Rosa and T. Seruya (eds). Amsterdam and Philadelphia: John Benjamins. 9–27.

Dollerup, Cay and Orel-Kos, Silvana. 2001. "Co-prints and Translation". *Perspectives: Studies in Translatology* 9 (2): 87–108.

Fabre, Daniel (ed). 1993. *Écritures ordinaires*. Paris: P.O.L.

Fabre, Daniel. 1997. *Par écrit: Ethnologie des écritures quotidiennes*. Paris: Éditions de la Maison des sciences de l'homme.

Folkart, Barbara. 1991. *Le conflit des énonciations. Traduction et discours rapporté*. Québec: Balzac.

Geertz, Clifford. 1973. *The Interpretation of Cultures. Selected essays*. New York: Basic Books.

Gouanvic, Jean-Marc. 1999. *Sociologie de la traduction. La science-fiction américaine dans l'espace culturel français des années 1950*. Arras: Artois Presses Université.

Hansen, Gyde (ed). 1999. *Probing the Process in Translation. Methods and results*. Copenhagen: Samfundslitteratur.

Heilbron, Johan and Sapiro, Gisèle (eds). 2002a. *Actes de la recherche en sciences sociales* 144. "Les échanges littéraires internationaux".

Heilbron, Johan and Sapiro, Gisèle. 2002b. "La traduction littéraire, un objet sociologique". *Actes de la recherche en sciences sociales* 144: 3–6.

Hermans, Theo. 1999. *Translation in Systems. Descriptive and System-oriented Approaches Explained*. Manchester: St Jerome Publishing.

Inghilleri, Moira. 2003. "Habitus, Field and Discourse: Interpreting as a Socially Situated Activity". *Target* 15 (2): 243–68.

Inghilleri, Moira. 2005. "The Sociology of Bourdieu and the Construction of the 'Object' in Translation and Interpreting Studies". *The Translator* 11 (2): 125–145.

Koskinen, Kaisa. 2000. "Institutional Illusions: Translating in the EU Commission". *The Translator* 6 (1): 49–65.

Koskinen, Kaisa. 2006. "Going into the Field. Ethnographic Methods in Translation Studies". In *Übersetzen – Translating – Traduire: Towards a "Social Turn"?*, M. Wolf (ed). Münster and Hamburg etc.: LIT. 109–118.

Knorr-Cetina, Karin and Preda, Alex (eds). 2004. *The Sociology of Financial Markets*. Oxford: Oxford University Press.

Kußmaul, Paul. 1995. *Training the Translator*. Amsterdam and Philadelphia: John Benjamins.

Lane-Mercier, Gillian. 1998. "Le travail sur la lettre: politique de décentrement ou tactique de réappropriation". *TTR* XI (1): 65–88.

Lane-Mercier, Gillian. 2001. "L'impossible unicité: le conflit des subjectivités et des réceptions". In *Faulkner: une expérience de retraduction*, A. Chapdelaine and G. Lane-Mercier (eds). Montréal: Presses de l'Université de Montréal. 131–178.

Latour, Bruno. 1989. *La science en action*. Paris: La Découverte.

Latour, Bruno (ed). 1997. *Nous n'avons jamais été modernes*. Paris: La Découverte.

Latour, Bruno. 2002. *La fabrique du droit. Une ethnographie du Conseil d'État*. Paris: La Découverte.

Latour, Bruno and Woolgar, Steven. 1988. *La vie de laboratoire. La production des faits scientifiques*. Paris: La Découverte.

Levine, Susan Jill. 1993. *The Subversive Scribe*. Saint Paul: Graywolf Press.

Massardier-Kenney, Françoise. 1994. "Translation Theory and Practice". In *Translating Slavery. Gender and Race in French Women's Writing, 1783–1823*, D.Y. Kadish and F. Massardier-Kenney (eds). Kent (Ohio): The Kent University Press. 11–25.

Ménard, Marc. 2001. *Les chiffres des mots*. Montréal: Sodec.

Nouss, Alexis and Laplantine, François. 1997. *Le métissage: un exposé pour comprendre, un essai pour réfléchir*. Paris: Flammarion.

Observatoire de la culture et des communications du Québec. 2004. *État des lieux du livre et des bibliothèques*. Québec: Gouvernement du Québec.

Pym, Anthony. 1998. *Method in Translation History*. Manchester: St Jerome Publishing.

Quebecor Inc. 2004. Quebecor Communication Services, http://www.quebecor.com. Visited May 2007.

Robinson, Douglas. 1998. "22 Theses on Translation", http://home.olemiss.edu/~djr/pages/writer/articles/html/22theses.html. Visited May 2007.

Simeoni, Daniel. 1995. "Translating and Studying Translation: The View from the Agent". *Meta* XL (3): 445–60.

Simeoni, Daniel. 1998. "The Pivotal Status of the Translator's Habitus". *Target* 10 (1): 1–39.

Simon, Sherry. 1999. *L'hybridité culturelle*. Montréal: L'île de la Tortue.

Sturge, Kate. 1997. "Translation Strategies in Ethnography". *The Translator* 3 (1): 21–38.

Sturge, Kate. 1998. [Review:] "James Clifford: Routes. Travel and Translation in the Late Twentieth Century". *The Translator* 4 (2): 375–379.

Venuti, Lawrence. 1998. *The Scandals of Translation. Towards an ethics of difference*. London and New York: Routledge.

Wolf, Michaela. 1999. "Zum 'sozialen Sinn' in der Translation. Translationssoziologische Implikationen von Pierre Bourdieus Kultursoziologie". *Arcadia* 34 (2): 262–75.

Wolf, Michaela. 2000. "The 'Third Space' in Postcolonial Representation". In *Changing the Terms. Translating in the Postcolonial Era*, S. Simon and P. St-Pierre (eds). Ottawa: University of Ottawa Press. 127–145.

Wolf, Michaela. 2002. "Culture as Translation – and Beyond. Ethnographic Models of Representation in Translation Studies". In *Crosscultural Transgressions. Research Models in Translation Studies II. Historical and Ideological Issues*, T. Hermans (ed). Manchester: St Jerome Publishing. 180–192.

Bridge concepts in translation sociology

Andrew Chesterman
University of Helsinki, Finland

Translation sociology brings back the notion of quality to centre-stage in translation studies, and at the same time adds to the field's social relevance. A sociological approach allows us to highlight "bridge concepts" which connect textual, cognitive and cultural perspectives, and can thus help to unify the discipline. These bridge concepts include the notion of causality; translation practice, discourse and *habitus*; and translation norm, brief, and strategy. By making explicit the links between different kinds of causality, this approach may even take a few steps towards the goal of consilience: the idea of uniting different branches of knowledge.

Introduction

This paper outlines a conceptual map of contemporary translation studies in which the sociological point of view is central. A number of key concepts are presented which play a bridging role between different research perspectives and may thus be useful in tying together the various parts of the research area. Perhaps the most important of these is the notion of causality, which implies a move beyond descriptivism. As soon as we begin to ask why, rather than what, we open up new avenues of research questions. (Recall the title of Toury 1995: *Descriptive Translation Studies and beyond.*)

We can also make translation research more relevant to the needs of society, in particular to the needs of professional translators. It is often pointed out that much translation research appears to lack social relevance (see e.g. Fraser 1996, Chesterman and Wagner 2002: Chapter 1).

Consider, for instance, the issue of translation quality, which is of obvious social relevance. Contemporary corpus research on translation universals has paid relatively little attention to the implications of this research for translation quality. In a major recent collection of papers on translation universals (Mauranen and Kujamäki 2004) the subject index lists only four references to quality in the whole book. The dominant paradigm for this corpus research is a descriptive one. Indeed, over the past two or three decades, descriptivism has become a major slogan in translation studies as a whole. The idea started out as a reaction to what was labelled the "prescriptivism" of so-called traditional work, which aimed to tell translators what they should do rather than simply analyse and describe what they do do. One result of this trend has been the way that the notion of quality has been seen as belonging to the applied branch of the field rather than the descriptive branch (following the Holmes map, originally published in Holmes 1987: 16). However, Holmes was also one of the first scholars to talk about the need for a translation sociology (1988: 95), as part of descriptive studies. If translation sociology includes the description of translation effects, that is translation reception, quality assessment can become a natural part of the descriptive branch. This point of view is a causal one: translations *cause* effects, including those we call quality assessments.

Translation sociology is a relatively new area within translation studies, staking out new research questions for instance between textlinguistics and cultural studies. A Popperian can easily see this as a response to the problems resulting from the current research paradigms. Translation sociology is particularly fruitful as a source of what I would like to call "bridge concepts". By this, I mean concepts which capture overlaps between other notions, and thus enable us to cross borders and set up new viewpoints.

Why might such bridge concepts be useful? There are two main reasons. First, as I argue below, translation studies is becoming increasingly fragmented, as it extends its already interdisciplinary field of interest into other neighbouring areas. If we wish to maintain some kind of coherence in the field, we need to look for ways of connecting different approaches. This may mean developing more abstract concepts, and/or shaping research around bridge concepts, in the search for a greater degree of consilience (see the concluding section). Second, it is often the case that both significant new research problems and fruitful insights and hypotheses arise in border areas, where fields meet. A good example is the new research on consciousness, which draws on neuropsychology, cognition research, philosophy, and other fields. "Consciousness" is thus itself a bridge concept. Another is the sociobiological study of human behaviour. Disciplines often develop via hybrids, as for instance psycholinguistics and sociolingustics have flourished within the mother discipline of linguistics. Bridge concepts may help us to focus on such potentially useful hybrids.

I will now outline the position of translation sociology in relation to other research perspectives, and then proceed to examine some of the bridge concepts it can offer.

Four perspectives on translation studies

When the cultural turn arrived in the 1980's (see e.g. Bassnett and Lefevere 1990), an opposition was set up between linguistic and cultural approaches.[1] Then came the new cognitive paradigm, mainly in the 1990's, looking at what went on in the translator's head via think-aloud protocols (see e.g. the special issue of *Across Languages and Cultures* 3.1, 2002, and the annotated bibliography of Jääskeläinen 2002.) This new interest was marked by a focus on aspects of the translation process rather than the product. But now we have a fourth perspective or level: the social one, also with a focus on processes. Translation studies is becoming increasingly interdisciplinary, and the risk is that it will also become increasingly fragmented – unless we can build links between the fragments. My focus in what follows is not the historical development of these perspectives (see e.g. the references cited), but their synchronic relations in contemporary research.

The linguistic level focuses on texts, as linguistic data in written or oral form; it looks at the relations between translations, their source texts, parallel non-translated texts in the target language, and other translations. It is thus interested in concepts such as equivalence, naturalness and fluency, and in the possibility of finding universal or very general features of translations as texts of a distinctive kind.

On the cultural level, the focus is on ideas (or memes, within a meme-pool; see Chesterman 1997), on the transfer of cultural elements between different repertoires or polysystems. Central issues are questions of ideology, cultural identity and perception, values, relations between centre and periphery, power, and ethics.

Research on the cognitive dimension is interested in the decision-making processes in the translator's mind, in the influence of such factors as the translator's emotions and attitudes, the amount of professional experience, the time available, the routine or non-routine quality of the translation task. The focus is on the cognitive processing, which is inferred from observation. This is the sphere of the translation act (Toury 1995: 249).

Sociological research includes such topics as the translation market, the role played by the publishing industry and other patrons or agents, the social status and roles of translators and the translator's profession, translating as a social practice, and what Toury (1995: 249) has called the translation event. This can be defined as starting with the client's request for a translation and ending with its reception by other agents on various levels. Between these two points come many different work phases involving interaction with both human and non-human resources (see e.g. Mossop 2000, 2001). The sociological focus is thus mainly on

---

1.   This opposition was partly an artificial one: see e.g. Pym (1999), Tymoczko (2002).

people and their observable actions. Sociological issues of translation have been raised earlier by both translation scholars (see e.g. Lefevere 1992; Hermans 1999; Wolf 2002) and sociologists (see e.g. Heilbron and Sapiro 2002).

Although these four areas of translation studies can thus be roughly separated, there is of course much research that cannot be carried out within one approach only, and overlaps are common. As will be illustrated below, overlaps and bridges can in fact be significant, in that they explicitly make links between different perspectives. The first bridge concept discussed here is the notion of causality.

Causality

I have elsewhere (e.g. 2000) suggested that translation studies makes use of three kinds of models of translation: comparative models, process models and causal models. These can be related to our four main perspectives as follows.

Comparative models are on the textual level. They model translation first as a relation between two texts, source and target. Central concepts are those of equivalence (or similarity) and shifts. Later versions of this model relate translations to parallel non-translated texts in the target language (cf. corpus research).

Process models have been proposed for the cognitive level, Toury's translation act. They show input to and output from the black box, and the flow between various assumed modules in the decision-making process. Process models have also been proposed for the sociological level, specifying the various phases in the observable translation process from the initiation by the client, via preparation, drafting and revision, to the final payment (e.g. Sager 1993).

Causal models aim to show cause and effect relations, not just temporal sequences. On one hand, translations are seen as caused or influenced by various causal conditions; and on the other hand, translations themselves are causes of effects, such as quality judgements by clients or readers, as mentioned above (see e.g. Chesterman 2000).

Some process models might be called *implicitly* causal, for they obviously assume a causal relationship between the process and the final product. International ISO, DIN and most recently CEN standards, for instance, specify aspects of the translation process in great detail, on the assumption that if the various phases are carried out "correctly" the final product will be of "acceptable quality", according to these standards.

Explicit causal models have been proposed to link all four levels, and they are the most relevant model type for the topic of this paper. Causal models relate textual features of translations to some features outside the translation. These features are either assumed to be causal conditions or subsequent effects. Different translation theories have foregrounded different kinds of causes. Textual theories can focus on source texts as causes, skopos theory focuses on the aim of the translation as a cause, cultural approaches focus on cultural causal conditions such as norms, and so on.

Translations have multiple causes, of course. The different kinds of causal conditions at different levels approximately correspond to Aristotle's four types of causes: the efficient cause, the material cause, the final cause and the formal cause (cf. Pym 1998: 148–149):

COGNITIVE	efficient cause (translator's mind and body)
TEXTUAL	material cause (target language + source text; computer etc.)
SOCIAL	final cause (*skopos*, translator's aim to earn a living, client's requirements)
CULTURAL	formal cause (translation norms, expectations)

In terms of a simple causal chain, for instance, we could say: this translation is like this, it contains these particular features, because of the decisions that this translator took; the translator worked like that partly because of the nature of the source text, the client's instructions and the ridiculously short deadline; the client specified these conditions because of the norms governing translation work of this kind in this society at this time, which are themselves determined e.g. by commercial values.

For example, in the Helsinki Metro there is the following notice, in Finnish, Swedish and English:

Metron hätäkeskus puh. ...
Metrons nödcentral tfn. ...
Emergency centre of the Metro tel. ...

The English is grammatical but unexpected, rather long-winded, with a contextually untypical use of the postmodification structure. Perhaps it was not translated by a native speaker, or not by a professional translator. Perhaps Helsinki City Transport did not think it was necessary to hire a professional. Their priorities were perhaps elsewhere... I note with interest that later notices in the same Metro now have the more natural phrase "Metro emergency centre", so perhaps someone has commented critically on the earlier text.

Discussion of causality in the human sciences needs some caveats. The general notion of a cause must of course be interpreted flexibly here, if we wish to avoid deterministic formulations. Most potential causes in translation research are general contributory conditions; even vague influences can be regarded as exerting a causal pressure in this loose sense. Within the infinite set of potential contributory conditions, however, some may stand out as seeming more influential than others. In von Wright's terms (2004/1971:85), we could say that translation research can provide "quasi-causal" explanations. Quasi-causes are not nomic (i.e. not based on a lawlike regularity), but they can explain why a given event was possible, and they can make it easier to understand why the event (or, say, textual feature) occurred. They can reduce our surprise; the event then seems to "make sense".

It is often observed, moreover, that all external causes of translations, or particular features in translations, only exert a causal force by virtue of their being channelled or filtered through the translator's mind. Cultural and sociological pressures and values, norms and instructions, only have an effect on the target text via the individual translator's cognition, since the text itself is only produced by the translator's agency (see further Chesterman 2002). On the theoretical level, this is visible in the criticism directed against polysystem theory, viz. that its concepts (system, polysystem) are too abstract to be able to function as real causes (Pym 1998: Chapter 7; Hermans 1999: Chapter 11). If translation sociology places people centre-stage, and uses a causal model, it can also highlight genuine human agency and give space to the translator's subjectivity.

Practice, discourse and *habitus*

What other bridges are available between these four different perspectives? Traditionally, we have been accustomed to seeing the textual perspective as central and primary, with the other perspectives more relevant to establishing the background conditions and consequences of the texts themselves. Indeed, this is the way I framed the causal model above. But what questions arise once the social perspective is placed at the centre? This means starting with a focus on people and what they do. If we take this viewpoint, three bridge concepts can be highlighted which help us to conceptualize connections between the social perspective and the other three.

One concept that covers both social and cultural aspects is that of the translation *practice*, understood as the set of translation events within a given temporal, institutional and cultural setting, influenced by and itself affecting cultural values and traditions. Between the social and the textual we have *discourse*, linking texts to their communicative context of production and reception. Discourse is a notoriously slippery term. I am not using it here in its narrow linguistic sense of "language beyond the sentence". Rather, I refer to the sense "language use in context" (see e.g. Brown and Yule 1983), and also more generally to the way in which the term is used to designate the wider context of a social practice (see e.g. Fairclough

1992). For instance, the term "discourse of translation" is already current, describing the ways people (including translators) talk and write about translation and thus contribute to the public image of the profession. In the former sense, we can say that the discourse conditions of a communicative act include all aspects of its situational and functional setting. Both senses include issues of power and institutional status.

Between the social and the cognitive, perhaps overlapping also with the cultural, we have the *habitus*, Bourdieu's term for the totality of professional dispositions and attitudes of agents within a given field or practice. The translator's *habitus* is what Simeoni (1998) refers to as the translator's mindset, or cultural mind, "the elaborate result of a personalized social and cultural history" (Simeoni 1998: 32). The *habitus* thus mediates between personal experience and the social world. The *habitus* is acquired via "inculcation in a set of social practices" (Inghilleri 2005: 70).

Professional *habitus* and practice thus affect each other. And much of this mutual shaping takes place via communication, via discourse. We also have critical discourse analysis, probing the hidden values and power structures underlying discourse. Practice analysis covers many sociological aspects of translation events. It focuses on what people (translators) do: how they work, how they organize their time, their workplace procedures, their interactions with other team members or experts, their use of resources, project management, quality control procedures, and so on. It thus covers a wider field than discourse analysis, which focuses mainly on language use rather than actions more generally. If we are interested in pinpointing weaknesses (for instance, weaknesses in quality control procedures or time management or task distribution) and identifying instances of "best practice", we are doing what we could call critical practice analysis. This could be defined as practice analysis in relation to the value of quality. *Habitus* analysis does not yet seem to be a current term, although there is some research on the typical personalities of translators and interpreters (see e.g. Kurz, Basel, Chiba, Patels and Wolfframm 1996). But what we could call critical *habitus* analysis is surely what we do in the training of future translators. This involves the formation and development of a professional *habitus*, socialization into the profession, the adoption of appropriate attitudes and values, and so on. Shifting the concepts of practice and *habitus* to centre-stage might inspire more research in these areas. A *habitus* is, admittedly, difficult to change; but not impossible.

Norms, brief, strategies

We can now ask more specifically how translation causality works, or, more specifically, how practice, discourse and *habitus* are manifested.

Translation practice is crystallized in translation *norms*. Norms entered translation studies primarily via Toury's applications of Even-Zohar's work on polysystems, but they are also central notions in sociology (see e.g. Giddens 1997). As values, intersubjectively agreed and established, they are cultural phenomena. But they are manifested in observable social behaviour, including the activity of translating. As ideas, they exist in the cultural sphere (according to the way I framed this sphere above, in contrast to the social one), but their prescriptive force, their causal influence, is seen in social practices and in their products, including of course translations.

The discourse conditions of a translation are manifested in the translation *brief*, the client's specification, the instructions. I take the brief to include the source text, the *skopos*, the resources, deadline, fee, etc. – all the task conditions relevant to a given translation. The brief (presumably) affects the way the translator thinks about a particular task, the way in which decisions are made during the process. Skopos theory has made the task specification a central notion, but much remains to be discovered about the precise nature of the relation between given features of a specification, given features of the cognitive process of translating, and given features of the resulting translation.[2]

Simeoni (1998) motivates his re-examination of the translator's *habitus* by the need for a better conceptualization of the translator's choices and the factors affecting a translator's individual style (Simeoni 1998: 1). In addition to the *habitus*, the factors obviously include the translator's competence, the translation's *skopos*, the task conditions (time, resources, text type, the language pair concerned, etc.) and the wider translation tradition as a whole, within which the translator works. The decisions made as a result of the joint influence of these and other relevant factors are manifested in the translator's *strategies*, which lead to the use of particular textual techniques, resulting in various kinds of equivalences and shifts. In this sense, strategies correspond to what some other scholars have called "global strategies" (Séguinot 1989), applying to the whole of a text or to a recurring kind of translation problem. Examples are decisions concerning foreignization or domestication; the use or avoidance of footnotes; general principles for dealing with very long sentences or names or metaphors, in a given text-type; attitudes to the use of loanwords; attitudes to norms; general principles regarding working meth-

---

2.   The question of how translations of the same source text vary when the specification varies is precisely the subject of Norberg (2003).

ods, drafting and revision. Strategies exist in the minds of individual translators, but they may of course be widely shared. The attitudes and professional dispositions which constitute the *habitus*, in the context of the constraints and demands of a particular translation task, are thus made visible in a translator's global strategies for that translation.

The causal conditions thus affect the textual profile of translations via the translation norms and the details of the translation brief, and the translator's choice of strategies. Strictly speaking, as mentioned earlier, the influence of norms and the brief takes effect via the translator's attitudes and responses to them.

Reactions, responses, repercussions

Translations are not just consequences of causal conditions of various kinds. They also act as causes themselves, they produce effects. Research on translation reception has not yet adopted standard terminology, so I shall venture to suggest some here. This is precisely where quality assessment enters the picture. As soon as we look at translation effects in a causal model, we realise that quality assessment is an integral part of such a model.

When you read a translation, the first effect it has on you must be a cognitive one: relevance theory talks of the "cognitive effects" of any act of communication. You might think "what an odd sentence", for instance, whereas closer examination might lead you to think "the translator must have made a mistake here", or even "what a wonderful translation", or "I really must read some more Japanese poetry". To refer to the effects of the textual (i.e. translations themselves) on the cognitive (i.e. the mental and emotional reactions of readers), we could thus use the term *reactions*. At the collective level, people's reactions to translations contribute to their shared mental image of what translations are like, and perhaps also of what translators are like – to the extent that they are reacting to the translations *as translations*, of course. But even if people are not aware that a given text is a translation, they nevertheless react to it as a text; and these reactions themselves are of relevance to translation research.

You might, of course, be content just to "react" mentally or emotionally to a given translation. But your reaction might also prompt you to say or do something, such as write to the newspaper to complain about the latest translation of the Bible, write a book review, draw a red line under the offending item, or make a note to offer further work to such an excellent translator. These observable acts of behaviour we could call *responses*. Responses manifest feedback. If the responses are communicative acts, they will also fall under the general notion of discourse. Indeed, we already talk about the "discourse of translation", meaning the way people talk and write about translation and thus create and reinforce the public image of the profession. Part of this image is formed and reflected by representations of translators and interpreters in literature. This sense of "image" can also be related to Bourdieu's *habitus,* as argued by Williams (2005). Discussing the rewriting of the city of Rome as a cultural construct, he suggests that the "image" of Rome helps to "define the *horizon of expectation* both of the reader and the rewriter" (2005: 80; emphasis original). The image, argues Williams (2005: 81) "functions in a manner akin to Bourdieu's '*habitus*'", in the sense that it reactivates the effects of past practices via acquired dispositions. Put simply, one's image of Rome is formed in part by what one has e.g. read about Rome, as one's dispositions are conditioned by one's previous experiences. Translations themselves (and other texts etc.) affect the discourse of translation, which is both affected by, and itself affects, the public image of translation and the *habitus* of translators.

Seen in this light, translation quality assessment is no more than a combination of particular reactions and responses, effects caused by a given translation. It also follows that, as I have argued elsewhere, prescriptive statements are none other than predictive hypotheses of such translation effects (Chesterman 1999). In this way, quality assessment fits naturally into the general study of translation effects, and there need be no gulf between old-fashioned prescriptivists and modern descriptivists.

To describe the effects of translations at the cultural level, we might then speak of *translation repercussions.* The Collins English Dictionary defines a repercussion as "a result or consequence, esp. one that is somewhat removed from the action or event which precipitated it" – a definition which fits very well with the sense I am suggesting here. Examples of translation repercussions might be the canonization of a literary work, changes in the evolution of the target language, changes in norms and practices, changes in the perception of cultural stereotypes. Thus defined, reactions, responses and repercussions are also bridge concepts, linking the textual perspective to the other perspectives.

The effects of translations, thus analysed, may of course be similar to the effects of any other text. The categories outlined above are not specific to translation.

Consilience

My general objective in choosing to discuss the topic of bridge concepts is to promote the idea of consilience. Consilience literally means "jumping together", but its derived meaning denotes the unity of all knowledge. Edward O. Wilson's book on the subject, *Consilience,* appeared in 1998. Although he first made his scientific reputation as an authority on ants, Wilson is perhaps most famous today as the founder of the science of sociobiology, which uses ideas and hypotheses derived from biology to examine and explain the social behaviour of human beings. In particular, Wilson has sought to apply Darwin's theory of evolution to social and cultural change. (He is not responsible for the rise of so-called social darwinism, which is based on a misunderstanding of Darwin's ideas. See e.g. Dennett 1995; Segerstråle 2000.) Wilson's attempt to sketch out the ways in which different sciences can be linked, not only with each other but also with the humanities, is of amazing scope and vision. Consilience, as a concept, highlights the significance of interdisciplines (or transdisciplines or pluridisciplines...), which allow us to cross boundaries between traditional fields. As Wilson points out, the most powerful explanations are often those that relate different fields. For Wilson, the idea of consilience symbolizes a vision of the unity of all human knowledge, an ideal goal. He does not give consilience a sociological context, nor does he relate the goal of linking different fields to any kind of Bourdieusian analysis of power struggles between fields. However, his work has certainly given rise to these kinds of struggles (see Segerstråhle 2000). I find this ideal inspiring, and I have used the notion of consilience as a useful way of referring to my general aim of explicating the relations between different parts of translation studies.[3]

What is the relevance of all this for translation studies? It has now become a commonplace to say that translation studies is an interdiscipline. From the consilience point of view, it is precisely this interdisciplinarity that is the strength of the field. As an interdiscipline, modern translation studies announces itself as a new attempt to cut across boundaries in the search for a deeper understanding of the relations between texts, languages, societies and cultures. On one hand, we seem to need conceptual borders, because without them, in other words without categories, we cannot think at all. But at the same time we can try to overcome or at least challenge these categorical borders, by exploiting notions that set up alternative categories. In time, bridge concepts may become primary ones, no longer seen as mere bridges between other concepts that are themselves regarded as primary. If this happens, and the conceptual centre of gravity thus shifts, the whole research paradigm of a given field changes. Exciting times...

References

Bassnett, Susan and Lefevere, André (eds). 1990. *Translation, History and Culture*. London and New York: Pinter.

---

3. For earlier versions of parts of this article, see Chesterman (2005a) and Chesterman (2005b).

Brown, Gillian and Yule, George. 1983. *Discourse Analysis*. Cambridge: Cambridge University Press.

Chesterman, Andrew. 1997 *Memes of Translation. The Spread of Ideas in Translation Theory*. Amsterdam and Philadelphia: John Benjamins.

Chesterman, Andrew. 1999. "The Empirical Status of Prescriptivism". *Folia Translatologica* 6: 9–19.

Chesterman, Andrew. 2000. "A Causal Model for Translation Studies". In *Intercultural Faultlines. Research Models in Translation Studies I. Textual and Cognitive Aspects*, M. Olohan (ed). Manchester: St Jerome Publishing. 15–27.

Chesterman, Andrew. 2002. "Semiotic Modalities in Translation Causality". *Across Languages and Cultures* 3 (2): 145–158.

Chesterman, Andrew. 2005a. "Towards consilience?". In *New Tendencies in Translation Studies*, K. Aijmer, Karin and C. Alvstad (eds). Göteborg: Göteborg University. 19–27.

Chesterman, Andrew. 2005b. "Consilience in Translation Studies". *Revista Canaria* 51: 19–32

Chesterman, Andrew and Wagner, Emma. 2002. *Can Theory Help Translators?* Manchester: St Jerome Publishing.

Dennett, Daniel C. 1995. *Darwin's Dangerous Idea*. London: Penguin.

Fairclough, Norman. 1992. *Discourse and Social Change*. Cambridge: Polity Press.

Fraser, Janet. 1996. "Mapping the Process of Translation". *Meta* XLI (1): 84–96.

Giddens, Anthony. 1997. *Sociology*. Cambridge: Polity Press.

Heilbron, Johan and Sapiro, Gisèle (eds). 2002. *Actes de la recherche en sciences sociales* 144. "Les échanges littéraires internationaux".

Hermans, Theo. 1999. *Translation in Systems. Descriptive and System-oriented Approaches Explained*. Manchester: St Jerome Publishing.

Holmes, James S. 1987. "The name and nature of translation studies". In *Translation Across Cultures*, G. Toury (ed). New Delhi: Bahri Publications. 9–24. Also published as: Holmes 1988: 67–80.

Holmes, James S. 1988. *Translated! Papers on Literary Translation and Translation Studies*. Amsterdam and Atlanta: Rodopi.

Inghilleri, Moira. 2005. "Mediating Zones of Uncertainty. Interpreter Agency, the Interpreting Habitus and Political Asylum Adjudication". *The Translator* 11 (1), 69–85.

Jääskeläinen, Riitta. 2002. "Think-aloud Protocol Studies into Translation: An annotated bibliography". *Target* 14 (1): 107–136.

Kurz, Ingrid, Basel, Elvira, Chiba, Doris, Patels, Werner and Wolfframm, Judith. 1996. "Scribe or Actor? A Survey Paper on Personality Profiles of Translators and Interpreters". *The Interpreters' Newsletter* 7: 3–18.

Lefevere, André. 1992. *Translation, Rewriting, and the Manipulation of Literary Fame*. London and New York: Routledge.

Mauranen, Anna and Kujamäki, Pekka (eds). 2004. *Translation Universals: Do They Exist?* Amsterdam and Philadelphia: John Benjamins.

Mossop, Brian. 2000. "The Workplace Procedures of Professional Translators". In *Translation in Context. Selected contributions from the EST Congress, Granada 1998*, A. Chesterman, N.Gallardo San Salvador and Y. Gambier (eds). Amsterdam and Philadelphia: John Benjamins. 39–48.

Mossop, Brian. 2001. *Revising and Editing for Translators*. Manchester: St Jerome Publishing.

Norberg, Ulf. 2003. *Übersetzen mit doppeltem Skopos*. Uppsala: Uppsala Universitet.

Pym, Anthony. 1998. *Method in Translation History*. Manchester: St Jerome Publishing.

Pym, Anthony. 1999. "Translation Studies Beyond 2000". In *Translation and the (Re)Location of Meaning. Selected Papers of the CETRA Research Seminars in Translation Studies 1994–1996*, J. Vandaele (ed). Leuven: CETRA. 443–449.

Sager, Juan. 1993. *Language Engineering and Translation*. Amsterdam and Philadelphia: John Benjamins.

Segerstråle, Ullica. 2000. *Defenders of the Truth. The battle for science in the sociobiology debate and beyond*. Oxford: Oxford University Press.

Séguinot, Candace. 1989. "The Translation Process: an Experimental Study". In *The Translation Process*, C. Séguinot (ed). School of Translation, York University: H.G. Publications. 21–53.

Simeoni, Daniel. 1998. "The Pivotal Status of the Translator's Habitus". *Target* 10 (1): 1–39.

Tirkkonen-Condit, Sonja and Jääskeläinen, Riitta (eds). 2002. *Across Languages and Cultures* 3 (1). Special Issue "Translation and Cognition".

Toury, Gideon. 1995. *Descriptive Translation Studies and beyond*. Amsterdam and Philadelphia: John Benjamins.

Tymoczko, Maria. 2002. "Connecting the Two Infinite Orders. Research Methods in Translation Studies". In *Crosscultural Transgressions. Research Models in Translation Studies II. Historical and Ideological Issues*, T. Hermans (ed). Manchester: St Jerome Publishing. 9–25.

von Wright, Georg Henrik. 2004/1971. *Explanation and Understanding*. Ithaka and London: Cornell University Press.

Williams, Scott G. 2005. "Rewriting Rome in post-1945 German-language Literature". *Across Languages and Cultures* 6 (1): 79–93.

Wilson, Edward Osborne. 1998. *Consilience. The Unity of Knowledge*. London: Little, Brown and Company.

Wolf, Michaela. 2002. "Translation Activity between Culture, Society and the Individual: Towards a Sociology of Translation". In *CTIS Occasional Papers* 2, K. Harvey (ed). Manchester: UMIST. 33–43.

PART IV

Constructing a sociology of translation studies

Overview and perspectives

Between sociology and history*

Method in context and in practice

Daniel Simeoni
York University, Canada

The recent emergence of a sociological outlook in translation studies seems to have been the result of a convergence of factors. It developed both in translation studies proper, in the wake of the DTS model of inquiry and also, in sociological circles, on account of a new interest for the space occupied by translations in the literary field. At the same time, this configuration of interests has taken place without much attention being paid to the uneasy relationships between sociologists and historians since the end of the nineteenth century. The first part of this paper is an attempt to locate the interdisciplinary space where a socio-translation studies could establish itself. The second section outlines a historical case study in which sociological concepts contribute a particular interpretation of a typically subaltern figure in the history of translations in Europe: the first complete play by Shakespeare translated in Italian, *Giulio Cesare* (1756), by Domenico Valentini. Together, the two sections will allow some insights about the issue of method in socio-historical case studies.

Between sociology and history I: A comparative background for a socio-translation studies in the making

The cultural turn in translation studies fostered fruitful exchanges with transdisciplinary cultural studies. It has also brought back to the fore two disciplines of the traditional human and social sciences – history and, more recently, sociology. This return to disciplinary thinking in translation studies is far from easy to grasp. The rapprochement with academic sociology, for example, may be less

* This paper marks a stage in a research that was made possible by the Social Sciences and Humanities Research Council of Canada (grant #410-2003-1112). I wish here to renew my thanks to the Federal Adjucating Committee that saw the interest of this research not only for the case study at hand, but for reflecting on a field of translation studies whose borders tend increasingly to overlap with those of other disciplines.

apparent in English-speaking countries and in other places around the world than in continental Europe. It is in a European context after all that novel approaches to translation were able to develop in the late 1990s in ways that made it amenable to the sociological discipline. Furthermore, where signs of interest for sociological theory have turned up in translation studies in places other than Europe, it was often at the instigation of scholars originally trained and active in, or with strong personal connections to the European tradition. Finally, the sociological models that have inspired this renewal of interest were derived from European works, in particular, the kind of social thought associated with the works of Pierre Bourdieu and Norbert Elias.

This contextualization provides a key to exploring differences of appreciation and judgment in the increasingly varied scholarly work developing here and there in the international field of translation studies. Among the most apparent divides today is the one between, on the one hand, an aggregate of European practices of scholarship (whatever differences exist internally among them) and, on the other, the vast expanse of work developing elsewhere, impelled by the extraordinary pressures brought about by the spread of the cultural studies movement on North American campuses and, outward from there, wherever world Englishes prevail: Australia, Canada, India, South Africa, Hong Kong etc. and, in part, England. In this particular geopolitical context, virtually all disciplines – history, anthropology, political science, geography etc., as well as the academic study of translation – have incorporated elements of the cultural studies movement. Mapping that circulation of ideas and the resulting practices in terms of the methods being used is not easy, but it is an indispensable step on the long and winding road of conceptualizing translation as an original object of study. For one thing, the institutional map does not coincide with the more complex positions of scholars active in those institutions. Secondly, it is always questionable to rationalize differences among scholarly ways of thinking in terms of aggregates, whether in terms of national or in larger, regional blocks. The risk is great also to see a return to essentialism in such homogenized groupings. But this is no reason why a comparative analysis should not be attempted along those lines, in order to make sense of the different approaches to method in our field. Ideally, we would obtain a kind of *Homo academicus* of translation studies, applicable beyond national fields. The map need not be fixed. Indeed, it constantly evolves.

Meanwhile, to understand the logic behind those intellectual linkages and ruptures, I have found it useful to think in terms of "scholarly localisms". Consistently, the history of disciplines in the English-speaking world has differed from that of their continental European counterparts. With the English language now achieving status of *lingua franca*, we might think that a convergence of sorts is taking place. Instead, we can observe distinct, still largely regional traditions hiding behind the dominant, ubiquitous use of English.

There is an abundance of signs that such scholarly localism exists in the international field of scholarship, particularly in the humanities and social sciences. Localisms may have flexible borders – "provincialism" is a relative notion – but their power of attraction is undisputable. How could it be otherwise? The opposite would mean that, by some miraculous stroke of luck, scholars are immune to the determinations that bear on what might be called the subjects of their investigations and which they profess to unveil. Translation studies is no exception. For example: the massive contribution of a particular group of Tel Aviv scholars to the field is likely to be less spontaneously recognized outside the continental European tradition (see e.g. Trivedi 2005). No doubt the genealogy of polysystemics played a role in provoking those differing appreciations. I am thinking of the still largely undiscussed assumptions among that group of Israeli scholars regarding the positive part played by nation states in the institution of translation, or the fact that the genealogy in question can be traced to a small number of European scholars outside translation studies, at a time when the establishment and achievements of modern nation states were looked upon in a generally favourable light. Such imaginary constructions as nineteenth-century nation states were being seriously questioned when translation studies developed – simultaneously with the new cultural history, cultural studies, women's studies, as well as a considerably revamped anthropology. But the ways in which those "new" areas of study crystallized out of the cradle of former disciplines were clearly marked by the personal and regional histories of the individual scholars who, in so doing, gave impetus to the global paradigmatic change taking place in the human sciences. Many among that group viewed themselves at the time as children of the Enlightenment.

In this context, to envisage the contribution that sociology can make to the field of translation studies is an open invitation to a discussion of method. "Method" is understood here as a body of scholarly practices, inherited – consciously or not – from the traditional disciplines. Both the historical method and the sociological method emerged in the nineteenth-century in relation to one another, antagonistically. Or rather, the sociological method developed out of, against certain practices of inquiry that had been the preserve of the historian. Not only that, but for eighty-odd years, a dispute prevailed between the representatives of each discipline as to which was more "scientific" in its approach of social phenomena.

The nineteenth-century historians who inherited the practices of inquiry of philologists and antiquarians of earlier times were first to impose their discipline as a model of truth-oriented research in what would later become known as social science. Primary documents, not secondary sources, provided the test case to distinguish between historians and other commentators of past events. The method consisted explicitly of four operations: analysis, categorization, definition and drawing relations between those definitions. It was designed to keep its practitioners away from "abstractions and metaphysical considerations". Of course, the historian's task so defined ignored the unconscious of its own practices, i.e. that it was guided, more often than not, by national, even nationalist concerns. But over all, such principles for doing sound research remained stable – and unchallenged – across the continent for over a century.

This characterization is fairly accurate for what happened until the emergence on the map of sociological inquiry, just before the turn of the twentieth century. That emergence was not sudden. The term itself – "sociology" – had existed for several decades, since the founder of positivism, Auguste Comte, projected the new science as the towering block on the edifice of scientific inquiry in 1848. In France, the 100-year period extending from Comte to Braudel (from the mid-nineteenth to the mid-twentieth century) can be read as an on-going, recurrent conflict between historians and sociologists around the issue of which discipline should be viewed as the dominant one on the social-science pyramid. In terms of method, new expectations were raised, to the effect that the student of past events could no longer be satisfied with simply recording the truth of events in primary sources. In a period of exacerbated nationalisms, the task became even more urgent for those who studied society in the present. Rules, or laws, became the ultimate goal pursued by the expert, beyond the mere description of facts. Even if the order was constantly pushed back until further proof was obtained, the objective remained the disclosure of the ways in which the national society under scrutiny worked. Operating principles and schemata, unearthed from the magma of current events, were devised to introduce, *ceteris paribus*, a degree of predictive value. Or so the theoretical discourse went, similar in spirit to the project known to us today as Descriptive Translation Studies when it began to materialize in the early 1970s.

The issue goes well beyond the case of translation studies. Can a new field of studies appear on the map of legitimate research (even more so on the "disciplinary" map) all equipped, not only with its methods but with its agreed conventions of doing science? The history of disciplines can be illuminating. It is common knowledge that the discipline of sociology was born out of the primacy of that of modern history but also, beyond that, of the earlier development of political theory, moral philosophy and economics (or social mathematics), not to mention the political and cultural climate of the times.[1] Similarly, what were the disciplin-

---

1. See e.g. for the case of French and European sociologies Heilbron (1990), Mucchielli (1998).

ary models and methods out of which translation studies started developing a scientific approach to its object? I would suggest that there is not one such body of antecedent scholarly practices to translation studies but several – linguistics, semiotics, philosophy, anthropology, sociology, history to name but the most obvious – which in itself may not be very different from the case of other social sciences before it, except that, unlike other specializations officially recognized today in the various institutional bodies regulating academic life, the aggregate formed by those previous disciplinary formations has not resulted in a coherent, semi-autonomous body of knowledge specific to the study of translation. It does not mean that it will not happen, but it has not succeeded yet.

Therefore, it is of some importance to try and understand why, thirty years or so after the introduction of the label "translation studies" and despite the establishment of not only professional but scholarly organizations, regional and worldwide, and a fair number of proposals intended to put some order in the diversity of research practices attested in the field (most prominently the excellent Williams and Chesterman 2002), there remains no commonly accepted method comparable to the "historical method" or the sociologist's method or *métier*, or principles of understanding of the kind developed by linguists who moulded their definition of "language" into a category that had nothing to do with the commonsense use of the word. It is against this constructed background that it may be useful, at this point in the evolution of our own area of knowledge development, to reflect on earlier examples of disciplinary formations, both to learn from their past difficulties and to become more aware of our own specificity. I have already written on those issues (Simeoni 2004) regarding the relations between (i) the way the "language of translation" has tended to be understood by practising translators and by theoreticians of that language, and (ii) the basis upon which the science of linguistics developed at the end of the nineteenth century. In the first section of this paper, I reflect in a similar way on the cases of sociology and its former competing model, history, and their mutual maturing in relation to each other. It may be from such a combination of former practices that translation studies may find a solid substrate for its future development. The focus of this section therefore, is not strictly on current attempts by Translation scholars to develop a sociological approach to facts of translation that could be amenable to translation studies as it has evolved but, more indirectly, to offer some thoughts on the history of two disciplines with longer standing which, sometimes, seem to appropriate the object of translation studies without paying much attention to the body of knowledge developed on the subject by TS scholars. The intent, therefore, is to contribute a preliminary reflection on the place of translation studies in the human sciences. For this reason, the argument developed in these pages is, inevitably, more conceptual than documentary. Which explains the limited number of references to translation scholarship proper or to the considerable work accomplished by many in this area. In no way should this be interpreted as a criticism of those contributions.

Today, perhaps on account of the fact that both history and sociology have had to face opposition from external sources, their methodological discourses have changed. The more classic polarities, as in (i) sociology being concerned with the present *versus* history dealing with the past, or (ii) sociology, a "nomothetic" science in search of behavioural laws, *versus* history's concern with the "idiographic" based on a principle of unrepeatability of events, or again, (iii) sociological data being more prone to statistical, quantitative treatment than historical facts drawn from primary data discoverable in archives etc., those systematic oppositions have become less clear-cut, giving way to less conflictual relationships.

What led to this relative peace? Firstly, while it is true that the internationalization of disciplines began long before the 1970s, it has taken gigantic proportions since then. There seems to be significant cultural variation between e.g. British, Italian, Indian or Latin American historians and sociologists in terms both of their research objects and methods. This is still a largely unexplored terrain in the social sciences in general but echoes of distinct preferences can be observed at international meetings of the professions. The variation is even more striking in written publications where norms of scholarship sometimes defy comparison (see e.g. Boutier 2001 for an illuminating description of what keeps distinguishing scholarly articles in France and in Italy, even within the confines of the historical discipline and, consequently, between cognate cultures and languages of exposition).

Secondly, the expansion of the Cultural studies program in the Anglo-American sphere of influence and of the "new" cultural history in Europe have undermined the monopoly exercised by historians and sociologists on issues of history and society. "New cultural history" is a term that may require some clarifying. As I use it, the phrase refers to a widespread practice of scholarship in Europe for nearly a quarter of a century (e.g. Burke 2004). Importantly, it is not to be confused with the so-called *New Cultural History* movement developed in North America (e.g. Bonnell and Hunt 1999). There are many overlaps between the new cultural historians of Europe and some cultural studies figures in North America but if one wanted to distinguish between the two practices of research by focusing on a single criterion of differentiation, it would probably be the following: Cultural studies practitioners tend to be more directly motivated politically than their European counterparts in the way they construct their objects of research, while new cultural historians seem to be primarily motivated by a desire to explore and promote the symbolic values of sociocultural objects and events without necessarily situating the latter in an overt political agenda and, most evidently, without marking their difference vis-à-vis their predecessors in the tradition as aggressively. This is not to suggest that new cultural historians are less politically committed in their personal interventions on current affairs. For prototypical examples of the two practices compare e.g. the works of Edward Said (1994) versus those of Carlo Ginzburg (see e.g. Ginzburg 1991).

Thirdly, the anthropological turn of the 1970s, with its interests in the study of cultural artefacts viewed as historically situated "texts", further sapped the primacy of the two disciplines, introducing new ways of understanding values in society and, crucially, relativizing the principle of literalness in the treatment of primary sources. This is yet another dimension differentiating Cultural studies and the new cultural history which would justify further work on the basis of the scholarly localism hypothesis. Most historians today have integrated in their approach or method of investigating past events the idea that access to "truth" is inevitably mediated by the time when history is actually being written. But there is a limit to the notion that every representational discourse, fictional or scientific, is constructed, beyond which new cultural historians will not go.

Fourthly, with the national – even nationalist – background of both disciplines losing much of its appeal after World War II, European historians and sociologists have been looking more and more fervently beyond the borders of Europe for their inspiration. This may be a reason why differences between European scholarship in cultural history and Anglo-American postcolonial studies are easily overlooked: The diversity of approaches tends to be minimized as readers and publishers prefer to focus on the similarity of titles. European social scientists have been looking beyond their *national* borders too, more systematically than in the past – the construction of a new European space, with a European community of scholars called on to complement the economic cooperation of member states, has provided the impetus for this border-crossing. The map has changed so remarkably in this respect that it is not rare for today's historians and sociologists to make use of the same concepts, so much so that an orthodox use of those itinerant, cross-disciplinary concepts no longer makes much sense Notions like those of "anomia", "status", "*habitus*", "field", etc., popularized by e.g. Durkheim, Weber, Elias or Bourdieu are examples of such migratory concepts, which it is not unusual to see used today by cultural, and even social historians. They have become common property and as such, can be adapted to any particular use the "outsider" will have for them. One does not have to follow Wallerstein on every score in his generalized criticism of the compartmentalization of disciplines (Wallerstein 2004) to observe that, with so many disciplinary initiatives overlapping, there is a sense that we may soon be heading towards a new global historical social science where the more sociologically-oriented translation studies may want to find its place, with implications as regards the exact nature of method in their ranks. The trend towards that new global social science is probably more advanced outside

Europe but certainly in the restricted triad of the classic social sciences – history, sociology, anthropology – the same evolution can be seen taking place in the academic institutions of Europe.

And yet, despite this generalized centripetal movement of globalization in the humanities and social sciences, something of the original divide between historians and sociologists seems to linger on. The distinction is most perceptible in those rare personal exchanges where representatives of the two sides congenial enough to each other's doubts and preferences have made their thoughts public (e.g. Bourdieu and Chartier 1989). When speaking of what is done and expected in the discipline of which s/he is part, the sociologist often gives an impression that he has answers – and if not, specific hypotheses which require testing. His blueprint is largely laid out even before he embarks on his quest. That is because he has a "theory" to guide him. While the historian, beyond the case on which s/he has been working, is more hesitant to reach beyond... questions. "Hypotheses" in the *métier d'historien* still present themselves as intuitions, limited to the case at hand. Could it be a matter of posture, or stance vis-à-vis the object? If so, the resulting features would be difficult not to trace to the history of the disciplines. Positionings toward what constitutes "proper" method are not rare either in the field of translation studies. It might be useful for us then to reflect on the precedents of the other disciplines – from the *Methodenstreit* in the human sciences at the end of the nineteenth-century to its multiple reincarnations in the twentieth century, either between particular disciplines or even within a single academic area. Two forms of *scholarly habitus* then, would seem to cohabit in the perspective of a much-needed discussion of "method in translation studies" based on the precedents of European social science: the personal (inevitably cultural) and the disciplinary.

Between sociology and history II: A minor case of "ab-normative" heresy in eighteenth century Italy – Valentini's *Giulio Cesare*

Where does the foregoing section leave us if we switch now to the practical issue of empirical work in cultural translation studies? In the second part of this paper, I briefly describe a case that I have been constructing and doing field research on, hoping to show that no empirical work can develop without theoretical underpinnings – a fairly obvious statement by now – but also, in my opinion, that sociohistorical empirical work can accomodate epistemological reflections involving considerations on the history of disciplines. In other words, cases are interesting not only for what they bring to the mill of existing theories. They are most suggestive when they raise questions beyond proven findings, not necessarily to criticize or disqualify previous work and substitute new models to former theories, but to open up alternative interpretations equally plausible *simultaneously*. In translation studies more than in any discipline, past or new, it is essential, in my opinion, to develop the prospect of a method pliable to multiple angles of interpretation. Specifically, those interpretations ought not to be seen in "either/or" exclusionary terms but in the context of mutually compatible frames of understanding where difference is the result of distinct historical traditions.

The case I will be briefly addressing here had rarely been studied when I set out to work on it: Graf (1911), Collison-Morley (1916), Crinò (1932), Rosa (1964), Petrone Fresco (1993) together make up 35 pages of evaluative criticism. A little-known figure of the Senese cultural scene, Domenico Valentini (1688?-1762) was the author of the first complete translation of Shakespeare's *Julius Caesar* in Italian. His translation was also the first complete one of the Shakespearian corpus in Italy and the second one in Europe after von Borck (1704–1747), the Prussian ambassador to Britain, initiated the long journey of European Shakespeares in London in 1741 (see Bertana 1901:73). Valentini's version was published in Lucca on the printing presses of Agostino Bindi in 1756 (Valentini 1756). He was already an aged man, with little to show to his credit – a mere collection of short essays and discourses in Latin and Italian and of translations from authors of the pre-Enlightenment period.

All things considered, the case seems as a-typical as can be, resisting conceptual treatment along the lines of any "theoretical" approach to translation and, for that reason, challenging generalization. The author had had substantial experience in circulating foreign works in Italian, all of them from the English language.[2] This was "Übersetzung aus zweiter Hand" in von Stackelberg's words (1984), i.e. through the mediation of existing French translations, following or-

---

2. See the second part of his collected works printed two years before his *Giulio Cesare* (Valentini 1754). Twelve copies of this rare volume were printed (see Pecci *Scrittori senesi*. ms. at the Biblioteca Comunale di Siena). Two only survive, one in Lucca at the Biblioteca Statale nel Convento Santa Maria Nera, the other at the Österreichische Nationalbibliothek, Vienna. I am grateful to Professor Mario Rosa for providing me with this precious information shortly after my personal copy of the *Raccolta* was destroyed. The intermediary translations included in the volume were from Simon Ockley's *Vita di Maometto*, based on a French translation (1748) of *The History of the Saracens* (1708–1718); a series of *Caratteri* from Temple Stanyan's *Grecian History* (1739), translated by Diderot in 1742; several chapters from the *Spectator* of Steele et Addison again translated out of their French version, *Le spectateur ou le Socrate moderne*; and an extract of Samuel Shuckford's *The Sacred and Profane History of the World Connected from the Creation of the World to the Dissolution of the Assyrian Empire at the Death of Sardanapalus, and to the Declension of the Kingdoms of Judah and Israel under the Reigns of Ahaz and Pekah* (1727), translated into French in 1752.

dinary practice in Europe in the eighteenth century.[3] Valentini's decision to do a *Giulio Cesare* was a far less banal initiative. He did not know a word of English and no previous translation of the work existed in French. In the 60-page preface he appended to the play, he acknowledges that he was helped in this project by a number of (unidentified) visitors from England who – presumably – were on their Grand tour. He presents himself quite candidly as "co-translator" (*contraduttore*). What is remarkable to us in retrospect is that he produced what can be considered today as the closest rendering of a foreign text in translation in his day and age.[4] It is the proximity of the two texts, "source" and "target", which makes that particular translation a practice violating local norms. After all, when Scipione Maffei protested vehemently in 1745 (Maffei 1991/1745) at the way Voltaire had translated his 1714 verse tragedy *Merope* in 1744 under the title *La Mérope française*, the countermodel he had in mind was not the one applied by Valentini. The *Giulio Cesare* went further; it was a truly modern transposition, more in line with the kind of discourse on translation that German theologians were to propose at the newly-founded University of Berlin toward the end of the Napoleonic wars (see e.g. Schleiermacher 1973/1813). But that was fifty years later. Also, it is doubtful that Valentini, passionate as he was, could have had the kind of nationalist agenda that his successors had (even if the cover page of his Lucchese translation specified that the translation was turned "*in Lingua Toscana*"). On the one hand, the non-recognition of Valentini in his own times and his invisibility in the history of translations confirm the target-oriented paradigm. Violating the norms is always an option. But the price for that is heavy. End of story. Or is it? What if we started looking at his case in a less definitive manner, from the perspective of the conflict of disciplines?

The *Giulio Cesare* appears to be a case for historians all through – the times, the context, the lack of representativeness of Valentini's version make it an exception, likely to attract historians of the *Settecento*, perhaps, for what it reveals of the tensions and uncertainties of the political culture in the *Granducato* under the

---

3. See also Toury (1995), Chapter 7, for cases of translation from English into Hebrew mediated by German.

4. Shakespeare's fame was just beginning to bloom in Europe after Pope's and Theobald's reconsiderations of his work in England. When Valentini translated *Julius Caesar* despite his ignorance of the English language, his critics seized upon the opportunity for delegitimizing his work. Yet it was not the first time that playwrights had been translated by Italian authors who did not know the source language. However, in all such cases, the end-result was a rewriting of the original product in keeping with eighteenth-century norms. In Valentini's, it was the proximity of the two versions which was the scandal. Interestingly, that proximity was hardly noted at the time – it was the quality of Shakespeare's text which was stigmatized, which entailed the complete disqualification of the translation and of its author.

Reggenza lorenese,[5] but certainly not to serve as an illustration of a general trend for newer translation norms to crystallize, eventually. Such an extrapolation can be performed of course, but in this case, anachronism would show through, as in the first works by cultural historians of the Italian pre-Enlightenment, aiming to demonstrate the continuity between that movement and the later *Risorgimento* (see e.g. Venturi 1969). That latter kind of approach can be useful in the early stages of reconsidering a period long neglected by the specialists of a discipline, but it cannot last. To go back to the discussion of traditional differences between historians and sociologists, Valentini's life history leaves us with lots of questions; few responses can be generated by hypotheses based on former casework.

However, the recent rapprochement of disciplines under external pressures from the new cultural history and also, perhaps, from non-European cultural studies elsewhere, suggests that the same case could also be studied in a sociological perspective. Based on the rare, disparate elements recoverable from the archives, Valentini's *habitus* can be reconstructed from his life history. Valentini was a typical *miraculé* – Bourdieu's catch-word for those who have managed to extract and disentangle themselves from the social determinations that, logically, should condemn them to a life of servitude and squalor (this was the eighteenth-century). He spent his early childhood in utter poverty, was brought to the city of Siena on his merits by a nobleman (a Borghese, no less) who recognized that the child could make good use of schooling in an elite institution. He ranked first among his peers at the close of his studies, graduating with a prestigious scholarship (*sussidio Mancini*), then was confirmed as a brilliant subject by the prominent figures of the local cultural scene, most notably Uberto Benvoglienti. He obtained his doctorate in theology at the age of 24, was ordained priest and nominated professor of Law and Theology at the renowned seminar of Alessandro Zondadori in 1719.[6] In 1732, he was elected President of the *Accademia Fisiocritica* for a two-year mandate (see *Accademia Fisiocritica* [2005]). Prior to that, he had been elected to the position of Custodian of the Meridian line at the same institution. In the mid-1730s, he is known to have been in Florence, serving as private instructor to the Prince of Craon, son of the then plenipotentary representative of the Emperor

---

5.   On this larger cultural context, see Mario Rosa's early treatment of the text of *Giulio Cesare* (Rosa 1964: 13–20), in which he identifies traces of a direct relationship of influence between the rare explicitations performed by Valentini on the source text, including a systematic darkening of the figure of Caesar, and the harsh government of the Duchy by the Comte de Richecourt following the departure for Vienna of the plenipotentiary Prince de Beauvau Craon.

6.   See his obituary by Lami (1763).

for Tuscany. His career culminated in 1741 with his election to the coveted title of Chair of ecclesiastical history at the University of Siena.[7]

By all standards, this was a truly outstanding itinerary. How could a child born in utter poverty at the end of the seventeenth century on the confines of the State of Siena, in a small isolated village located twenty leagues or so south of the town, raise himself to such a rank? In addition, Siena at the time was undergoing the most severe demographic and economic depression. The fact that Valentini's early, secondary socialization did not succeed in erasing the traces of his primary family environment raises interesting questions about the exact nature of his *habitus* and, by implication, that of the cultural elite in Tuscany. He would *never* be accepted by his peers in the cultural field, let alone by the Florentine republic of letters who considered him a *parvenu* at best, not to say a fraud.[8] His translation of Shakespeare would not simply be ignored by the most renowned players on the cultural scene, it was downright stigmatized for its being faithful to an unacceptable author.[9] For us, 250 years later, the innovations Valentini brought to the practice in translating the *Julius Caesar*, without being entirely exceptional if measured against the known range of possibilities, anticipated a behaviour that would achieve norm-status half a century later. We are left with the mystery of what might have motivated him. Anything beyond that, making him a precursor of later practices for example, would be mere rhetorical sleight-of-hand, pertinent perhaps to recast the scene two generations later, or to initiate a new inquiry into a little-known period, or for theoretical purposes, those natural providers of essentialization by simplification, but not to clarify the case in its specific context.

I have assumed that Valentini's case presented an impossible challenge for traditional sociology until recently. As long as he keeps being viewed as an exception in his surroundings (which he was), Valentini is a subject for historians. Had he been more representative of his times, he would serve as a classic case for a sociology of translation agents (dis)positioned in their web of relations. But I have also suggested in the previous paragraph that a treatment of his biography in

---

7. This was a prestigious position at the time, albeit in a remote post – prior to that he had even managed to land a position in one of the more prestigious universities, Torino, as Chair of Canonical law, upon recommendation by the most renowned scholar in the peninsula, Ludovico Muratori from Modena. He decided not to accept the nomination, much to the surprise of some of Muratori's correspondents (see Muratori 1978).

8. See Lami (1763, col. 197): "non seppe tanto ben condursi...". Also letter from Pecci to Lami, 11 febbraio 1756 (*Carteggio* Lami/Pecci, Biblioteca Riccardiana [281]).

9. Here again, Lami's judgment in the *Novelle letterarie* set the pace (Lami 1756). See also the Jesuit critic Zaccaria's appraisal of his performance seven years later (Zaccaria 1763, 1:42–43, Biblioteca Universitaria di Bologna).

a sociological perspective could be undertaken, provided we understood him as a *miraculé* of sorts. *Miraculés* of the social order of ordinary suppression, by definition, were never a dominant group at any given time in any social context, even prior to modern societies' accession to nation-state status.

One can safely assume that there were and still are Valentinis among translators, in Italy and elsewhere in Europe. It is interesting to ask: What makes such cases exceptions to rules of behaviour they do not adhere to? Not a deliberate will on their part to violate the rules – here by producing a faithful translation of a little known author, at a time when the *Belles infidèles* still largely prevailed. Nothing in the archives supports this hypothesis of a deliberate engagement.

Valentini produced an a-typical translation just by being himself, an iconoclast by default, i.e. by virtue of being objectively ignorant of the benefits associated with a rightful attitude to norms, social or literary, or of the rules of erudition still flourishing in that region of Europe in the late 1750s. He was "ignorant" in the sense that he ignored them; he was not capable of applying them even though he probably knew them. For he was an avid reader of anything new – journals, gazettes, books – and he was in correspondence with the best critics of the times. He had succeeded in training himself to the highest level of local recognition, but those who counted in Florence, in Pisa and beyond that in Vienna, to a certain extent even in Siena as the Sienese circles became more and more assimilated,[10] snubbed him until his death.[11] He did die a solitary death. Could it be that his "abnormal" or, to coin a new concept, his "ab-normative" behaviour – both in court society, in the smaller circles of power, and in the field of publishing (also, by extension, in his translation preferences) – was a matter of perception? A plain *stigma* deriving from his unacceptable social background? The methodological difficulty in enlarging the scale from his personal life – beyond his individual case – would be a function, not only of the scarceness of similar situations but also, wherever other cases plausibly exist, of the rarity of traces documenting such departures from the norms. It is the treatment of posterity, i.e. by the ensuing scholarly tradition that need be questioned. In Valentini's case, Chair of ecclesiastical history as he was, all his personal papers disappeared. As a result, much of the data has been lost. Or it has remained hidden, preserved haphazardly, mostly in the form of brief allusions to his whereabouts and his often extraordinarily whimsical decisions, in copies of letters by his better-known contemporaries, ad-

10. This is the sense of Pecci's impatience with Valentini – both were natives of Siena but they belonged, by birth, to totally different spheres. As Pecci grew to be the correspondent of the *Novelle letterarie*, he became more and more concerned with his association with Valentini.

11. See his last letter to Lami on Dec. 17, 1762, a few days before his death (*Carteggio*, Biblioteca Riccardiana, ms. 3760, cc. 135–136).

dressed to third parties, copies hardly legible that had been quickly drafted by some famous figure prior to mailing his correspondence, only to keep a trace of his precious messages which, he must have anticipated, would be of interest to future generations.

With the growing interest in the lower classes in the 1960s, historians realized it was no longer possible to write a social history of the times – anywhere and in any location – by focusing on the rich and powerful and their acts of glory. A similar awareness has taken longer to emerge in orthodox sociologies, possibly because the structural grids which those sociologies shared among them, despite differences between and within national traditions, prevented them from seeing beyond, and through, "the view from above". Surveys and large mappings of a given period have tended to be more "democratic" in this regard than studies of direct, personal cases – with few noticeable exceptions such as the so-called *Letters from Jenny* edited by Gordon Allport in 1965.[12] Those precedents of the two most representative social sciences being long alienated from the study of common people should be meditated when looking at the literature focusing on the history and sociology of translation. Portraits of translators are fast becoming a genre in translation studies. Such biographies, when they reach beyond the anecdotal, ought to attract interest to other minor (in the sense of "ab-normative") figures. Further, if sociobiographical approaches were to develop systematically, not as a new "paradigm" for translation studies but in complement to the survey model currently preferred, methodological issues will arise that may complicate the empirical work, but hopefully also facilitate the discussion between those concerned with maintaining the tradition of orthodox sociologies, with a view to generalizing their findings out of well-defined, sample-based studies, and others more inclined to studying isolated cases selected from the start for their (assumed) lack of representativeness.

Method building in the history and sociology of translation

Orthodox sociologies as they developed before the generalized cultural turn of the late 1970s have had some difficulty in adjusting themselves to global societal changes since then. Attempts have been made to scale up the concept of "field", originally devised and constructed on the basis of state-national features, to give it international currency. In many ways, those sociologies remain the dominant

---

12. See e.g. my early attempt at a sociological treatment of this well-known life history of a sub-altern figure. The *Letters from Jenny* up to that time had been analyzed in a different disciplinary framework as a case for psychology (Simeoni 1995).

models for cultural translation studies in Europe, including target-oriented studies of translational practice. What has worked best so far has been, first, the systematic use of large surveys (see e.g. Heilbron and the research undertaken by several members of the *Centre de sociologie européenne*) or, when more specific cases have been dealt with, studies of prominent figures in the local national pantheon, whether the prominence was that of the translator or of the author being translated. The poor, the marginal, those least representative of their countries and of their times, probably make up the majority of cases but it seems fair to say that they have hardly been given justice by the specialists. Valentini is interesting because everything in and around him locates him at the lower end of the scale: his early social origins, his choice of a marginal author (in 1756, Shakespeare was still a minor figure at best in continental Europe) and, obviously, his heretical practices as a translator.

The lesson, here again, comes from cultural history.[13] Translation scholars tell us that choices faced by common translators in history have been either to mimic the dominant model of the day – "stick to the norms" – or fall into oblivion. This is indeed what has happened in most cases wherever "ab-normative" translational behaviour was involved. The protagonists do not receive any form of recognition (even negative). They are ignored. They simply do not exist. But the real issue lies elsewhere. Cases are "never given"; they constitute elaborations against a background of commonly accepted circulating ideas. Therefore it is less a question of what happened in reality than a matter of how cases are constructed. The question is: How much of the ordinary neglect of "ab-normative" behaviour has been a result of a self-fulfilling, pre-judgmental appreciation by the scholarly gaze? Translators as social agents are perceived today anywhere along a continuum of practice marked by varying degrees of agency. Either they are seen as norm-carriers alternating between the (rarely) innovative and the (often) perpetuating or, they are described as failed producers, relegated to the lowest rung on a scale of visibility. This perspective is also true when analysis is performed historically, sometimes hundreds of years after the facts. But it is also a highly selective, partial, massively incomplete description of reality. The scholarly judgment in this case has been an artefact of the way we focus on what we are looking at. The focus is largely a function of those commonly accepted, ceaselessly circulating ideas that characterize the time of the observation. Instead of emphasizing the extent of adhesion to

---

13. For an example of what cultural history "from below" can do, see e.g. Ginzburg's biography (1999) of Domenego Scandella, called Menocchio, the sixteenth-century peasant miller sentenced to death by the Inquisition. A highly readable text turned international best-seller, this biography is also an exemplary case study of the spread of Reformation ideas in the peripheral areas of Europe.

norms by social agents, what prevents us from considering the host of competing options at their disposal as *heretical versions*, worthwhile to study for what they reveal of the society that surrounded them at the time of their accomplishment? Ultimately, this is a question for the field of translation studies itself. Why has the normative paradigm taken root so persuasively, in the way it has taken shape? Why not the concept of deviance, for instance, a common response to social order in general, just as identifiable as normative compliance and, as shown in specialized literature, equally amenable to sociological treatment?

Should this shift of perceptions occur, the study of translations would likely join ranks with the practices developed by the new cultural history – whether its "method" was derived from the precedents of the historical tradition or of sociology, past or present. The research generated would not invalidate existing approaches, survey-based or singular product-/agent-focused. But it would certainly open new territories. The potential for popularizing the subject and making the profession better known and esteemed would be enormous. The impact of norms would also be clarified, although not as carriers of institutional pressures to the advantage of all successful cultural agents and, ultimately, of nations. Norms would begin to be perceived in a less consensual manner. They could be seen as powerful, mostly anonymous forces imposed on agents, shaping their beliefs and, ultimately, the *habitus* of the profession, leaving alternative sources of creation untapped. Those redefined "norms" would convey a delicate proportion of habituation and dis-habituation, a complementary process that not every subject could endorse and incorporate, however skilled or talented s/he were. Options such as those favoured by Valentini could be reevaluated, and revalued, as signs of the ordinary heresy triggered by the violent mismatch between the primary social background of those involved, and the dominant order of the day. That would be a far cry from the *stigma* of social incompetence and fraudulent behaviour laid out on his performance by his contemporaries, a *stigma* unwittingly perpetuated by literary studies and translation scholarship.

References

Accademia Fisiocritica [2005] http://www.accademiafisiocritici.it/pages/mm496.jsp. Visited May 2007.
Allport, Gordon W. 1965. *Letters from Jenny.* New York: Harcourt, Brace & World Inc.
Bertana, Emilio. 1901. "Teatro tragico italiano del secolo XVIII prima dell'Alfieri". *Giornale Storico della letteratura italiana*, supplemento 4. Torino: Ermanno Loescher.
Bonnell, Victoria and Hunt, Lynn. 1999. *Beyond the Cultural Turn: New Directions in the Study of Society and Culture.* Berkeley: University of California Press.

Bourdieu, Pierre and Chartier, Roger. 1989. "Gens à histoire, gens sans histoire". *Politix* (Presses de la Fondation Nationale des Sciences Politiques) 6: 53–60.

Boutier, Jean. 2001. "Les outils des historiens sont-ils universels?" *Correspondances, Bulletin scientifique de l'IRMC.* Also published as: *Le goût de l'enquête. Pour Jean-Claude Passeron,* Fabiani, Jean-Louis (ed). 2001. Paris: L'Harmattan. 81–83.

Burke, Peter. 2004. *What is Cultural History?* Cambridge: Polity Press.

Collison-Morley, Lacy. 1916. *Shakespeare in Italy.* Stratford-on-Avon: Shakespeare Head Press.

Crinò, Anna Maria. 1932. "La prima traduzione italiana di un dramma di Shakespeare". *Rassegna Nazionale* (ottobre). Reprinted in 1950, *Le traduzioni di Shakespeare in Italia nel Settecento,* A.M. Crinò. Roma: Edizioni di storia e letteratura. 41–56.

Ginzburg, Carlo. 1991. *Il giudice e lo storico.* Torino: Einaudi.

Ginzburg, Carlo. 1999. *Il formaggio ei vermi. Il cosmo di un mugnaio del '500.* Einaudi: Torino.

Graf, Arturo. 1911. *L'Anglomania e l'Influsso inglese in Italia nel secolo XVIII.* Torino: Loescher.

Heilbron, Johan. 1990. *Het ontstaan van de sociologie.* Amsterdam: Prometheus (English translation: 1995, *The Rise of Social Theory.* Trans. Sheila Gogol. Minneapolis: University of Minnesota Press).

Lami, Giovanni. 1756. *Novelle Letterarie pvbblicate in Firenze L'anno MDCCLVI.* Tomo XVII. Firenze: Stamperia della SS. Annunziata.

Lami, Giovanni. 1763. *Novelle Letterarie pvbblicate in Firenze L'anno MDCCLXIII.* Tomo XXIV. Firenze: Stamperia di Gaetano Albizzini.

Maffei, Scipione. 1991/1745. "Risposta alla lettera del Signor di Voltaire". In *The Complete Works of Voltaire. Vol. 17.* Oxford: The Voltaire Foundation Taylor Institution. 355–387.

Mucchielli, Laurent. 1998. *La découverte du social. Naissance de la sociologie en France.* Paris: La Découverte.

Muratori, Ludovico. 1978. *Edizione Nazionale del Carteggio di L.A. Muratori. Centro di Studi Muratoriani, Modena, vol. 44,* Carteggi con Ubaldini Vannoni, a cura di Michela L. Nichetti Spanio, Leo S. Olschki, Firenze.

Petrone Fresco, Gaby. 1993. "An Unpublished Pre-Romantic 'Hamlet' in Eighteenth-Century Italy". In *European Shakespeares. Translating Shakespeare in the Romantic Age,* D. Delabatista and L. D'hulst (eds). Amsterdam and Philadelphia: John Benjamins. 111–128.

Rosa, Mario. 1964. *Despotismo e libertà nel Settecento. Interpretazioni "repubblicane" di Machiavelli.* Bari: Laterza.

Said, Edward. 1994. *Culture and Imperialism.* New York: Vintage Books.

Schleiermacher, Friedrich. ²1973/1813. "Über die verschiedenen Methoden des Übersetzens". In *Das Problem des Übersetzens,* H.J. Störig (ed). Darmstadt: Wissenschaftliche Buchgesellschaft. 38–70.

Simeoni, Daniel. 1995. "The Stylistics of Life Histories: Taking Jenny at Her Word(s)". *Current Sociology* 43 (2/3): 27–39.

Simeoni, Daniel. 2004. "La langue de traduction". *La linguistique* 40 (1): 67–82.

Stackelberg, Jürgen von. 1984. *Übersetzungen aus zweiter Hand.* Berlin and New York: Walter de Gruyter.

Toury, Gideon. 1995. *Descriptive Translation Studies and beyond.* Amsterdam and Philadelphia: John Benjamins.

Trivedi, Harish. 2005. "Translating Culture versus Cultural Translation". In *In Translation. Reflections, Refractions, Transformations,* P. St-Pierre and P.C. Kar (eds). Delhi: Pencraft International. 251–260. Also published as: Trivedi, Harish. 2007. "Translating Culture versus Cultural Translation". In *In Translation. Reflections, Refractions, Transformations*, P. St-Pierre and P.C. Kar (eds). Amsterdam and Philadelphia: John Benjamins. 277–287.

Valentini, Domenico. 1754. *Raccoltà di vari componimenti latini ed italiani [...] colla giunta d'alcuni saggi di traduzione sopra diversi soggetti*. Lucca [Benechini] MDCCLI.

Valentini, Domenico. 1756. *Il Giulio Cesare Tragedia istorica di Guglielmo Shakespeare Tradotta dall'Inglese in Lingua Toscana dal Dottor Domenico Valentini Professore di Storia Ecclesiastica nell'Università di Siena*. In Siena l'Anno MDCCLVI. Nella Stamperia di Agostino Bindi.

Venturi, Franco. 1969. *Settecento Riformatore. I. Da Muratori a Beccaria*. Einaudi: Torino.

Wallerstein, Immanuel. 2004. *The Uncertainties of Knowledge*. Philadelphia: Temple University Press.

Williams, Jenny and Chesterman, Andrew. 2002. *The Map. A Beginner's Guide to Doing Research in Translation Studies*. Manchester: St Jerome Publishing.

Zaccaria, Francesco Antonio. 1763. *Annali letterari d'Italia, vol. 1, parte 1*. Modena: A spese di Antonio Zatta.

Y a-t-il place pour une socio-traductologie?

Yves Gambier
University of Turku, Finland

Translation studies has become an (inter)discipline but under which conditions? This paper deals with the necessity for the creation and development of socio-translation studies. Three main elements are presented: the need for the self-analysis of scholars, the need for a historiography of the field, and the need for an analysis of institutions and publications which shape and identify the discipline.

La traductologie qui englobe divers types de recherche et d'efforts en théorisation touchant la traduction (au sens générique ou prototypique du terme c'est-à-dire incluant la traduction, les différents modes d'interprétation, la localisation, la versionisation en audio-visuel, la production documentaire multilingue, etc.) a un long passé comme ensemble de réflexions mais une brève histoire comme "discipline" universitaire et comme "domaine" de connaissance. Elle se développe selon des ressorts, des critères, des motivations encore largement inexplorés. L'exposé qui suit, programmatique, tente de cerner la nécessité et les conditions de la place éventuelle d'une socio-traductologie.

Certaines questions (section 1) m'ont amené à l'élaboration d'un tel concept. Quelles seraient alors les orientations de cet effort de réflexivité (sections 2 et 3)? La problématique soulevée peut être considérée à la fois comme impossible – comment dire de l'intérieur mais avec distance le "domaine" de la traductologie, sans dénoncer, sans insinuer? – et comme nécessaire, pour objectiver l'autorité, la légitimité de cette même traductologie.

Questions de départ

La traductologie a connu bien des tournants depuis une petite vingtaine d'années: culturel, idéologique, post-moderne, sémiotique, cognitif, sociologique, etc. Ces tournants sont-ils des hésitations épistémologiques, des virages opportunistes

pour obtenir une reconnaissance, des essais méthodologiques? Après un bouil-
lonnement intellectuel et éditorial, assiste-t-on à un essoufflement, à une pause,
alors même que les technologies de l'information et de la communication (TIC),
la globalisation avec une nouvelle géographie des marchés de la traduction, les
normes de qualité rendent les pratiques plus visibles, plus compétitives, plus pro-
ductives, plus flexibles? La traductologie voit-elle son objet lui échapper?

A ces questions s'en ajoutent d'autres qui lentement ont été posées ces dern-
iers temps et qui ne lui sont sans doute pas propres. D'autres sciences humaines se
sont interrogées de façon similaire mais l'émergence assez récente de la traductologie les rend plus aigues, sinon plus urgentes, d'autant que le "domaine" n'a pas
partout une reconnaissance assurée, n'est pas forcément un mode de consécration
pour ses agents.

–   La prétention scientifique de la traductologie lui impose-t-elle d'être sans en-
    jeux sociétaux, sociaux? Ou du fait même de traiter des situations de métis-
    sage, d'entre deux, sa neutralité est-elle intenable, une illusion à dépasser?
–   A quelles conditions l'interdisciplinarité s'opère-t-elle? Pourquoi la traducto-
    logie emprunte-t-elle, plus qu'elle n'est elle-même source d'emprunts? (Gam-
    bier 2006).
–   Comment fonctionne la recherche traductologique? N'est-elle le fait, majori-
    tairement, que d'enseignants-chercheurs et qu'incidemment de chercheurs à
    temps plein affiliés à des institutions publiques? En d'autres termes, la tra-
    ductologie est-elle impulsée surtout par des soucis de carrière académique,
    sans autre pertinence évidente (Gambier 2005).
–   Comment décide-t-on d'un thème de conférence, d'article, de thèse? Ce
    n'est un secret pour personne qu'il y a des répétitions de problématique dans
    les travaux publiés, des récurrences thématiques dans les rencontres inter-
    nationales. Ainsi, la traduction littéraire continue d'occuper le devant de la
    scène quand bien même elle ne représente qu'un infime volume des traduc-
    tions réalisées au quotidien, que par exemple il y a eu trois colloques succes-
    sifs sur l'interdisciplinarité entre septembre et mi-novembre 2002, qu'il y a
    nombre d'écrits aujourd'hui qui prennent prétexte de la traduction audiovi-
    suelle, etc.
–   Comment en vient-on à la traductologie? Les motivations ont-elles évolué en-
    tre la génération florissante des années 1980 et celle de maintenant, tandis que
    le cadre institutionnel et les références ont changé? Aux chercheurs hybrides
    dans leurs langues (de travail et d'étude) et leurs cultures (d'éducation et de
    formation) voit-on se succéder des chercheurs d'un autre type? Dans cette
    perspective, l'influence éventuelle de l'*habitus* des chercheurs sur la structure
    et l'évolution de la traductologie devient une question plus que pertinente.

– Le recours à une lingua franca n'est-il pas paradoxal ou même intenable pour un "domaine" qui veut traiter de la communication multilingue et multiculturelle? Il ne s'agit pas de mentionner seulement le "problème", en introduction de colloque ou de numéro spécial – en passant, mais de le traiter en théorie et en pratique. Quelques rares articles rappellent ce paradoxe, sinon cette contradiction (par ex. Snell-Hornby 1997 et 2000; Dollerup 1997; Baumgarten, House and Probst 2004).

Ces quelques questions qui implicitement mettent en corrélation tendances en traductologie et profils de traductologues m'ont amené peu à peu, depuis deux-trois ans, à envisager une socio-traductologie, afin de mieux appréhender comment la traductologie s'est constituée en "domaine" ou champ institutionnalisé de recherche, de critique, d'enseignement. Une "école", un enseignement, un modèle, une théorie, ce sont des mises en perspectives liées nécessairement à des contextes, à des formations antérieures, à des expériences, à des dispositifs de transmission. Le besoin d'une socio-traductologie a aussi mûri avec les réflexions et engagements d'un Pierre Bourdieu, entre autres. Une telle socio-traductologie est présentée ci-dessous selon deux grandes perspectives, d'une part l'historicisation de la traductologie (section 2), d'autre part les institutions et les activités contemporaines du champ (section 3).

Pour une historicisation de la traductologie

Deux orientations principales vont être présentées dans ce qui suit: le besoin d'une auto-analyse des chercheurs et le besoin d'une historiographie du champ.

Réflexivité nécessaire

Depuis *la Reproduction* (1970) et *la Distinction* (1979), une certaine vulgarisation a transformé bien des concepts bourdieusiens en termes-fétiches (champ, *habitus*, capital symbolique, disposition, pouvoir symbolique, légitimité culturelle, etc.). A partir de situations diverses, Bourdieu a tenté d'expliquer comment les hiérarchies entre cultures, goûts, manières d'être opposaient, distinguaient les groupes sociaux; d'autres sociologues, à sa suite, comme Lahire (2004), ont mis en évidence que ces mêmes hiérarchies traversaient aussi les individus dans leurs pratiques quotidiennes et leurs préférences. C'est dire que éducation, culture, littérature, édition, art, photographie, médias, économie (pour ne citer que des champs analysés par Bourdieu et ses collègues), ne sont pas étudiés pour la seule logique de leur fonctionnement interne ni leur simple instrumentalisation au service des dominants; ils sont décrits, détaillés comme lieux et occasions de rapports de force entre agents, transfigurés en rapports de sens. Une telle entreprise a cherché à dépasser les antinomies longtemps établies entre interprétation et explication, structure et histoire, liberté et déterminisme, individu et société, subjectivisme et objectivisme.

L'autre aspect de cette sociologie de Bourdieu, souvent passé sous silence mais éclairant ses postures politiques des années 1990, est la permanente interrogation sur la position paradoxale du sociologue vis-à-vis de ce qu'il observe, commente, fait, écrit. Certains ont douté de la pertinence, de la légitimité scientifiques des efforts de Bourdieu sous prétexte qu'il avait ses revues (*Actes de la Recherche en sciences sociales, Liber* (1989–1998)), sa collection (Liber), son Centre de recherche (*Centre de sociologie européenne*), sa chaire au Collège de France (1982–2001), ses éditions (Raisons d'agir), confondant ainsi critique scientifique et dénigrement, remise en cause des processus de domination et invective. Il n'en reste pas moins que ses constantes réflexions sur ce que peuvent le sociologue et la sociologie – depuis *Le métier de sociologue* (1968) jusqu'à *Esquisse pour une auto-analyse,* en passant par ses ouvrages de 1980, 1981, 1982, 1992, devraient nous aider à penser l'identité et le statut du chercheur qui peut être et informant (traducteur ou sujet-praticien suivant des normes) et chercheur (traductologue ou sujet épistémique), c'est-à-dire juge et partie.

Cette situation paradoxale n'est pas propre à la traductologie, transdiscipline réflexive dont l'épistémologie est coextensive au discours de recherche qu'elle tient: elle rejoint par exemple l'ethnographie (voir parmi les travaux les plus récents, entre autres, Buzelin 2004). Jusqu'où l'expérience pratique dupe-t-elle et change-t-elle l'approche et le dire du théoricien? Jusqu'où ce dernier peut-il, doit-il s'appuyer sur son rôle de traducteur? L'objectivité visée est-elle conciliable avec la loyauté envers son groupe socio-professionnel, avec le savoir pratique incorporé? Il pourrait être toujours tentant pour les traductologues de reproduire la vision idéologique que les traducteurs ont de leur propre pratique (Kalinoswki 2002).[1] Pour ne pas d'une part réduire l'activité du traducteur à des conditions sociales d'apparition et d'exercice et pour ne pas d'autre part occulter son travail de ces mêmes conditions sociales, le traductologue a à se retourner sur sa propre trajectoire, ses choix de chercheur, pour comprendre les sources de ses positions et de ses prises de position (voir p.ex. Gouanvic 1999) – sources qui mêlent état du champ traductologique à un moment donné et origines, formation de l'individu. C'est ce que Bourdieu s'est appliqué à lui-même dans sa leçon d'"auto-socio-ana-

---

1.   Bien évidemment, la question de cette "tentation" est nettement plus complexe. Bourdieu lui-même parlerait dans ce contexte sans doute d'une homologie entre le champ de la traduction et celui de la traductologie.

lyse" lors de son dernier cours au Collège de France (publié en 2001). Une analyse de la sorte est analogue à celle de l'ethno-analyse des Boas, Malinowski, Mead, Leach... ou comment penser contre ses propres conditionnements et habitudes, reconnaître ses sources antérieures, discuter les objections faites, expliciter et mesurer les enjeux de ses discours, etc.

Ni confession, ni autobiographie, un tel effort crée la distance pour appréhender la genèse, l'usage de certains concepts en traductologie, pour mettre à jour les impensés, les "inconscients académiques" dissimulés dans tout ce qui va de soi, touchant par exemple les catégories de perception, les emprunts interdisciplinaires, les méthodes d'enquête, les logiques institutionnelles, les propositions spéculatives, les prétendus modèles explicatifs, le recours non questionné à une lingua franca, etc. Berman (1989) a été sans doute l'un des premiers a posé les jalons pour la saisie à la fois des tâches et des discours de la traductologie. La compréhension de nos opérations, des représentations qu'on se fait de nos pratiques, y compris de nos pratiques discursives, relève d'une socio-traductologie encore à construire, pour rompre à la fois avec un certain idéalisme et avec le relativisme qui restreint les recherches et les chercheurs aux déterminismes socio-historiques. Les travaux sur l'*Homo academicus* (1984) et *la Noblesse d'Etat* (1989) pourraient aider à la mise en place d'une telle socio-traductologie, sinon l'inspirer, puisque la traductologie est aussi (avant tout?) une discipline universitaire, prise dans un espace de positions, de productions, de pouvoirs établis. Cela n'implique pas qu'il faille rester entre universitaires. La recherche orientée vers l'action (Action Research/Recherche action), faisant appel à d'autres agents sociaux en interaction et négociation, peut être aussi une solution de réflexion sur ses réflexions (Gambier 2005). Les projets de socio-biographie (Simeoni 1995), les autoportraits de traducteurs littéraires (Lauber 1996), les récits de vie sous forme d'interview audiovisuelle sont également d'autres moyens de mise à jour des logiques à l'œuvre dans les efforts traductologiques.

Une historiographie de la traductologie encore à élaborer

Bien des dichotomies hantent les réflexions traductologiques, comme par exemple l'opposition entre texte de départ et texte d'arrivée, équivalence et acceptabilité, domestication et étrangéité, traduction libre et traduction littérale, facteur linguistique et facteur culturel, recherche en traduction (processus abstrait des conditions matérielles, culturelles, sociales de travail – par exemple études sur corpus, TAP/ think aloud protocol ou verbalisation concourante) et recherche sur la traduction (produit qui circule, avec des effets escomptés et donnés), approche descriptive (plutôt centrée sur la cible, la réception) et approches dites engagées ("commited approaches", comme celles féministe, post-coloniale. Cf. Brownlie 2003), etc.

Une mise en perspective historique, s'interrogeant sur les situations socio-culturelles des chercheurs, prenant en considération les emprunts conceptuels et méthodologiques à d'autres disciplines (linguistique textuelle, psycholinguistique, sémantique, neurolinguistique, anthropologie, sémiotique, études interculturelles, etc.), permettrait d'appréhender hypothèses, problématiques, notions-clés, modèles ne se répandant pas "comme des gènes", ne se propageant pas par imitation (Chesterman 1997: Ch. 1 et 2), comme si une proposition théorique n'était qu'une réaction à une autre proposition antérieure, selon une logique de dominos. Une telle évolution linéaire, reprise dans des ouvrages comme ceux de Venuti (2000) et de Munday (2001), aussi différents qu'ils soient, laisse perplexe: peut-on à la fois insister sur la contextualisation de toute traduction et théoriser en occultant les conditions hic et nunc qui justifient cette théorisation? (Delabastita 1991). Les modes d'approche et de légitimation du champ sont-ils pareils, de l'Europe à la société chinoise, de l'Amérique du Nord à la communauté indienne, de la fédération russe aux Caraïbes, à l'Afrique? Par ailleurs, la traductologie doit-elle reprendre à son compte la conception d'une histoire qui a dominé longtemps par exemple en littérature – histoire perçue comme continuité chronologique avec filiations, croisements, dettes, etc., à la manière d'une évolution biologique? Quelle est la conception de l'histoire dans une approche systémique de la traduction – linéaire, en reflet, romantique, dialectique, nationale, cyclique? Répondre à cette question, c'est aussi répondre à propos de la place et du rôle du traducteur, par exemple par rapport aux normes: en est-il simple reproducteur, conservateur, transgresseur? (Toury 1995: 255–258). C'est également envisager la place et le rôle du traductologue, dans le devenir de sa "discipline" – avec ses permanences et ses changements, ses catégories et ses représentations, ses a priori et ses innovations, ses paradigmes et ses hésitations, ses critères de preuve et ses lieux de transmission (D'hulst 1990).

La traductologie pour le moment a la mémoire assez courte, ayant marginalisé sa propre histoire, avant même les polémiques qui ont tourné autour de son appellation à la fin des années 1970. Mais à l'auto-socio-analyse des chercheurs doit faire écho désormais l'élaboration d'une archéologie des discours en traductologie, d'une historiographie du champ qui ne soit pas cumulative et fractionnée (Lambert 1993; D'hulst 1995). L'élaboration d'encyclopédies, de "readers", d'anthologies est un signe en ce sens.

D'autres orientations d'une socio-traductologie sont possibles, notamment celle portant sur les institutions et les activités contemporaines du champ.

Instances et productions en traductologie

Le champ de la traductologie, avec ses mécanismes de reconnaissance, d'acceptation, de consensus, d'autorité s'est mis en place, assez récemment. Rappelons qu'un champ scientifique est "un champ social comme un autre avec ses rapports de force et ses monopoles, ses luttes et ses stratégies, ses intérêts et ses profits" (Bourdieu 1976: 89). Il est "le lieu d'une lutte de concurrence qui a pour enjeu spécifique le monopole de l'autorité scientifique" (ibid.), c'est-à-dire le pouvoir d'imposer une certaine définition du domaine, d'en délimiter les problèmes, les méthodes. Une telle notion rompt avec une vision de la "communauté scientifique" où personne ne chercherait à imposer la valeur de ses produits, son autorité de producteur légitime. Dans cette lutte, les agents investissent selon leur capital socio-symbolique (titres universitaires, rang hiérarchique, possibilités d'obtention de fonds de recherche, invitations, consultations, distinctions honorifiques, accès aux moyens d'édition, etc.); les chances de profit orientent les stratégies sociales et intellectuelles de placement, incluant les sujets de recherche, les lieux de publication, les prises de position idéologiques et épistémologiques. Une perspective de la sorte exclut de ne considérer que les énoncés ou idées des intervenants (discours théoriques, arguments méthodologiques, controverses, analyses).

Pour parvenir à circonscrire positions et stratégies, divers entretiens et enquêtes sont à mener, divers corpus sont à rassembler – sur les auteurs et leurs thèmes de prédilection, leurs supports éditoriaux préférés, sur les revues et les structures d'édition en général, sur les institutions d'enseignement et de recherche avec leur répartition géo-linguistique, sur les équipes de recherche avec leur organisme de tutelle, sur les thèses dirigées et soutenues avec leurs directeurs, les membres des jurys, les modes d'évaluation, etc. L'analyse qualitative et quantitative de ces corpus devrait éclairer la cartographie dynamique du champ – avec des courants, des flux, des alliances... auxquels on se rattache ou pas. (cf. travaux sur la recherche en interprétation de conférence par Gile 1995; Tommola 1997). D'évidence, l'agent cartographe est doté d'un certain pouvoir ou autorité pour lancer ces analyses et participe lui-même au jeu.

Pour promouvoir sa relative autonomie comme (inter)discipline, la traductologie a dû se donner des instances. L'expansion de celles-ci doit répondre à quelques questions comme celle de leur distribution (internationale, transnationale, régionale et nationale) et celle de leur spécialisation (par exemple, traduction/localisation). Peut-on parler, et à quelles conditions, de "centres" et de "périphéries" pour ces instances?

Parmi les institutions, on peut citer à titre d'exemples:

- Les *associations*, comme ACT/CATS (Association canadienne de traductologie, 1987), CEATL (Conseil européen des associations de traducteurs littéraires, créé en 1990), EST (European Society for Translation Studies, 1992), ABRAPT (au Brésil, 1992), The Nida Institute au sein de l'American Bible Society (2002), AIETI (Associación Ibérica de Estudios de Traducción e Interpretación, 2003), ATSA (American Translation Studies Association, 2003), IATIS (International Association for Translation and Intercultural Studies, 2004). On peut ajouter certaines associations sœurs comme LISA (Localisation Industry Standards Association), EAMT (European Association in Machine Translation), etc. Comment ces associations définissent-elles leurs relations d'acceptation, de consensus, de cooptation, d'exclusion?
- Les *écoles doctorales* internationales, organisées sur des périodes intensives, comme celles de CERA depuis 1989, à Leuven (devenue CETRA en 1995), en Grande-Bretagne (co-organisée par l'University College London (UCL), Manchester et Edimbourg, depuis 2003), à Sarrebruck depuis 2004, etc., auxquelles on peut joindre la dizaine de formations doctorales permanentes à Tarragona, Paris, Warwick, Dublin, Ottawa, etc.
- Les *centres ou collèges de traducteurs* (littéraires), présents dans la plupart des pays européens, par exemple en Allemagne (à Straelen), Belgique (à Seneffe), Espagne (à Tarazona), France (à Arles), Grèce (à Athènes), Irlande (à Annaghmakerring), Portugal (à Albufeira), etc. Ces collèges favorisent le travail des professionnels et leurs réflexions sur leur activité, en leur offrant résidence et parfois soutien financier pour une période déterminée.
- Les *lieux de formation/d'enseignement* (écoles, instituts, départements) (Caminade 1995, dont l'analyse date maintenant un peu). Il serait intéressant de noter les directions du changement ces dix dernières années au moins, notamment après l'essor des nouvelles technologies, les élargissements de l'Union Européenne en 1995 puis en 2004, la réforme des cursus suite à la Déclaration de Bologne. Ces facteurs d'évolution, acceptée ou subie, ont peut-être modifié le rapport de la traduction et de la traductologie aux disciplines comme les langues étrangères (appliquées), la linguistique. Ils ont peut-être aussi transformé les liens entre formation des traducteurs et développement de la recherche, en particulier avec la division des études en deux cycles distincts. Dans ces lieux, quelles sont les procédures de nomination, de promotion des enseignants, des chercheurs? Y a-t-il des chercheurs à temps plein et à quelles conditions? En tout cas, ces lieux de formation se sont multipliés partout sur la planète, de la Chine à l'Estonie, du Nigéria aux Emirats Arabes Unis.
- Les *rencontres internationales,* plus ou moins régulières ou rituelles (colloques, conférences, congrès, symposiums, séminaires). Sur quels thèmes portent-elles? Quels sont leurs objectifs déclarés? Qui les organise et pour

quelles raisons? Quels sont les effets de rattachement encore fréquent de la traductologie aux départements de langues, de littérature comparée, de linguistique, sur le choix des thèmes, sinon même la rhétorique des appels à communication? Ces rencontres donnent-elles toujours lieu à publication? Quels sont leurs critères de choix pour désigner les orateurs de plénière, les intervenants en sessions? La répartition chronologique et géographique de ces rencontres obéit-elle à une logique? Comment évoluent leur topographie, leur fréquence? Quels sont le sens et l'étendue de leur internationalité?

– Les *organismes de subvention*, au niveau international (par ex. UNESCO), européen, national, universitaire. D'où viennent les fonds? Quelle est la fonction de certaines fondations? Qui reçoit des aides financières pour la recherche et pour quel type de projet? Comment sont financées les publications régulières?

Aux instances, plus ou moins stables, s'ajoute la production d'écrits institutionnalisés et institutionnalisants – les deux ensembles concourant à la dynamique et à la régulation du champ, au moins en le rendant visible (distribution des textes, statistiques des publications, index des citations, etc.).

– Qui écrit? De jeunes chercheurs et doctorants? Des professeurs en titre? Quelle est leur formation initiale? Ont-ils dorénavant reçu une formation en traduction? Quelle est leur posture auctoriale ou comment se mettent-ils en scène, selon l'ethos de la rhétorique? Comment affirment-ils leur crédibilité, leur autorité?

– Quelle est ou quelles sont les langues de rédaction? de publication?

– Quels types d'énoncé se présentent comme efforts de théorisation? (articles, ouvrages, actes de colloque). Le métalangage en traduction pose-t-il problème? Quelle place occupent désormais les réseaux, les listes de discussion, les publications en ligne… dans ces efforts? La technologisation des pratiques bouleverse-t-elle les discours des traductologues?

– Y a-t-il des thématiques dominantes selon certains lieux et pour quels auteurs?

– Quels travaux sont les plus référencés, les plus cités? Peut-on à partir de ces indices et analyses scientométriques définir des tendances, des "écoles", des lignes de force (et de fracture), privilégiant un sous-domaine de la traductologie, une méthodologie, une approche conceptuelle? (cf. Gile 2000; Pöchhacker 1995a, 1995b, sur l'interprétation). Y a-t-il des réseaux de diffusion interne?

– Qui sont les referees ou évaluateurs et consultants, les membres des comités de rédaction, de lecture? Comment se formulent leurs évaluations, leurs dé-

cisions? Quels sont leurs critères de sélection, de révision? Reçoivent-ils des directives et de qui?
- Qui rédige des comptes rendus d'ouvrage?
- Comment circulent les théories? Peut-on déduire des flux de dissémination, des influences? Qu'est-ce qu'on traduit de ces théories et dans quelles langues?

D'évidence, les modes de traitement, de circulation, de réception des écrits ne répondent pas uniquement à des conditions marchandes et techniques. La scientificité de ces textes doit aussi être établie, selon des exigences précisées à la fois par des pairs et par des agents extérieurs (maisons d'édition, pouvoirs publics).

Sont à considérer parmi les écrits dont les origines et les initiateurs seraient à décrire:

- Les *revues,* nombreuses à avoir été lancées dans les années 1990, loin derrière leur ancêtre *Meta* (1955): *TTR* 1988, *Target* 1989, *Perspectives: Studies in Translatology* 1993, *Terminology* 1994, *The Translator* 1995, *Interpreting* 1996, *Across Languages and Cultures* 2003, etc. Quelle est la durée moyenne d'existence de ces périodiques? Quelle est l'étendue de leur diffusion (nombre d'abonnements, de lecteurs)? Ont-ils une politique rédactionnelle explicite? Quelles sont leurs visées et ambitions affichées? Quelle est la composition de leurs comités?
- Les *collections,* comme celles des éditions John Benjamins, Routledge, Multilingual Matters, etc. Quelles sont la fréquence et la régularité de leurs publications? Comment évoluent leurs comités éditoriaux?
- Les *anthologies* et les *manuels d'introduction* qui se sont multipliés également dans les années 1990, entre *Reading in Translation Theory* (édité par Chesterman en 1989) et Venuti (2000). S'agit-il d'un signe de maturité ou un nouveau signe de la mode du digest et du zapping? Cette accumulation soudaine, rapide de textes "fondamentaux", de pensées concentrées préfigure-t-elle le sommeil dogmatique de la traductologie? Ou ne recouvre-t-elle que des intérêts d'auteurs pris dans la concurrence universitaire et dans l'inflation éditoriale?
- Les *dictionnaires et encyclopédies* de traductologie, édités par exemple par Shuttleworth & Cowie en 1997, Baker en 1998, Snell-Hornby et al. aussi en 1998, Classe en 2000, Kittel et al. en 2004 et Brown en 2006. Est-ce une manière de synthétiser un champ éclaté, de rassembler ce qui est discontinu? d'affirmer sa place et sa légitimité et aux yeux de qui?
- Les *bibliographies* dont les premières sont déjà sorties dans les années 1970, suivies plus tard par exemple par *Abstracts in Translation Studies* depuis 1998,

Translation Studies Bibliography en ligne depuis 2004, sans compter les essais dispersés en Cédéroms pour recueillir les titres de mémoires de maitrise, les thèses. La traductologie doit aussi se soumettre à l'épreuve des titres des banques de données bibliographiques, prétendant couvrir les Humanités, les sciences du langage, etc. Comment, dans ces bibliographies et bases, le nombre de références en traductologie a-t-il évolué dans le temps, globalement et par sous-domaines, par langues étudiées et langues de rédaction?

Pour conclure

La triple réflexivité, esquissée ici sur et par le traductologue, dans le cadre d'une historiographie du champ, et par l'analyse des instances en traductologie, peut et doit servir à mettre à jour les points aveugles de la traductologie, ses points de vue, ses points de mire, ses points de tension et de rupture. Elle répondra à la question ambiguë "mais que font les traductologues?" (cf. Gadet 2004, à propos des sociolinguistes en France), dépliant ce qu'ils ont tendance à occulter, à refouler, à passer sous silence, à délaisser ou à reporter. Elle pourrait déranger en mettant en évidence l'idéologie des chercheurs et leur mode de fonctionnement mais aussi permettre de développer un réseau international de traductologues (Gambier 2005), relevant ainsi le défi à la fois de la mondialisation des recherches et des TIC.

Références

Baumgarten, Nicole, House, Juliane and Probst, Julia. 2004. "English as Lingua Franca in Covert Translation Processes". *The Translator* 10 (1): 83–108.

Berman, Antoine. 1989. "La traduction et ses discours". *Meta* XXXIV (4): 672–679.

Bourdieu, Pierre. 1968. *Le métier de sociologue*. En collaboration avec J.-C. Passeron et J.-C. Chamboredon. Paris: Mouton/Bordas.

Bourdieu, Pierre. 1970. *La reproduction*. Paris: Minuit.

Bourdieu, Pierre. 1976 "Le champ scientifique". *Actes de la recherche en sciences sociales* 2–3: 88–104.

Bourdieu, Pierre. 1979. *La distinction*. Paris: Minuit.

Bourdieu, Pierre. 1980. *Le sens pratique*. Paris: Minuit.

Bourdieu, Pierre. 1981 *Questions de sociologie*. Paris: Minuit.

Bourdieu, Pierre. 1982. *Leçon sur la leçon*. Paris: Minuit.

Bourdieu, Pierre. 1984. *Homo academicus*. Paris: Minuit.

Bourdieu, Pierre. 1989. *La noblesse d'Etat. Grandes écoles et esprit de corps*. Paris: Minuit.

Bourdieu, Pierre. 2001. *Science de la science et réflexivité*. Paris: Raisons d'agir.

Bourdieu, Pierre and Wacquant, Loïc. 1992. *Réponses: pour une anthropologie réflexive*. Paris: Seuil.

Brown, Keith (ed). 2006. *Encyclopedia of Language and Linguistics*. Oxford: Elsevier.

Brownlie, Siobhan. 2003. "Distinguish some approaches to translation research: The issue of interpretative constraints". *The Translator* 9 (1): 39–64.

Buzelin, Hélène. 2004. "La traductologie, l'ethnographie et la production de connaissances". *Meta* XLIX (4): 729–746.

Caminade, Monique. 1995. "Les formations en traduction et interprétation. Perspectives en Europe de l'ouest". *TTR* VIII (1): 247–270.

Chesterman, Andrew. 1997 *Memes of Translation. The Spread of Ideas in Translation Theory*. Amsterdam and Philadelphia: John Benjamins.

Classe, Olive (ed). 2000. *Encyclopedia of Literary Translation into English*. London: Fitzroy Dearborn Publishers.

Delabastita, Dirk. 1991. "A False Opposition in Translation Studies: Theoretical versus/and Historical Approaches". *Target* 3 (2): 137–152.

D'hulst, Lieven. 1990. "Pourquoi et comment écrire l'histoire des théories de la traduction?", *Actes du 12ème Congrès mondial de la FIT*. Belgrade: Prevodilac. 57–62.

D'hulst, Lieven. 1995. "Pour une historiographie des théories de la traduction". *TTR* VIII (1): 13–33.

Dollerup, Cay. 1997. "Issues Today, Challenges Tomorrow: Translation and English as the International Lingua Franca". In *The Changing Scene in World Languages: Issues and Challenges*, M.B. Labrum (ed). Amsterdam and Philadelphia: John Benjamins. 83–106.

Gadet, Françoise. 2004. "Mais que font les sociolinguistes?". *Langages et Société* 107: 85–94.

Gambier, Yves. 2005. "Pertinence sociale de la traductologie?". *Meta* L (4) (CD).

Gambier, Yves. 2006. "Pour une socio-traduction". In *Translation Studies at the Interface of Disciplines*, J.F. Duarte, A. Assis Rosa and T. Seruya (eds). Amsterdam and Philadelphia: John Benjamins. 29–42.

Gile, Daniel. 1995. *Regards sur la recherche en interprétation de conférence*. Lille: Presses Universitaires de Lille.

Gile, Daniel. 2000. "The History of Research into Conference Interpreting. A Scientometric Approach". *Target* 12 (2): 297–321.

Gouanvic, Jean-Marc. 1999. *Sociologie de la traduction. La science-fiction américaine dans l'espace culturel français des années 1950*. Arras: Artois Presses Université.

Kalinowski, Isabelle. 2002. "La vocation au travail de traducteur". *Actes de la recherche en sciences sociales* 144: 47–54.

Kittel, Harald, Frank, Armin Paul, Greiner, Norbert, Hermans, Theo, Koller, Werner, Lambert, José and Paul, Fritz (eds). 2004. *Übersetzung/Translation/Traduction. Ein internationales Handbuch zur Übersetzungsforschung. An International Encyclopedia of Translation Studies. Encyclopédie internationale de la recherche sur la traduction. Volume 1*. Berlin and New York: Mouton de Gruyter.

Lahire, Bernard. 2004. *La culture des individus. Dissonances culturelles et distinction de soi*. Paris: La Découverte.

Lambert, José. 1993. "History, historiography and the discipline: A programme". In *Translation and Knowledge*, Y. Gambier and J. Tommola (eds). Turku: Centre for Translation and Interpreting: 3–25.

Lauber, Cornelia. 1996. *Selbstporträts. Zum soziologischen Profil von Literaturübersetzern aus dem Französischen*. Tübingen: Narr.

Munday, Jeremy. 2001. *Introducing Translation Studies. Theories and Applications*. London and New York: Routledge.

Pöchhacker, Franz. 1995a. "Those who do... A profile of Research(ers) in Interpreting". *Target* 7 (1): 47–64.

Pöchhacker, Franz. 1995b. "Writing and Research in Interpreting. A Bibliographical Approach". *The Interpreters' Newsletter* 6: 17–31.

Simeoni, Daniel. 1995. "The Stylistics of Life Histories: Taking Jenny at Her Word(s)". *Current Sociology* 43 (2/3): 27–39.

Snell-Hornby, Mary. 1997. "Lingua franca and cultural identity. Translation in the Global Village". In *Transferre necesse est. Proceedings of the 2nd International Conference on Current Trends in Studies of Translation and Interpreting, 5–7 September, 1996, Budapest, Hungary*. K. Klaudy and J. Kohn (eds). Budapest: Scholastica: 27–36.

Snell-Hornby, Mary. 2000. "'McLanguage': The identity of English as an issue in translation today". In *Translation und Text. Ausgewählte Vorträge von Mary Snell-Hornby*, M. Kadric and K. Kaindl (eds). Wien: WUV. 35–44.

Tommola, Jorma. 1997. "Interpretation Research Policy". In *Conference Interpreting. Current Trends in Research*, Y. Gambier, D. Gile and C. Taylor (eds). Amsterdam and Philadelphia: John Benjamins. 69–88.

Toury, Gideon. 1995. *Descriptive Translation Studies and beyond*. Amsterdam and Philadelphia: John Benjamins.

Venuti, Lawrence (ed). 2000. *The Translation Studies Reader*. London and New York: Routledge.

Notes on contributors

Agorni Mirella is Associate Professor of English Language and Translation at the Università Cattolica del Sacro Cuore in Milan, Italy. Her research interests lie in the field of translation theory, history of translation, translation pedagogy and travel writing. She has published several articles on these topics, and is the author of *Translating Italy for the Eighteenth Century: Women, Translation and Travel Writing* (2002) and *La traduzione: teorie e metodologie a confronto* (2005). mirella.agorni@aliceposta.it

Buzelin Hélène completed a PhD in French literature and translation from McGill University in 2002. She has taught translation at the Université du Québec (Trois-Rivières) and at York University (Toronto). Since August 2003, she has been Assistant Professor at the Department of Linguistics and Translation of Université de Montréal. Her research interests are social and cultural aspects of literary translation, with a special focus on post-colonial contexts. Her current research deals with the role of networks and intermediaries in the production process of literary translation. She is the author of *Sur le terrain de la traduction* (2006) and has also published various articles in translation studies and literary journals. helene.buzelin@umontreal.ca

Chesterman Andrew moved to Finland in 1968 and has been based there ever since, at the University of Helsinki, where he has mostly taught English and translation theory. His current position is in the Department of General Linguistics, where he is Professor of multilingual communication. His main research interests are in contrastive analysis, translation theory, translation norms and ethics, and translator training. He was CETRA Professor in 1999, and has an honorary doctorate from the Copenhagen Business School. Main books: *Memes of Translation* (1997); *Contrastive Functional Analysis* (1998); (with Wagner, E.) *Can Theory Help Translators? A Dialogue between the Ivory Tower and the Wordface* (2002); and (with Williams, J.) *The Map. A Beginners' Guide to Doing Research in Translation Studies* (2002). chesterm@mappi.helsinki.fi

Gambier Yves Docteur en linguistique, Professor and Head of the Centre for Translation and Interpreting, University of Turku, Finland. Main interests: translation theory, translation history, screen translation, socioterminology, sociolinguistics, language policy, bilingualism, discourse analysis, training of teachers in translation and interpreting. Has published more than 140 articles and edited or co-edited 18 books. Main publications: *Communication audiovisuelle et transferts linguistiques / Audiovisual Communication and Language Transfers*, special issue of *Translatio*, 1995; *Transferts linguistiques dans les médias audiovisuels*, Ed. du Septentrion, 1996; *Language Transfer and Audiovisual Communication. A Bibliography*, Turku, 1997; *Translating for the Media*, Turku, 1998; *(Multi)Media Translation. Concepts, Practices and Research*, John Benjamins, 2001. Guest-editor of the special issue of *The Translator* 9:2, 2003, *Screen translation*; guest-editor of the special issue of *Meta* XLIX: 2, 2004, *La traduction audiovisuelle*. Membership of Editorial Boards of journals (*Koinè, Terminology, Sendebar, Hermeneus, TTR*) and collections: Benjamins Translation Library (John Benjamins); Scandinavian University Studies in Humanities and Social Sciences (Peter Lang), Traductologie (PU d'Artois). Member of a number of Associations. President of the European Society for Translation Studies (EST) 1998–2004.
yves.gambier@utu.fi; gambier@utu.fi

Gouanvic Jean-Marc is a professor in the Département d'études françaises at Concordia University (Montréal), where he teaches translation studies and translation. In 1987, he founded the translation studies journal *TTR* with Robert Larose. His research and publications deal with the sociology of translation of American literature in France from 1820 to 1960, as informed by Pierre Bourdieu's social theory. In 1999, he published *Sociologie de la traduction: la science-fiction américaine dans l'espace culturel français des années 1950*, and in 2007 *Pratique sociale de la traduction: le roman réaliste américain dans le champ littéraire français (1920-1960)*. He has recently published articles on the translation/adaptation of American literature for youth into French: on James Fenimore Cooper, Harriet Beecher Stowe, Mark Twain, Jack London, James Oliver Curwood. He is currently working on the translation of the American detective-novel into French (1920–1960).
jmgouan@alcor.concordia.ca

Heilbron Johan is a sociologist at the Centre de sociologie européenne (CNRS, EHESS, MSH) in Paris, and at Erasmus University in Rotterdam. He is also a member of ESSE (Pour un espace des sciences sociales européen). His research interests are mainly in economic sociology, the sociology of culture and transnational cultural exchange, and in the historical sociology of the sciences. Recent

publications are *The Rise of Social Theory* (1995), *The Rise of the Social Sciences and the Formation of Modernity* (with Magnusson, L. and Wittrock, B., 1998, paperback 2001), *Pour une histoire des sciences sociales. Hommage à Pierre Bourdieu* (co-edited with Lenoir, R. and Sapiro, G., 2004). In the sociology of translation he published "Towards a Sociology of Translation: Book translations as a Cultural World System" (in: *European Journal of Social Theory* 2, 1999), and edited, with G. Sapiro, two issues of *Actes de la recherche en sciences sociales* (n° 144 and 145, 2002) on translation and the circulation of ideas.
johan.heilbron@wxs.nl; heilbron@msh-paris.fr

Hermans Theo studied at the universities of Ghent (Belgium), Essex and Warwick (UK). He is currently Professor of Dutch and Comparative Literature at University College London (UCL) and member of the advisory board of *The Translator*. His research interests are in translation theory and history, comparative literature, Renaissance studies, Dutch and Flemish literature. He has published on various historical and methodological aspects of translation studies. Recent books include *Translation in Systems. Descriptive and System-oriented Approaches Explained* (1999), (ed.) *Crosscultural Transgressions* (2002), (ed.) *Translating Others* (2006, 2 vols.).
ucldthe@ucl.ac.uk

Prunč Erich has a PhD in Slavonic Studies and Comparative Literature; research project „Lexical Inventory of the Slovene Popular Language in Carinthia"; in 1988 appointment as a Full Professor to the newly established chair of translation studies at the University of Graz; 1988–2003 Head of the Department of Translation Studies at Graz University. Main research interests: history of translation studies, literary translation, translation ethics. Recent books include *Einführung in die Translationswissenschaft* (2001) and *Entwicklungslinien der Translationswissenschaft. Von den Asymmetrien der Sprachen zu den Asymmetrien der Macht* (2007).
erich.prunc@uni-graz.at

Sapiro Gisèle is research director at the CNRS (Centre de sociologie européenne), Paris and member of ESSE (Pour un espace des sciences sociales européen). After a BA and an MA in philosophy and comparative literature at Tel-Aviv University, she turned to sociology and prepared her PhD dissertation at the Ecole des hautes études en sciences sociales in Paris, with P. Bourdieu. Out of this dissertation on the French literary field during WWII, she published *La Guerre des écrivains, 1940–1953* (1999). Recent publications include *Pour une histoire des sciences sociales. Hommage à Pierre Bourdieu* (co-edited with Lenoir, R. and Heilbron, J., 2004) and several articles on the sociology of translation, such as: "Forms of polit-

icization in the French literary field", in *Theory and Society* 32, 2003 and "The literary field between the state and the market", in *Poetics* 31: 5–6, 2003. In 2002, she edited, with J. Heilbron, two issues of *Actes de la recherche en sciences sociales* (n° 144 and 145) on international cultural exchanges and the circulation of ideas.
sapiro@msh-paris.fr

Simeoni Daniel is Associate Professor of Translation Studies at York University (Toronto), member of the Doctoral program in Humanities and, since 2001, Director of the Graduate program in Translation. His publications are in linguistics, translation studies and the sociology of translation. His current research is divided between an on-going sociobiographical study of D. Valentini, the Italian translator of Shakespeare's *Julius Caesar* in 1756 and, more reflexively, the issue of method in translation studies and the human sciences in multicultural environments.
dsimeoni@yorku.ca

Wolf Michaela has an MA in Translation Studies and a PhD in Romanic languages. She is Associate Professor at the Department of Translation Studies, University of Graz, Austria. Areas of research are sociology of translation, aspects of cultural studies in translation, translation history, postcolonial translation, feminist translation.

She edited various books, e.g. *Übersetzungswissenschaft in Brasilien. Beiträge zum Status von 'Original' und Übersetzung* (1997); *Übersetzung aus aller Frauen Länder. Beiträge zu Theorie und Praxis weiblicher Realität in der Translation* (2001), *Übersetzen – Translating – Traduire: Towards a "Social Turn"?* 2006, and is the author of a series of articles in books and reviews. Currently she is preparing a book on the translation activity in the late Habsburg Monarchy.
michaela.wolf@uni-graz.at

Author index

Subject index

Benjamins Translation Library

A complete list of titles in this series can be found on *www.benjamins.com*

47 **SAWYER, David B.:** Fundamental Aspects of Interpreter Education. Curriculum and Assessment. 2004.
    xviii, 312 pp.

46 **BRUNETTE, Louise, Georges BASTIN, Isabelle HEMLIN and Heather CLARKE (eds.):** The Critical
    Link 3. Interpreters in the Community. Selected papers from the Third International Conference on
    Interpreting in Legal, Health and Social Service Settings, Montréal, Quebec, Canada 22–26 May 2001. 2003.
    xii, 359 pp.

45 **ALVES, Fabio (ed.):** Triangulating Translation. Perspectives in process oriented research. 2003. x, 165 pp.

44 **SINGERMAN, Robert:** Jewish Translation History. A bibliography of bibliographies and studies. With an
    introductory essay by Gideon Toury. 2002. xxxvi, 420 pp.

43 **GARZONE, Giuliana and Maurizio VIEZZI (eds.):** Interpreting in the 21st Century. Challenges and
    opportunities. 2002. x, 337 pp.

42 **HUNG, Eva (ed.):** Teaching Translation and Interpreting 4. Building bridges. 2002. xii, 243 pp.

41 **NIDA, Eugene A.:** Contexts in Translating. 2002. x, 127 pp.

40 **ENGLUND DIMITROVA, Birgitta and Kenneth HYLTENSTAM (eds.):** Language Processing and
    Simultaneous Interpreting. Interdisciplinary perspectives. 2000. xvi, 164 pp.

39 **CHESTERMAN, Andrew, Natividad GALLARDO SAN SALVADOR and Yves GAMBIER (eds.):**
    Translation in Context. Selected papers from the EST Congress, Granada 1998. 2000. x, 393 pp.

38 **SCHÄFFNER, Christina and Beverly ADAB (eds.):** Developing Translation Competence. 2000.
    xvi, 244 pp.

37 **TIRKKONEN-CONDIT, Sonja and Riitta JÄÄSKELÄINEN (eds.):** Tapping and Mapping the Processes
    of Translation and Interpreting. Outlooks on empirical research. 2000. x, 176 pp.

36 **SCHMID, Monika S.:** Translating the Elusive. Marked word order and subjectivity in English-German
    translation. 1999. xii, 174 pp.

35 **SOMERS, Harold (ed.):** Computers and Translation. A translator's guide. 2003. xvi, 351 pp.

34 **GAMBIER, Yves and Henrik GOTTLIEB (eds.):** (Multi) Media Translation. Concepts, practices, and
    research. 2001. xx, 300 pp.

33 **GILE, Daniel, Helle V. DAM, Friedel DUBSLAFF, Bodil MARTINSEN and Anne SCHJOLDAGER
    (eds.):** Getting Started in Interpreting Research. Methodological reflections, personal accounts and advice
    for beginners. 2001. xiv, 255 pp.

32 **BEEBY, Allison, Doris ENSINGER and Marisa PRESAS (eds.):** Investigating Translation. Selected papers
    from the 4th International Congress on Translation, Barcelona, 1998. 2000. xiv, 296 pp.

31 **ROBERTS, Roda P., Silvana E. CARR, Diana ABRAHAM and Aideen DUFOUR (eds.):** The Critical
    Link 2: Interpreters in the Community. Selected papers from the Second International Conference on
    Interpreting in legal, health and social service settings, Vancouver, BC, Canada, 19–23 May 1998. 2000.
    vii, 316 pp.

30 **DOLLERUP, Cay:** Tales and Translation. The Grimm Tales from Pan-Germanic narratives to shared
    international fairytales. 1999. xiv, 384 pp.

29 **WILSS, Wolfram:** Translation and Interpreting in the 20th Century. Focus on German. 1999. xiii, 256 pp.

28 **SETTON, Robin:** Simultaneous Interpretation. A cognitive-pragmatic analysis. 1999. xvi, 397 pp.

27 **BEYLARD-OZEROFF, Ann, Jana KRÁLOVÁ and Barbara MOSER-MERCER (eds.):** Translators'
    Strategies and Creativity. Selected Papers from the 9th International Conference on Translation and
    Interpreting, Prague, September 1995. In honor of Jiří Levý and Anton Popovič. 1998. xiv, 230 pp.

26 **TROSBORG, Anna (ed.):** Text Typology and Translation. 1997. xvi, 342 pp.

25 **POLLARD, David E. (ed.):** Translation and Creation. Readings of Western Literature in Early Modern
    China, 1840–1918. 1998. vi, 336 pp.

24 **ORERO, Pilar and Juan C. SAGER (eds.):** The Translator's Dialogue. Giovanni Pontiero. 1997. xiv, 252 pp.

23 **GAMBIER, Yves, Daniel GILE and Christopher TAYLOR (eds.):** Conference Interpreting: Current Trends
    in Research. Proceedings of the International Conference on Interpreting: What do we know and how?
    1997. iv, 246 pp.

22 **CHESTERMAN, Andrew:** Memes of Translation. The spread of ideas in translation theory. 1997.
    vii, 219 pp.

21 **BUSH, Peter and Kirsten MALMKJÆR (eds.):** Rimbaud's Rainbow. Literary translation in higher
    education. 1998. x, 200 pp.

20 **SNELL-HORNBY, Mary, Zuzana JETTMAROVÁ and Klaus KAINDL (eds.):** Translation as Intercultural
    Communication. Selected papers from the EST Congress, Prague 1995. 1997. x, 354 pp.

19 **CARR, Silvana E., Roda P. ROBERTS, Aideen DUFOUR and Dini STEYN (eds.):** The Critical Link: Interpreters in the Community. Papers from the 1st international conference on interpreting in legal, health and social service settings, Geneva Park, Canada, 1–4 June 1995. 1997. viii, 322 pp.

18 **SOMERS, Harold (ed.):** Terminology, LSP and Translation. Studies in language engineering in honour of Juan C. Sager. 1996. xii, 250 pp.

17 **POYATOS, Fernando (ed.):** Nonverbal Communication and Translation. New perspectives and challenges in literature, interpretation and the media. 1997. xii, 361 pp.

16 **DOLLERUP, Cay and Vibeke APPEL (eds.):** Teaching Translation and Interpreting 3. New Horizons. Papers from the Third Language International Conference, Elsinore, Denmark, 1995. 1996. viii, 338 pp.

15 **WILSS, Wolfram:** Knowledge and Skills in Translator Behavior. 1996. xiii, 259 pp.

14 **MELBY, Alan K. and Terry WARNER:** The Possibility of Language. A discussion of the nature of language, with implications for human and machine translation. 1995. xxvi, 276 pp.

13 **DELISLE, Jean and Judith WOODSWORTH (eds.):** Translators through History. 1995. xvi, 346 pp.

12 **BERGENHOLTZ, Henning and Sven TARP (eds.):** Manual of Specialised Lexicography. The preparation of specialised dictionaries. 1995. 256 pp.

11 **VINAY, Jean-Paul and Jean DARBELNET:** Comparative Stylistics of French and English. A methodology for translation. Translated and edited by Juan C. Sager, M.-J. Hamel. 1995. xx, 359 pp.

10 **KUSSMAUL, Paul:** Training the Translator. 1995. x, 178 pp.

9 **REY, Alain:** Essays on Terminology. Translated by Juan C. Sager. With an introduction by Bruno de Bessé. 1995. xiv, 223 pp.

8 **GILE, Daniel:** Basic Concepts and Models for Interpreter and Translator Training. 1995. xvi, 278 pp.

7 **BEAUGRANDE, Robert de, Abdullah SHUNNAQ and Mohamed Helmy HELIEL (eds.):** Language, Discourse and Translation in the West and Middle East. 1994. xii, 256 pp.

6 **EDWARDS, Alicia B.:** The Practice of Court Interpreting. 1995. xiii, 192 pp.

5 **DOLLERUP, Cay and Annette LINDEGAARD (eds.):** Teaching Translation and Interpreting 2. Insights, aims and visions. Papers from the Second Language International Conference Elsinore, 1993. 1994. viii, 358 pp.

4 **TOURY, Gideon:** Descriptive Translation Studies – and beyond. 1995. viii, 312 pp.

3 **LAMBERT, Sylvie and Barbara MOSER-MERCER (eds.):** Bridging the Gap. Empirical research in simultaneous interpretation. 1994. 362 pp.

2 **SNELL-HORNBY, Mary, Franz PÖCHHACKER and Klaus KAINDL (eds.):** Translation Studies: An Interdiscipline. Selected papers from the Translation Studies Congress, Vienna, 1992. 1994. xii, 438 pp.

1 **SAGER, Juan C.:** Language Engineering and Translation. Consequences of automation. 1994. xx, 345 pp.